Gabriele Klein & Franz Anton Cramer (eds.)
Materialities in Dance and Performance

Critical Dance Studies | edited by Gabriele Brandstetter and Gabriele Klein
Volume 70

Gabriele Klein (Dr. rer. soc.) is Professor of Ballet and Dance ("Hans van Manen Chair") at the University of Amsterdam since 2022. From 2002 to 2023 she held the chair of Sociology of Human Movement, Sports, Dance and Performance Studies at Universität Hamburg. She is PI of the Cluster of Excellence "Understanding Written Artefacts" at Universität Hamburg.

Franz Anton Cramer was research associate in the project "Choreographies of Archiving" directed by Gabriele Klein (2020–2023), as part of the Cluster of Excellence "Understanding Written Artefacts" at Universität Hamburg. Prior to that, he conducted research and archival projects at Universität Leipzig (Dance Archives), Centre national de la danse in Paris (CND), Tanzplan Deutschland / Dance Heritage (Berlin), and Paris Lodron Universität Salzburg.

Gabriele Klein &
Franz Anton Cramer (eds.)

Materialities in Dance and Performance. Writing Documenting Archiving

[transcript]

This publication was funded by the Deutsche Forschungsgemeinschaft (DFG, German Research Foundation) under Germany's Excellence Strategy – EXC 2176 "Understanding Written Artefacts: Material, Interaction and Transmission in Manuscript Cultures", project no. 390893796. It was developed in the context of the subproject "Choreographies of Archiving" in the EXC 2176, whose research was conducted within the scope of the Centre for the Study of Manuscript Cultures (CSMC) at Universität Hamburg.

Bibliographic information published by the Deutsche Nationalbibliothek
The Deutsche Nationalbibliothek lists this publication in the Deutsche Nationalbibliografie; detailed bibliographic data are available in the Internet at *dnb.dnb.de*

 This work is licensed under the Creative Commons Attribution - Non Commercial 4.0 (BY-NC) license, which means that the text may be may be remixed, build upon and be distributed, provided credit is given to the author, but may not be used for commercial purposes.
For details go to: *creativecommons.org/licenses/by-nc/4.0/*
Permission to use the text for commercial purposes can be obtained by contacting *rights@transcript-publishing.com*
Creative Commons license terms for re-use do not apply to any content (such as graphs, figures, photos, excerpts, etc.) not original to the Open Access publication and further permission may be required from the rights holder. The obligation to research and clear permission lies solely with the party re-using the material.

First published in 2024 by transcript Verlag, Bielefeld
© Gabriele Klein & Franz Anton Cramer (eds.)
Cover, Graphic Design & Typesetting by Andreas Steinbach, *buerobrueggmann.de*
Printed by Docupoint
Print-ISBN 978-3-8376-7064-6
PDF-ISBN 978-3-8394-7064-0
doi.org/10.14361/9783839470640
ISSN of series 2747-3120
eISSN of series 2747-3139
Printed on permanent acid-free text paper

Gabriele Klein & Franz Anton Cramer (eds.)
**Materialities in Dance and Performance.
Writing, Documenting, Archiving**

Writing as Choreographic Practice

8
Gabriele Klein & Franz Anton Cramer
Materialities in Dance and Performance. An Introduction

24
Jonathan Burrows **Scribbling Towards Something: Interview on the Written in Dance**

34
Lou Forster **What Dance Teaches Us about Reading: Four Events and an Interlude**

54
Gabriele Klein & Franz Anton Cramer
Choreographic Writing. Material Practice of Artistic Production

82
Bojana Kunst **Passing on the Legacy of Collaboration: Material Goods as Marginalia**

Documenting as Knowledge Production

104
Sasha Waltz **"I want to continue working on the body". Gabriele Klein and Sasha Waltz in Conversation**

118
Annet Dekker **From Documentary to Performative Documentation**

134
Axel Malik **The Scriptal Method and Choreography**

152
Sybille Krämer **Notational Iconicity, Spatiality, Time: The Creativity of Artificial Flatness**

Archiving as Performative Act

176
deufert+plischke **anarchivTANZ**

192
Aleida Assmann **Archiving the Body – Cultural Memory and the Practice of Intangible Cultural Heritage**

208
Sasha Portyannikova **Absent and Abundant Arte(povera)facts**

226
Cristina Baldacci **"Things that Death Cannot Destroy": The Afterlife and Performativity of Photographic Images (Linda Fregni Nagler)**

244
Timmy De Laet **Multiple Materialisms: Situating Dance between Enactivist and New Materialist Discourses**

270
Contributors

Materialities in Dance and Performance
Introduction

Gabriele Klein
Franz Anton Cramer

"Turn" – this term, which seems so beautifully dance-like, has characterised debates in the humanities, cultural studies, and social sciences since the 1960s. Various turns found their first impetus in 1967 through the anthology by the American philosopher Richard Rorty, which bears the term "The Linguistic Turn" (Rorty 1967) in its title – a term already introduced by the philosopher of science Gustav Bergmann in the 1950s. Rorty argues that language is an inescapable condition for all forms of thought, cognition and reflection. The *linguistic turn* becomes the prelude to all subsequent turns, be it the *performative* (Gotman 2022), *reflexive* (Lumsden et al. 2019), *postcolonial* (Devish and Nyamnioh 2011), *pictorial/iconic* (Curtis 2010), *body* (Gugutzer 2015), *spatial* (Warf and Arias 2009) or *material turn* (Bennett and Joyce 2010).

The literary and cultural studies scholar Doris Bachmann-Medick has convincingly traced the forms and characteristics of previous cultural turns in the history of humanities and social sciences (Bachmann-Medick 2016). According to her, these turns do not provoke radical paradigm shifts or fundamental theoretical transformations. Rather, they change previous research perspectives and systematic questions. They are therefore less epistemic ruptures than shifts in perspective, which nevertheless have consequences for theoretical concepts and methodological procedures. Moreover, all of these turns are characterised by interdisciplinary approaches and do not just take place within one discipline.

The material turn in dance and performance

This book deals with the "material turn", i.e. a turn towards things, objects, and the material; it asks how this turn becomes visible and reflected in contemporary dance and performance art.

The material turn marks a shift in perspective towards the thing-like and object-like in the humanities, cultural and social sciences. It has led to the establishment of new research areas such as science and technology studies (STS), new materialism, and material studies. It has also brought about a change of perspective in research on the arts. This can be observed in the performing arts, especially in dance and performance. Since the 2010s, dance and performance artists are increasingly working at the interface between human and non-human bodies. They present dance as no longer necessarily dependent on dancing human bodies and are dedicated to the permanence and sustainability of dance art by focusing on documentation and archiving.

While the material turn has occupied museum studies and archive research since the 1980s, dance and performance research has remained largely untouched by it. In the 1990s, it was the performative turn that had an impact here, with dance and performance being viewed primarily as ephemeral art forms. Accordingly, theoretical concepts such as presence, co-presence, aura, the event-like, and the singular are being sharpened (Lepecki 2016; Mersch 2002).

With the material turn, the focus in dance and performance research is also shifting from the ephemeral and momentary to the stable and permanent. Methodologically, this has resulted in a stronger focus on empirical and praxeological research and thus an opening of dance and performance studies to social science methodology. The material turn has also led to a rapprochement between the visual and performing arts. Dance and performance are not only seen as immaterial and thus in opposition to the materiality of visual arts and architecture. Rather, the question of the materiality of dance and performance itself arises.

The materiality of artistic practice

By focusing on practice, the material turn also draws attention to artistic work processes and thus to the concept of work. In contrast to the performative turn, which places the present and situatedness of performance at the centre, the work process also brings its materiality into focus and with it the documentation, archiving, and preparation of 'ephemeral art'. This is precisely what choreographer William Forsythe declared as his goal in his paradigmatic digital project *Synchronous Objects*[1]: recorded choreographic facts are to be presented and visualised in digital forms and formats, thereby transforming their artistic power, as it were. This approach was expanded in the *Motion Bank* project initiated by Forsythe, which has been continued at Mainz University of Applied Sciences since 2016. Here, the focus is on the fundamentals of digital dance research, the digital documentation of dance, and the use of digital technologies in dance practice. Digitality is intended to ensure the representation and archiving of processuality and multi-perspectivity.[2]

The increasing importance of the artistic working process for the representation and legitimisation of performative art is reflected in the fact that artistic working processes such as research, note-taking, documentation, and archiving are now obligatory components of project applications. In the past, they characterised the artistic work process, but were considered to be of little relevance for the recognition of the artwork and were not made public. While it has long been standard in academia that research processes must be traceable and documented and that research material must be preserved over a longer period of time, this has also been expected of artists since the concept of research found its way into art. But regardless of these requirements, many artists also see documentation and archiving as components of artistic research. For project funding, all artists are expected to disclose, document, and make their work processes accessible. This new attention to artistic work processes not only marks a departure from the notion of the unique 'work of art'. It also aims to recognise the work process as an integral part of artistic production. What possibilities, limits, and forms can documentation and archiving of dance and performance art have? What does data say about dance?

The material turn thus focuses on artistic practice, the working process, documentation, and the archive. At the same time, the concept of work, both in the sense of the final artefact and the activity used to produce it, is being realigned. This is also interesting from a sociological perspective: whether, how long, where, when, and with whom an artist works is no longer unimportant for the evaluation of their work.

Writing, documenting, archiving

But what significance does the materiality of the artistic work have for the aesthetic quality of a dance, a choreography, or a performance? And how can we draw conclusions about artistic quality from the documentation and archiving of material? These questions guided our research project "Choreographies of Archiving. A cross-cultural study of archiving practices in contemporary dance", which we conducted as part of the Hamburg Cluster of Excellence "Understanding Written Artefacts. Material, Interaction and Transmission in Manuscript Cultures"[3] at the Hamburg University from 2020 to 2023.

Overall, the cluster deals with the materiality of writing processes and written artefacts in different historical epochs and cultural contexts. Cluster research adopts a praxeological and material-oriented perspective, insofar as it deals with the question of how writing processes are interwoven with cultural objects and interact with human and non-human actors. The research focus of the cluster is therefore on the practices, techniques, materials and resources that are used in cultural schemes of writing.

The research project "Choreographies of Archiving" adopted a sociologically inspired praxeological perspective within this research framework. Since our object of research was contemporary dance, we also had a different view on the question of writing than classical philological disciplines: While the focus of the cluster is on (hand-)written artefacts and (hand)writing in all their different materialities, different historical times and different cultural spaces, we concentrated on writing practices in contemporary dance and their role for documentation and archiving as well as their significance for the creation and revival of choreographies. We assumed that both writing and choreography produce artefacts that manifest themselves materially in the generated form of writing or movement. It is this materiality that turns them into documents, makes archiving possible, transports the knowledge they contain through time and thus turns the documents into the cultural memory of dance.

Writing Our results show that contemporary choreographers do not understand and use writing in their artistic practice primarily as a documentary act or as an archival activity. Rather, writing is first and foremost a creative and temporary process that can be described as an intermediate stage between 'idea' and 'realisation'. At the same time, writing also has a memory function. Only the artist or their legal descendants decide what of the written material finds its way into the archive and is thus passed on. The archived and handed-down material that is released fulfils one purpose above all: on the one hand, it shapes the artistic self-image, and on the other hand, the release potentially provides the artists with access to the canon of (dance) historiography.

Despite this great importance for the individual and collective memory of dance, writing, unlike notation, is generally regarded as secondary by choreographers and researchers alike. Writing is seen as a pragmatic act of preparation and development of that which lies beyond the material, namely the movement, the dance, the choreographic artefact. Through our investigation of written artefacts by dance artists, we can show that written documents and the analysis of the writing processes and techniques used here make it clear that writing has a variety of functions and meanings for choreographic work, how the aesthetics of writing correspond to the aesthetics of movement and how the way of writing relates to artistic aesthetics. This brings the relationship between the materiality of the body and the materiality of writing as well as the material practices of writing and dancing to centre stage. In contrast to the investigation of handwritten writing practices, research into materiality in dance is confronted with a particular question: How does the materiality of the dancing body, its immediacy and presumed speechlessness relate to writing practices?

Documenting In contrast to written artefacts in other historical and cultural contexts, choreographic writing is fundamentally linked to a physical practice that shapes every writing both in its semantic content and in its materiality (Jeschke 2023). Dance and choreographic written artefacts provide indications of the creative power in artistic work processes. During their lifetime, contemporary choreographers create a personal archive that is generally not accessible to others and which they use primarily for pragmatic purposes: Most of all, it serves to revisit pieces or to reuse building blocks from earlier artistic work processes. However, many contemporary choreographers do not set up an archive at all – for time or financial reasons and also because the dynamics of the contemporary art market, which is orientated towards the new, only very rarely require a choreography to be revived.

Nevertheless, an "archival impulse" (Foster 2004) underlies both choreographic writing itself and the use and function of written artefacts. Thus, writing is intricately linked to archival practices. What is archived must also be described and recorded and thus receives an additional, organising level of writing. Digital media technologies such as digital writing, visual annotation of writing and moving images, or social media also modify and change archival practices. The use and appraisal of documents in the archive, in turn, depends on material aspects such as size, form, state of preservation or fragility.

Archiving Such entanglements of writing, documenting, and archiving have led, particularly in dance and performance research, to the concept of the archive and the practice of archiving being put to the test and the traditional understanding of archiving being scrutinised (Foellmer et al. 2019; Ayerbe 2017, 2018; Dekker 2018; Barbéris 2015; Cramer 2014). Accordingly, various variants of archiving have been established, which, for example, view the body as a living archive (Lepecki 2010; Wehren 2016) or document the affective content of the archive instead of viewing the actual archival materials as sources (Marshall and Tortorici 2022; Bissell and Haviland 2018; Palladini and Pustianaz 2017). The archivability of artistic dance depends less on the forms created than on the specific intentions underlying the artistic work. It is these intentions that the practice of writing contains and turns over to the archive for documentary use. Current research on the archival turn in dance and embodied practices (Yamomo 2019; Ortmann 2017; Giannachi 2016; Hahn 2007; Hamilton 2002) deals with the resulting archival materialisation of dance both in the performance and in the document.

The archive in dance – in its double meaning as a place and as a form of memory – is thus essentially a genuine component of artistic body practice. Dance scripts in their diverse forms organise a linear process and its medial representation in contrast to the simultaneity of the performance and its *hic et nunc* condition. In this understanding, the archive can no longer be seen as a documentary endpoint: the archive is an integral part of writing and physical practice. Writing, documenting and archiving practices, which are understood as the totality of possibilities for documenting and passing on dance and performance-related practical knowledge along with the experiences generated therein, manifest themselves in manifold ways. The contributions to this anthology bear witness to this.

On the architecture of the anthology

The term "materialities", which we emphasise in this anthology, examines the material from a certain perspective. In the practice of the performance-based arts, the material comprises the specific design of a piece using certain materials such as stage sets, props, and costumes in a certain form and texture on the one hand. On the other hand, these materials in their own materiality are closely linked to the material appearance of document, artefact, and archive. Every document is first and foremost material. "Materialities" refers precisely to this link between the artistic creation, distribution, perception and reception of artworks and their transmission and preservation, documentation and archiving, which always take place via storage media.

This anthology brings together contributions that focus on this question of material, matter, and the objective in their interaction with artistic and scientific actors and examine both choreographic practices and epistemic endeavours. The contributions are divided into three chapters, each chapter focuses on one of the topics mentioned in the title: I. WRITING AS A CHOREOGRAPHIC PRACTICE, II. DOCUMENTING AS KNOWLEDGE PRODUCTION and III. ARCHIVING AS A PERFORMATIVE ACT.

Each chapter opens with an artistic position that explains the respective characteristics and necessities of writing in and for the artistic process. In the first chapter, choreographer **Jonathan Burrows** answers our questions about the role of writing, writing support and archiving in his 20-year collaboration with composer Matteo Fargion. Dance scholar **Lou Forster** uses four case studies of situated reading to show how omnipresent the use of written artefacts has been in dance creation in Western Europe since the 1970s at the latest and ultimately since the beginnings of modern dance in the 1910s with Rudolf von Laban's kinetography. The dance scholars **Gabriele Klein** and **Franz Anton Cramer** examine choreographic writing and the visual and objective materialities of written artefacts in the process of choreographing. According to their thesis, writings in dance are part of the artistic work and allow the immaterial to become visible in the world even before the actual performance. The philosopher and performance theorist **Bojana Kunst** presents writing – in the form of handwritten notes in printed texts – as an example of collaborative creation in which a specific relationship between shared time and the object is established.

The second chapter deals with documentation as a form of knowledge production: documents bear witness to what has been and what we can know, but they can also produce new insights and configurations of materials. The choreographer **Sasha Waltz** opens this chapter. In an interview with Gabriele Klein, she explains how documentation is an essential part of her artistic working method, which she has developed anew in the piece *In C*. *In C* is based on a series of fixed choreographic and movement-related figures that are arranged, mixed, and presented in ever new ways. In order to pass this piece – or rather the ability to perform this piece – on to other dancers, she has produced a mixture of oral and documentary, in this case written and visual material, through which the dancers learn the technical and formal knowledge of *In C*. Learning the given material via documents is at the same time a recreation of dance knowledge on one's own body. Using the example of net-based media art, cultural and archival scholar **Annet Dekker** develops the concept of "generative documentation". She presents documentation as something that is always focused on what already exists as well as on what is possible in the future. In his artistic work, visual artist **Axel Malik** moves beyond the conventional concept of knowledge production. For him, the physical act of writing letter-like signs always refers to physical sensations, individual memories and cultural frameworks. His work thus not only enables new insights into habitualised gestures and routines but is itself a choreographic act. The philosopher **Sybille Krämer** uses Malik's images as one example to analyse the diverse potential of writing as a highly productive cultural technique. The artificial flatness of the writing medium makes it possible to decontextualise and make visible things that are not in the world as material entities but as mere concepts or speculations. Written (or drawn) elements stand for knowledge formations that are otherwise inaccessible to the senses or the mind.

The third chapter is dedicated to the archive and archiving as part of the performance. The artist duo **deufert+plischke** (Kattrin Deufert and Thomas Plischke), together with dramaturge **Karen Zimmermann**, present visual and text material that was created as part of their long-term project *Just in Time*. This project brings together written memories of individual dance experiences and collective dance events in the form of letters. This connection between material and immaterial forms of archiving and remembering is addressed by the English and cultural studies scholar **Aleida Assmann.** She focuses on the relevance of the material turn for the constitution and understanding of memory cultures and emphasises in particular the body as a performative archive. The dancer and archive researcher

Sasha Portyannikova deals with the effect of archiving ideologies, especially those that create a canon and often formulate dance history primarily through omission. Using the artistic practice of Linda Fregni Nagler as an example, art historian **Cristina Baldacci** shows how documents that have been abandoned take on new meaning, thereby illustrating that the archive is not the past but always already an instance of the new. Finally, theatre and dance scholar **Timmy De Laet** uses the production *Unfolding an Archive* by Belgian choreographer Zoë Demoustier as an example to examine the theoretical concepts and critical potential of new materialism and enactivism, in which the concepts of agency and material environment play a central role, and relates these to the concept of materialism in Marxist theory.

ACKNOWLEDGEMENTS

An anthology is always a collaborative process that could not be realised without the cooperation of many people and institutional support.

This book is based on the contributions given at the "Material Goods" conference. The conference was embedded in a four-day festival of the same name, which consisted of lectures, lecture-performances, panel discussions, artistic performances, and workshops.[4] These formats contributed to an understanding of materiality in dance and performance art from both an artistic and academic perspective. The participating scholars and artists were confronted with both research findings and embodied forms of thought and knowledge production, were able to question previous perceptions of writing as a cultural and social practice, experiment artistically with writing in the workshops and in this way reflect on writing as a cultural and artistic practice.

First and foremost, we would like to sincerely thank all contributors for their excellent cooperation and their contributions, which reflect the current debates and the continuing importance of this topic from various perspectives and research disciplines.

We also wish to thank all members of the cluster for their diverse inputs and the enriching discussions, which on the one hand offered us a broad interdisciplinary perspective far beyond the field of dance and performance research. On the other hand, we are also grateful for the opportunity to bring the perspective of the aesthetic and the body, dance and performance into the research network through our research perspective.

Our thanks also go to the student assistant Ken Q. H. Phan for the support in compiling the book. Andreas Steinbach is responsible for the layout and graphic design. We would like to thank him very much for the stimulating and uncomplicated co-operation.

Last but not least, we express our gratitude to all the choreographers with whom we had many intense discussions during the course of the project and who granted us access to their archive material and thus made our research possible in the first place.

Gabriele Klein & Franz Anton Cramer
HAMBURG / BERLIN, January 2024

---

1. *Synchronous Objects* was a digital choreographic research project initiated by choreographer William Forsythe and realised in collaboration with Maria Palazzi and Norah Zuniga Shaw at Ohio State University's Advanced Computing Center for the Arts and Design. Published online in 2009, the "interactive artwork" with its full title Synchronous Objects for One Flat Thing, reproduced "re-imagines the expressive possibilities of information in dance", as the website says, flowing "from dance, to data, to objects" (*synchronousobjects.osu.edu/* 10/11/2023).
2. The digital archive project *Motion Bank* (*motionbank.org/* 10/11/2023) was initiated by The Forsythe Company in 2010. Tools were developed to document and analyse choreographic thinking and complex movement sequences by displaying them simultaneously in multiple views. Since 2016, the project has continued as at Mainz University of Applied Sciences, Department of Design. See also Delahunta and Jenett 2016.
3. See *csmc.uni-hamburg.de/written-artefacts.html* (07/09/2023).
4. The festival and the international conference "Material Goods" took place in Hamburg from 30 January to 4 February 2023. It was a cooperation event between the Cluster of Excellence "Understanding Written Artefacts" and Kampnagel / Hamburg, the largest venue for performing arts in Europe. The curator was Gabriele Klein.

REFERENCES

Ayerbe, Nerea (2017): Documentando lo Efímero: reconsideración de la idea de presencia en los debates sobre la performance. In: Revista Brasileira de Estudos da Presença, vol. 7, nr. 3, pp. 437–458.

Ayerbe, Nerea (2018): The ephemeral and its materialisations. Towards a redefinition of performance art. In: MAP #9, Das Buch als Archivraum und Medium der Kunst, *perfomap.de/map9/archiv-fragen/the-ephemeral-and-its-materialisations* (15/06/2021).

Bachmann-Medick, Doris (2016): Cultural Turns: New Orientations in the Study of Culture. Berlin, Boston: de Gruyter.

Barbéris, Isabelle (ed.) (2015): L'archive dans les arts vivants. Performance, danse, théâtre. Rennes: Presses universitaires de Rennes.

Bennett, Tony and Patrick **Joyce** (eds.) (2010): Material Powers: Cultural Studies, History and the Material Turn. London and New York: Routledge.

Bissell, Bill and Linda Caruso **Haviland** (eds.) (2018): The Sentient Archive. Bodies, performance, and memory. Middletown: Wesleyan University Press and The Pew Center for Arts & Heritage.

Cramer, Franz Anton (2014): Experience as Artifact: Transformations of the Immaterial. In: Dance Research Journal, 46, no. 2, September 2014, pp. 24–31.

Curtis, Neal (2010): The Pictorial Turn. London: Routledge.

Dekker, Annet (2018): Enduring Liveness. An Imaginary Retrospective of Tino Sehgal's Constructed Situations. In: Exhibition Library, exhibition catalogue, Seoul: Seoul Museum of Art.

Delahunta, Scott and Florian **Jenett** (2016): A conversation on Motion Bank. In: MAP #6, Aufzeichnen. Verzeichnen. *perfomap.de/map6/medien-und-verfahren-des-aufzeichnens/a-conversation-on-motion-bank* (15/08/2021).

Devisch, René and Francis B. **Nyamnjoh** (eds.) (2011): The Postcolonial Turn: Re-Imagining Anthropology and Africa. Cameroon: Langaa Research and Publishing Common Initiative.

Foellmer, Susanne, Maria Katharina **Schmidt** and Cornelia **Schmitz** (eds.) (2019): Performing Arts in Transition. Moving between Media. Abingdon and New York: Routledge.

Foster, Hal (2004): An Archival Impulse. In October, Vol. 110, Autumn 2004, pp. 3–22.

Giannachi, Gabriella (2016): Archive Everything. Mapping the Everyday. Cambridge: The MIT Press.

Gotman, Kélina (2022): Theories of Performance: Critical and Primary Sources (4 Volumes). London and New York: Bloomsbury Academic.

Gugutzer, Robert (ed.) (2015): body turn: Perspektiven der Soziologie des Körpers und des Sports. Bielefeld: transcript.

Hahn, Daniela, Isa **Wortelkamp** et al. (eds.) (2019): Expanded Writing. Inscriptions of Movement between Art and Science / Expanded Writing. Bewegung (ein)schreiben zwischen Kunst und Wissenschaft. Berlin: Revolver Publishing.

Hahn, Tomie (2007): Sensational Knowledge. Embodying culture through Japanese dance. Middletown: Wesleyan University Press.

Hamilton, Carolin, Verne **Harris**, Jane **Taylor** et al. (eds.) (2002): Refiguring the Archive. Cambridge: Cambridge University Press.

Jeschke, Claudia (2023): Gedächtnistransfers, Spurensuchen – und Nijinsky. In: Tanz&Archiv, ForschungsReisen, nr 10, Tanz schreiben: Artefakte, Hypertexte – und Nijinsky. München: epodium 2023, pp. 56–90.

Lepecki, André (2010): The Body as Archive: Will to Re-Enact and the Afterlives of Dances. In Dance Research Journal 42 (2010) no. 2, pp. 24–48.

Lepecki, André (ed.) (2016): Singularities. Dance in the Age of Performance. London and New York: Routledge.

Lumsden, Karen, Jan **Bradford** and Jackie **Goode** (2019): Reflexivity: Theory, Method, and Practice. London: Routledge.

Marshall, Daniel and Zeb **Tortorici** (eds.) (2022): Archival Turning. The Life of the Historical in Queer Studies. Durham NC: Duke University Press.

Mersch, Dieter (2002): Ereignis und Aura. Untersuchungen zu einer Ästhetik des Performativen. Frankfurt a. M.: Suhrkamp.

Moore, Niamh, Andrea Salter, Liz Stanley und Maria Tamboukou (2016): The Archive Project. Archival Research in the Social Sciences. London: Routledge.

Ortmann, Lucie (2017): Artistic Processes of Archiving in Contemporary Dance. Tokyo/Singapore: Archive Box Project (2013-2016). In: MAP #8, Transformieren, Reinszenieren., 2017, *perfomap.de/map8/archiv.-geschichten-2013- re-inszenierung-und-praesentation/artistic-processes-of-archiving-in-contemporary-dance* (14/11/2023).

Palladini, Giulia and Marco **Pustianaz** (eds.) (2017): Lexicon for an Affective Archive. Bristol: intellect 2017.

Rorty, Richard (ed.) (1967): The Linguistic Turn: Recent Essays in Philosophical Method. Chicago and London: The University of Chicago Press.

Warf, Barney and Santa **Arias** (eds.) (2009): The Spatial Turn: Interdisciplinary Perspectives. London: Routledge.

Wehren, Julia (2016): Körper als Archiv in Bewegung. Choreografie als historiografische Praxis. Bielefeld: transcript, DOI: 10.14361/9783839430002.

Yamomo, meLê (2019): Theatre and Music in Manila and the Asia Pacific, 1869—1946. Sounding Modernities. Cham: Palgrave Macmillan.

Writing
Choreo
Practic

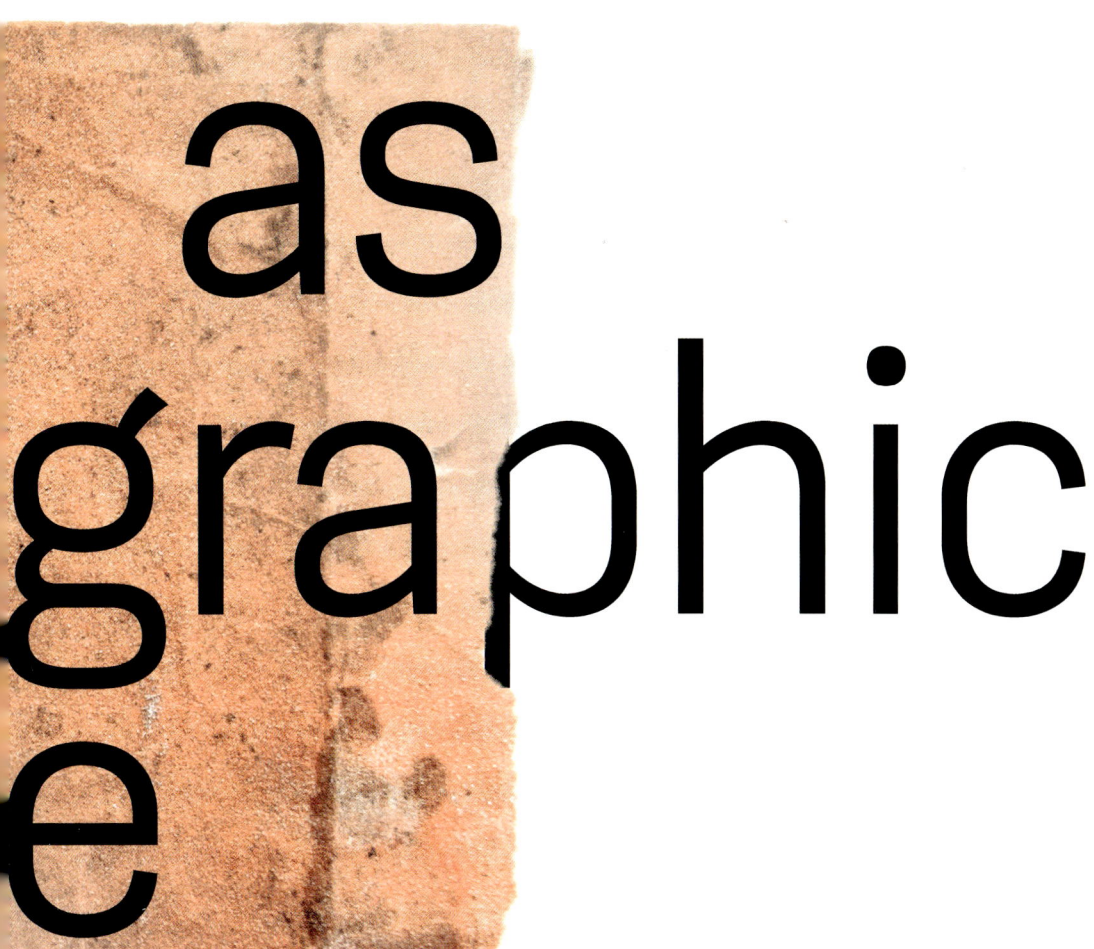

as
graphic
egge

Scribbling Towards Something: Interv[iew with] the Written in Da[rk] Jonathan Bur[...]

GABRIELE KLEIN & FRANZ ANTON CRAMER
What role do written records play in the development of your artistic work?

JONATHAN BURROWS Writing is always present as part of my daily practice, but I wouldn't describe the things I write as a 'record'. The nature of practice for me is that it's an unfolding process which accumulates and alters constantly in relation to whatever's going on for you, and within your changing context and environment. To try and capture that process in the form of a 'record' can risk disrupting the happy accidents that happen as things unfold. You might start to think you know what you're doing and then suddenly you're no longer doing it. So, for instance, when you're choreographing you sometimes arrive somewhere and it seems to make sense, but you've lost track of how you got there and somehow you needed to lose track in order to get there. I mean you write stuff down, but it's often a mess and it needs to be a mess.

Recently I tidied away 30 years of notebooks into a loft, and looking through them I mostly had no idea what any of the writing meant. It was all very specific to a particular period of questions and worries and possibilities from a moment that had passed. I wonder if other artists have had a similar experience and felt maybe liberated in the way I did. All that furious writing, but it turned out the real purpose of it was only to observe thoughts as they went by and then to let them fade into pointlessness. That was what I enjoyed about the "Material Goods" conference[1], that it focussed on the nature of the written as a form of graphic thinking and doing. The sense of scribbling your way towards something, and the recognition of the importance of the relationship between the sequenced activity of the writing hand and the way human beings map themselves into and through their imaginative landscape.

You have been working with composer Matteo Fargion for many years. What role do written records play in your collaboration?

Matteo Fargion and I have used scores in our performances for many years and the scores are visible onstage, so people tend to assume they represent a fixed record of the work. It's true that our scores don't change from one performance to the next, but the function of the scores is always and only to shape the performance

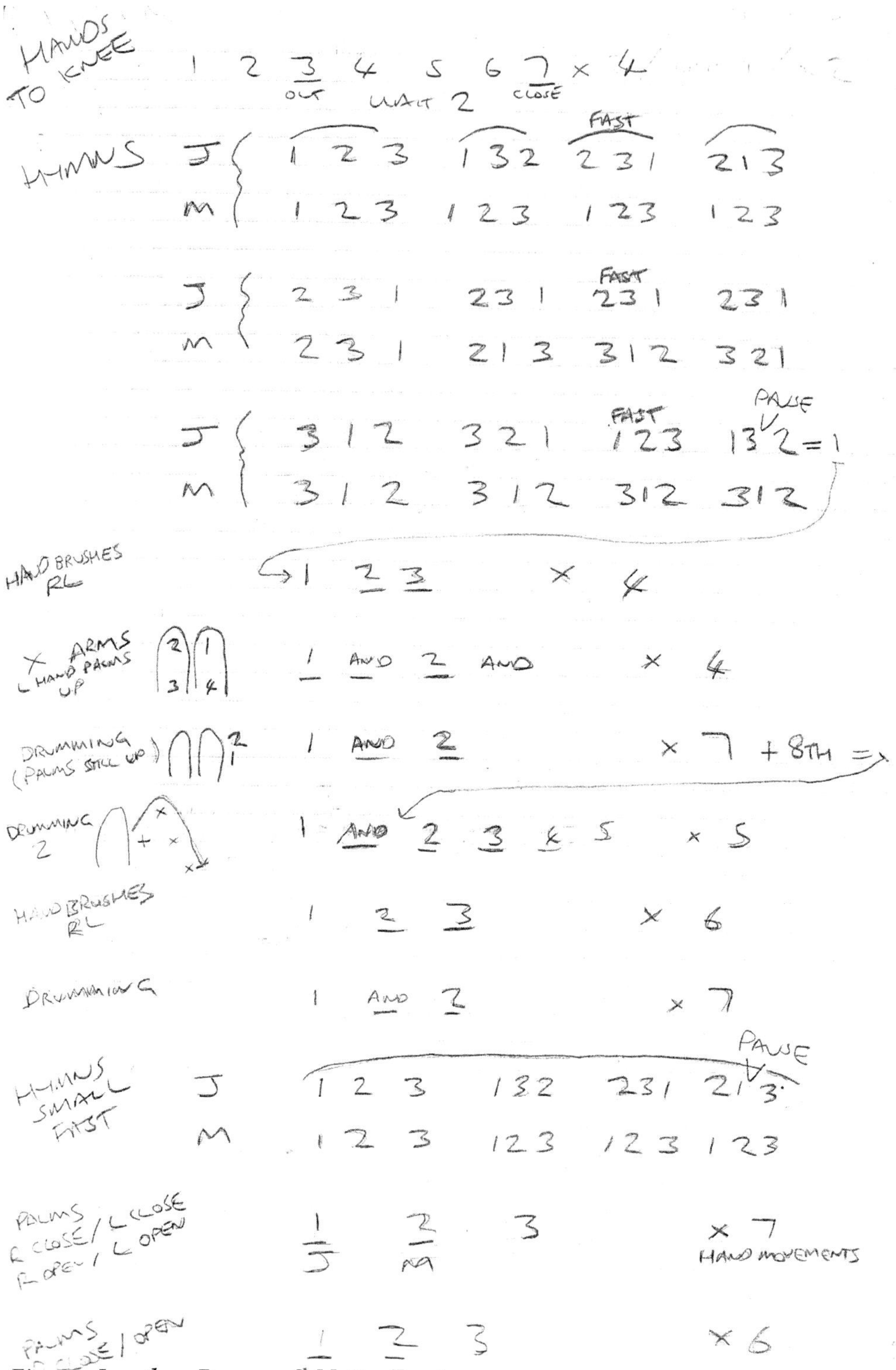

Fig. 1 — Jonathan Burrows & Matteo Fargion:
Parallel Scores for Both Sitting Duet, *2002*

HYMNS (SEPARATE:)

FAST
3|1 2 3   1 2 3   1 2 3   1 2 3
2 3 1 . 2 1 3   3 1 2   3 2 1
                FAST
3 1 2   3 1 2   3 1 2   3 1 2→

SMALL PETALS ×4   CROSS ×4   DRUM ×7   ×5   PETALS ×6
[:3/8 ♩♩ 4 :]   [:2/8 ♩♩ :]   [:4 7 :]   [4/8 7 E]   [:3/8 4 ♩ ♩:]

DRUM ×7   SMALL HYMNS
[:2/8 4 ♩♩ :]   FAST   1 2 3   1 2 3   1 2 3   1 2→

OPEN/CLOSE HAND ×7   R.H ×6
[3/8 7 ♩]   close open
R, L, R, L, R, L, R   [: 4 ♩♩ :]

BAMPTON   ×5   ×8   ×3   ×4
[:6/8 ♩ ♩ ♩ ♩ :]   [:3/8 ♩ 7 :]   [:6/8 ♩ ♩ ♩ ♩ :]   [:3/8 ♩ 7 :]

THIGH STROKE ×3   TAP   ×4
[:8/8 o :] |6/8 d.| |8/8 o| [:12/8 ξ ♩ ξ 3. 3. :] |24/4 – o|

SURRENDER
[:6/8 ♩ :] |5/8 d 4| |10/8 3 o| |8/8 o| [:5/8 ♩ 4. :] ×2

ROCKING ×5 WAIT 6   ×3 |16/8 – |

in a way that opens new possibilities. That's why we keep on performing the work over many years because it never quite arrives. There's always something that seems to be about to make sense in the gap between the written score and what we're doing.

Do you have your favourite writing materials? And if so, why do you prefer certain materials over others? (particular notebook, particular pen etc.)

When I was tidying my notebooks away I noticed all the different kinds of book I'd used over the years. There would be a long series of one particular make of notebook and then suddenly a mess of styles and sizes, from expensive hardbacks to very cheap notebooks, as though I'd bought the first thing I could find. With the expensive ones, it's like I was trying to make my practice more serious and consequential, and with the cheap ones it's as though I was searching for a more spontaneous and disposable way of doing things.

The notebooks also showed a constant alternation between things written in pencil which could be neatly rubbed out, or careless scribbling with a pen. I notice now perhaps that the careless approach is becoming more prominent as I get older because in the end, I guess you start to realise nobody will ever look at all your pointless scribbles and if they did they wouldn't understand them either. I think for me then, it's become more about physically doing the writing than about what it records for the future.

What practices do you have when you take written notes? Do you use notes for preparation or for follow-up to rehearsals, for example?

I'd say that my only practice in relation to rehearsal or performance notes is to frame the notes as questions and then to shut the book and forget the questions. Somehow the act of writing the questions plants a seed that does its work anyway and does it better when I don't try too hard to apply them.

What is the nature of your written records? Are these sketches, ideas, reflections, for example?

Every now and again I do a lot of drawing because I enjoy the connection between drawing and moving as a dancer and the way they both feel like non-languaged forms of writing. I also write lists of questions or observations as an occasional daily practice. These processes usually tail out fairly quickly, but they feed into what I'm doing and I pick them up again every so often. In terms of the relationship between writing and other aspects of practice, I more and more make no distinction between any of the kinds of stuff I do. I treat it equally and of equal importance. I'm inclined to follow a process of doing whatever I feel able to do next, for however long or short, without trying to make any obvious connection between the different things. So I might answer an email, rehearse some music, work on a new piece, edit an article, improvise a bit in my living room, think about teaching, play the harmonica and then maybe write some stuff in a notebook, and it all seems like a form of thinking by doing, which all feels like writing. None of it has much to do with performing, it's more like a way to wake myself up.

How do the writing tools you use influence your creative process?

I use different tools and ways to get into working and it's hard to say which of the actual physical objects I use directly influences what I'm doing. I mean by the time any influence has taken effect I've often forgotten where it came from. From my point of view, it would be more accurate to say that all the ways you work affect and become your creative process whatever they are, even if you don't know you're being creative, or even that you're working. Having said that I do get pleasure from the feel of some of the things I use, like a nice biro or the cat pencil case my daughter bought me, so that sensual information must be offering something.

Dance and music have a different history from written records or notations. What are the differences between writing, notating and drawing – as a choreographer/dancer or composer/musician?

I guess because I work with Matteo, a classical music composer, I have the reassurance that at some point while we're working the kind of clarity that comes from musical notation might also play a part and be helpful. It allows me to be the messy one, and if we're lucky our two parallel approaches keep things alive. In my own notes, I do borrow musical devices occasionally, or sometimes arrows and circles from Benesh Dance Notation, but mostly I just write names for movements in longhand as a way to remember

*Fig. 2 —
Jonathan
Burrows:
Notebook
Drawings,
1995*

them. Matteo and I have an unwritten principle that it's useful to leave things undiscussed, so the other person has room to do what they need to do in their own way. It doesn't particularly matter that the music he writes has the clarity of a formal notation whereas I'm messier and less efficient because both approaches coexist and information is passing accidentally all the time anyway. When we teach workshops we have to explain and analyse how we work, which makes it look like we're busy all the time explaining and analysing, but we did all that 30 years ago and now we just work and it's not necessarily clear where the boundaries are.

You have made pieces in which you use written documents, for instance *Both Sitting Duet* (first performed in 2002) and *Rewriting* (first performed in 2021). How relevant are these documents to the performance and to the aesthetics of the piece?

That's an interesting question and my first response is that there is a great pleasure in the way the score of *Both Sitting Duet* has become older as I got older. I like that the second page is no longer attached to the notebook. Maybe this awareness of the wearing out of the score has a certain aesthetic quality. But for me, the most important thing is the way it functions as a re-presentation of ongoing work towards the performance, not just in the six months it took to make it, but through the hundreds of performances we've done since then in all sorts of different spaces and contexts. All these spaces are somehow present as material traces or history in the worn-out paper. There are footprints on pages of my book and they're familiar when I see them. They remind me of coming back onto the stage at the end of a particular performance and running accidentally across the book as I passed. You might think of a score as a formal thing, but it feels personal. There's a lot of memory there.

Matteo's and your notebooks on the piece are different. Do you have individual recording procedures? Can Matteo read your records and can you read his?

I've recently started playing more live music, and although it's mostly folk tunes learned by ear, nevertheless the experience has slightly changed how I relate to how Matteo writes music. At the same time, I've become more alert to the extraordinary facility human beings have to memorise sequences of movement, which is something that happens all the time whether you're aware of it or not. So, I'm also increasingly trustful of my own brain and body as its own notation system. The ways Matteo and I work are different because I can't always read his music and he can't easily memorise movement, but we both do both and both are useful at different times.

Does the orientation on the written notes allow for improvisation?

The parameters for improvisation in the work tend to be based on the idea that Matteo and I can change whatever we're doing at any moment if we want to, so long as the other person knows we're changing. The changes usually have to do with timing, space or dynamics rather than order of events, but they can dramatically alter the sense of the moment. The important thing is that it's not about tricking the other person or the audience, it's more like tuning in to what's going on in the room and then intuitively allowing something else to happen that potentially was already happening in everyone's imagination. The audience for our work often divides into those who wonder why we're not improvising and those who think we are. At some level, we are improvising, but we're also following a score which gives us clues on what to do, so we can do it with a certain degree of freedom. That sounds paradoxical and the approach doesn't work for everyone, but it works for us so we do it. It's not really an aesthetic choice, it's just a meeting of our relative skills and backgrounds in ballet and classical music.

When you performed in Hamburg[2] the audience could look at your notebooks after the show. Why is this important to you?

It was very important from the beginning that reading the scores onstage didn't become a private element that excluded the audience, so we started inviting people to come onstage afterwards to look at the scores. This has grown now into a general sense that it's ok to walk onstage, and we often don't invite people anymore, they just come. For me that's the most exciting part of the performance, not because it breaks the fourth wall of the theatre, but because this moment of looking and talking together allows the performance to resonate between the performers and the audience in a different and interesting way. It's not about being democratic, it's just about recognising that the performance can't exist without the active presence and permission of the audience.

What do you archive from your collaborative pieces?

It's difficult to know what to archive really. I used to file away the advertising from every performance we did, and then one day while moving house I just dumped it in a bin. It was such a relief. For many years we regretted that we'd never photographed all the chairs we've sat on to perform *Both Sitting Duet,* but who would want to look at hundreds of photographs of chairs? That would just be a vanity project, as though every performance needed to be documented, rather than fading into oblivion. Our archiving consists now of looking after and sharing the scores and trying to keep and make available a reasonable video of each piece. I don't know if this counts as archive because it's just the bare bones, but I prefer it that way.

Here are four issues concerning the use of writing. Are they relevant to you?

1 **Writing as designing/modelling/sketching**

My experience is that when you watch a dance performance there's a layer of automatic languaged response which tips towards very obvious narrative interpretation of what's happening in front of you, and I think there's an echo of that voice in the way I write notes about my choreographic processes. I try to be careful not to let that narrative voice oversimplify what's going on, but at the same time sometimes the acceptance of obvious images is useful. It's part of the way we name the world as we move through it.

2 **Writing as a process of change**

The process of writing notes is sometimes about reflecting on what's already occurred and sometimes about looking for something new that might be added in the future. These two things tend to blur together. So, thinking about what's already happened seems to provoke possibilities for what might happen next.

3 **Writing as individual and/or collaborative practice**

I'm increasingly interested in co-teaching and co-writing, but only if everyone feels able to follow their own path within the collaboration. This reflects the way Matteo and I work. We try to resist the idea of a 'good' collaboration and look instead for ways to do things in parallel that leave each of us to our own devices and without too much distracting discussion.

4 Writing as memory stored externally

Even the most rigorously written score is meaningless without the performers who've embodied and are living that score, and it's the same with written materials. The best you can do with notes is to try and find a language that might provoke the memory of a quality, but it's a very blunt tool. I tend to use the same descriptive words over and over again, and each time I use them they subtly change. Or sometimes it's not a word at all, but rather the memory of a particular atmosphere. I go back often to an experience I had one evening when I was about 26 and I walked into an empty pub in the East End of London, and I leant on the bar and ordered a pint of beer. That was it, nothing happened, but there was a particular atmosphere that seemed to matter – and it still seems to matter. I've been in a lot of pubs since, but it's that one evening that holds the key. Having said that I've never written it down before so it'll be interesting to see what happens now.

Fig. 3 — Jonathan Burrows: Notebook Drawings, 1996

ACKNOWLEDGEMENT

The editors sent the questions to Jonathan Burrows at the end of February 2023 and he sent his answers, as arranged, by email in May 2023.

---

1. Jonathan Burrows and Matteo Fargion were invited to hold a four-day workshop titled "This Then That" as part of the conference event "Material Goods" in Hamburg. They were also part of the panel "Writing Practices in Performance Art", bringing together Jonathan Burrows, Matteo Fargion, Axel Malik and Ursina Tossi on Saturday, 4 February 2023, in the K2 venue at Kampnagel, Hamburg.

2. Jonathan Burrows and Matteo Fargion presented the double programme *Rewriting* and *Both Sitting Duet* at Kampnagel in Hamburg in the context of the festival "Material Goods".

What Dance Teaches Us about Reading: Four Events and an Interlude

Lou Forster

Document 1 — Simone Forti in Readers *(2017) by James Benning. Courtesy of the artist and neugerriemschneider, Berlin.*

"People declare as much, without, apparently, looking into the matter very closely. They seem able to dispense with the conscientious observer's scruples when inflating their bladder of theory."
Jean-Henri Fabre, *The Life of the Spider,* 1912

This quote from the naturalist and entomologist Jean-Henri Fabre (1823–1915) concludes James Benning's film *Readers* (2017) – four portraits of people reading, filmed in static shots and lasting around twenty-five minutes each. Set in their homes, Clara McHale-Ribot, a film student at CalArts, writer Rachel Kushner, sociologist Richard Hebdige and choreographer Simone Forti, engage in this daily and familiar activity, which the reader of these lines is performing in this very moment. The artist invites us to observe carefully these four scenes that are striking in their similarity: the readers assume a comfortable posture, focus their attention on the page and absorb themselves in it for several minutes until a numb limb, a page to turn, a noise or a thought prompts them to change position; then, impassively, silently and invariably, they resume their reading. Neither the books they read, which are quoted at the end of each sequence, nor the age or gender of the readers affect this activity. They share what Erving Goffman calls a "frame" – a common activity that appears remarkably stable here.[1] The readers portrayed by James Benning combine the same features – absorption, impassivity, immobility and silence – which were already present in Jean-Honoré Fragonard's painting *La Liseuse* (1770) almost 250 years earlier. They constitute the canonical representation of this form of silent and solitary reading, which acquired its modern characteristics during the eighteenth century.[2]

However, for a long time, this socially and historically situated form of reading was considered universal. While it is easy to understand that cooking, eating, playing, learning, healing or dancing can vary depending on cultures and contexts, reading, due to its prominent role as a vehicle and provider of knowledge in Western modernity, has long remained outside the scope of sociological, anthropological or historical survey. It was only in the early 1980s that various human sciences, whether it be the history of reading or what I would refer to, for the sake of clarity, as new literacy studies, shed light on reading's great diversity[3]. In 1982, the sociologist Shirley Brice Heath proposed in her seminal article "What No Bedtime Story Means: Narrative Skill at Home and School" to analyse "literacy events", these "occasions in which written language is integral to the nature of participants' interactions and their interpretive processes and strategies" (Brice Heath 1982: 50). These everyday events provide a flexible analytical frame analysis that allows the sociologist to compile a repertoire of situations that enrich the representations of this activity[4]. In doing so, she extracts reading from the abstract universalism that still characterised works on reading by the anthropologist Jack Goody in the late 1970s[5]. By describing reading as a practice embodied in gestures, spaces and habits, new literacy studies highlight the fact that there are different ways of reading and writing.

Reading within the field of dance suffers from an even stronger lack of understanding and visibility. Dance literacy as developed in Europe during the eighteenth century under the name of *chorégraphie* was abandoned a century later for complex historical reasons. The literacy event where a dancer deciphers, learns and then embodies a dance with a book in their hand before setting it aside and performing, has been forgotten, despite the diverse movement notation systems that have marked the history of this discipline since then[6]. The idea that this art by nature cannot be written and that dancers are illiterate, became firmly entrenched in the nineteenth century when the dominating figure of the dance world shifted from the choreographer or dance master to the ballerina.[7] Furthermore, all the related dance practices in which graphic artefacts play a significant role in teaching, rehearsing or performing have been rendered invisible.

The purpose of this article is to describe four literacy dance events – everyday or exceptional situations in which graphic artefacts play a decisive role in learning, embodying or performing a dance. I would like to demonstrate the significance of graphic artefacts in a discipline that is still largely perceived as lacking in written form. Moreover, by focusing on literacy events rather than texts, I want to highlight the importance for dance scholars to examine the materiality and pragmatics of documents that keep the traces of gestures and situations in which they have been used. They contribute to establishing a historical and cultural anthropology of dance through its reading practices. Lastly, by describing these different forms of reading, I aim to demonstrate how reading practices in dance have the potential to transform the representations of literacy in general, whose political, cultural and social significance goes beyond mere technical skill.

Document 2 – Class of Kinetography Laban at the Dansacademie (Rotterdam), 1970. Photograph by Cock Tholens. Médiathèque du Centre national de la danse – Albrecht Knust Papers – Donation Roderyk Lange, courtesy Lieneke de Boer

First literacy event: embodied reading

ROTTERDAM, 1970. In the studio of the *Dansacademie*, seven dancers read and dance. In their hands they hold a few pages that contain a dance transcribed in the system of movement analysis developed from 1928 by the Austro-Hungarian choreographer Rudolph Laban (1879–1958) and his collaborators. The teaching of the Kinetography Laban or Labanotation spread over the following decades, becoming one of the most widely used contemporary literate dance techniques. Photographer Cock Tholens captured an ordinary teaching situation where the dancers decipher and perform the same score in a dance studio. In the background, their teacher, Belgian Léa Dann (1906–1995), points out a detail that one of the dancers overlooked. This ordinary image selected by the photographer and preserved by Albrecht Knust (1896–1978), one of the inventors of this system, exemplifies the effectiveness of this notation that renders the complexity of movement, as evidenced by each dancer.

Similar photographic documents of literacy events can be found in various archival collections of choreographers, dancers, teachers and movement notators. In all of these images, Kinetography Laban appears not only as a form of writing (a system of signs organised by syntax) or as a technical skill but rather as an atypical teaching situation where each performer deciphers and memorises a dance individually. Focused on their scores, they dance both alone and with others, isolated yet inherently connected to their peers. The enigmatic nature of Cock Tholens's photograph lies in this elusive connection, contrasting with the conventional image of a dance class where all eyes are on the teacher demonstrating the dance. Here, the teacher is no longer a prominent figure; almost invisible in the image, she appears as the one who guides the dancers in their reading dancing. With her back turned, her face towards the page, Léa Dann has already almost vanished.

The embodiment of movement in these reading situations follows a path that Cock Tholens's image captures only as a snapshot. The reader progresses in two distinct directions. First, they focus on the centre of the staff, reading the page vertically from bottom to top to understand the evolution of weight transfers over time. Then, the reader progresses from the centre outward to coordinate movements of leg, back, arm and head, moving from the proximal (centre of the body) to the distal (extremities). Thus, the coordination, rhythm and flow of movement are gradually rediscovered by the dancer through the analytical decomposition that enabled its writing[8].

However, Tholens's photograph depicts an atypical dance situation: all the dancers know how to read. More often, rehearsals involving this notation have only a limited number of readers. They revolve around one or more specialists in writing, referred to from the 1950s onwards as movement notators[9]. These specialists translate their interpretation of the score to the dancers by demonstrating or explaining the movements they have previously embodied. In modern societies where literacy has become widespread since the late eighteenth century, this situation is atypical, constituting one of the cultural peculiarities of dance, where individuals who are neither the authors nor the performers play a prominent role in passing on choreographic works.

Within the field of dance, the role of these writing specialists has sparked intense controversies. Simon Hecquet and Sabine Prokhoris have described them as translators to highlight the essential role of transcribing a dance onto paper and incorporating it from a score (Hecquet and Prokhoris 2007). They oppose the technical approach to literacy promoted in the 1950s by Ann Hutchinson Guest (1918–2022) and the *Dance Notation Bureau,* which envisioned notators as mere stenographers[10]. While the term "translator" is slowly gaining acceptance in the field of dance, the understanding of Kinetography Laban has already evolved in relation to a poetics and politics of transmission and dissemination of choreographic works[11].

However, it seems to me that the concept of translation sidesteps the two essential issues raised by the social and cultural representation of reading practice. If the appropriate term, namely "literate dancer," does not correspond to the embodied approach of reading and writing proposed by Kinetography, it is primarily because this practice carries a conception of reading that is the opposite of the impassive, immobile and silent body with which reading has been associated in modernity. When Laban develops *Schrifttanz* in 1928, literally a "dance of script", he promotes an embodied approach to reading where the score (script) induces the reader into movement. For him, Kinetography and modern dance serve as a lever to transform the culture of writing in general. Developed within the context of the body culture *(Körperkultur)* – a cultural movement that encompasses both dance and gymnastics, as well as bodybuilding, nudism, and vegetarianism, advocating for a more direct relationship with nature – Kinetography aims to reform education through the formative dimension (Bildung) of reading dancing. Kinetography proposes to envision any kind of reading as a form of movement. However, this modernist programme championed by expressive dance *(Ausdruckstanz)* became unacceptable from 1933, when Laban and part of German modern dance compromised with Nazism[12]. Therefore, it is difficult to restore the cultural and social significance of *Schrifttanz* without considering its relation to the culture of writing it intended to transform. Dance literacy can only be recognised by transforming our general representation of reading and writing.

        Furthermore, the very term "literate dancer" establishes a division between performers who can read and those who are considered "illiterate". However, while most dancers do not possess this specific literate skill, they commonly engage in a plurality of writing practices. Dance studios and theatres are filled with a variety of graphic artefacts used by dancers and choreographers in their creative processes.

Document 3 — Rehearsal of Parts of Some Sextets *by Yvonne Rainer, New York, 1965. Photograph: Al Giese. Courtesy of the Getty Research Institute (ID no. 2006.M.24)*

Second literacy event: distributed cognition

NEW YORK, 1965. The eleven performers[13] of *Parts of Some Sextets* are rehearsing in the studio of choreographer Yvonne Rainer. In the foreground, Robert Morris (1931–2018) gathers information from a 2.20-meter-long sheet of paper posted on the wall[14]. It is a double-entry chart that indicates, for each performer designated by their initials, the choreographic materials (on the vertical axis) in relation to time (on the horizontal axis). In the photograph, Morris uses his finger to locate the next material he will perform, while behind him, four dancers engage in activities corresponding to that specific moment in the piece. Unlike the previous literacy event, Morris does not decipher the movement he is about to perform. Rainer created the 31 dance materials of *Parts of Some Sextets* in collaboration with the performers during rehearsals. They are designated on the chart using familiar terms such as "Looking Figure", "Bird Run" or "Bend Walk". The reading does not directly induce movement as *Schrifttanz* would. Instead, performers navigate the dramaturgical structure of the piece using this synoptic view. The literacy event that takes place during the last rehearsals of *Parts of Some Sextets* can be described as a technical gesture – extracting information to understand the order and timing of upcoming activities.

The document posted on the wall is one element of a broader technical apparatus that enables Rainer to organise the action of the dancers on stage. The duration of the piece is divided into 30-second intervals, a temporal module that is reflected in the chart. During the performance, the dancers use sentences from a text recorded on magnetic tape and played live as cues. Following this track, they can meticulously adhere to the 30-second intervals formalised by Rainer on paper[15]. In the final weeks of rehearsals, the performers also wrote their own notes based on the master displayed on the wall, summarising their individual scores. For example, Robert Rauschenberg gathered on three columns his dance activities, the number provided by the chart, and the cues from the recording. This note operates as an interface between the chart and the sound recording, allowing the performer to memorise his role[16]. Ultimately, during the performance, the entire action of *Parts of Some Sextets* took place on sight. The performers no longer referred to the chart, and the stage activities were perfectly coordinated without the audience being able to grasp the underlying mechanisms.

The cognitive artefacts of the piece, including chart, sound recording, performer's notes and memory, constituted a network. During the shows, human and non-human agents acted together. Critics compared the piece to an elusive, relentless and cold mechanism[17]. While Laban and his collaborators aim to emancipate dancers from their masters, Yvonne Rainer uses written artefacts to implement a system that dissociates the organicity of the dance activities from an indiscriminate temporal structure. The dances that are divided into 30-second modules are constantly interrupted. The distinct temporality of the performative material and the dramaturgy maintain a dialectic at the heart of the piece that enacts how the media, particularly television, depicts reality while simultaneously creating a division between it and what it represents[18].

The literacy event depicted by Al Giese's photograph is not unique to the field of dance. Sociologists and anthropologists have described situations in which reading operates in a similar manner on film sets, airplane or boat cabins, archaeological excavation sites, scientific laboratories or administrative departments of a city[19]. This research highlights what Edwin Hutchins describes as "socially distributed cognition", situations in which artefacts and individuals constitute a system that enables them to act upon their environment. In *Parts of Some Sextets,* Yvonne Rainer devised such a system to simultaneously represent its pernicious effects on human activities.

Document 4 – Performance of Both Sitting Duet *(2002) by Jonathan Burrows at the Kaaitheater (Brussels) in 2002. Four video stills. Video: Florian Jenett*

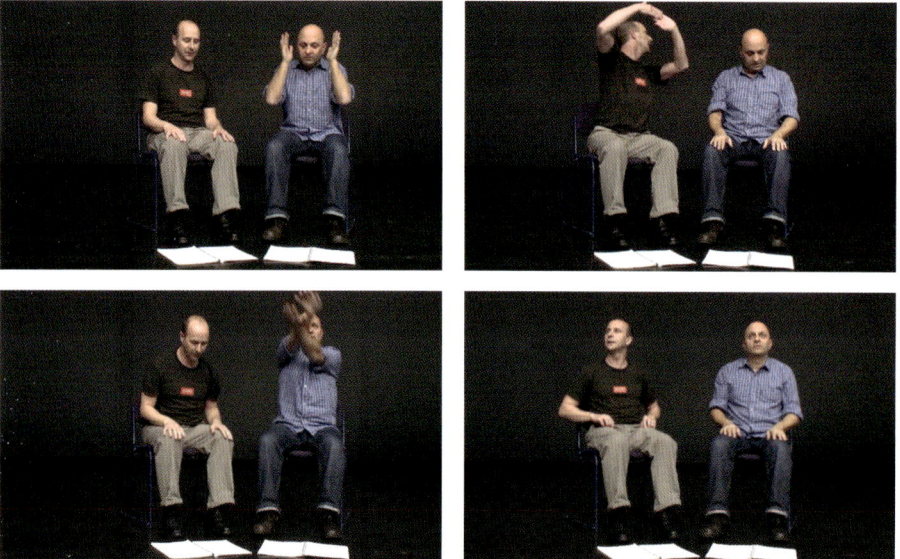

Third literacy event: attentional exercise

BRUSSELS, 2002. At the Kaaitheater, choreographer Jonathan Burrows and composer Matteo Fargion performed *Both Sitting Duet*. The performers remained seated during this 35-minute duet relying on the virtuosity of the upper body, particularly the arms and hands. The piece is a literal transposition, note by note and measure by measure, of Morton Feldman's composition for violin and piano, *For John Cage* (1984), in which sounds are substituted by gesture. During the performance, two spiral notebooks were placed on the floor. Matteo Fargion's score incorporated elements of musical notation (notes and chord notation), counts and textual instructions for gestures, while Jonathan Burrows only used counts to indicate the rhythm. The choreographer also added diagrams to specify the different areas of the laps with which his hands made contact. Although *Both Sitting Duet* didn't adopt Western solfeggio, the piece transposed the recital of classical music and the literacy event that constitutes one of its determining elements into the realm of dance. Matteo Fargion and Jonathan Burrows read and dance – these two actions being performed simultaneously or alternately. The scores serve as tools that facilitate the real-time execution of a rhythmically demanding composition[20]. They support a form of gesturing that is at once frank, eloquent and precise.

The literacy event performed in *Both Sitting Duet* has an ambivalent value in dance literacy. The promoters of Labanotation and other systems of recording movement looked at Western classical music as a model for dancers who may decipher their scores autonomously as musicians do. However, the classical music concert also represented for these same artists, the epitome of restricted bodies – performers sitting in front of their music stands, confined in their tuxedos or long dresses, compelled to subserviently read a score. This stilted situation was a repellent image for proponents of modern dance who advocated for *Schrifttanz* that would emancipate the reader through movement. *Both Sitting Duet* does not adopt this modernist stance. Jonathan Burrows doesn't choreograph the seated posture as a form of subjugation, as in the modern pieces ranging from *Lamentation* (1930) by Martha Graham, through *Rooms* (1955) by Anna Sokolow, or *Rosas danst Rosas* (1983) by Anne Teresa De Keersmaeker – works in which bodies struggle for liberty. Instead, the seated posture appears as a simple constraint that allows to focus on the virtuosity of the upper body of two seemingly ordinary individuals, an everyday situation shared by all the bodies in the room. Revealing the unsuspected expressive richness of quotidian movements of arms and hands, Jonathan Burrows and Matteo Fargion adopt the irreverent attitude of the neo-avant-garde toward the emancipatory ideals of modern dance. In this regard, *Both Sitting Duet* reclaims the heritage of the so-called "postmodern dance" and its use of the seated posture as one of the emblems of the pedestrian in Steve Paxton's *Satisfyin' Lover* (1967), Yvonne Rainer's *Chair Pillow* (1969) or David Gordon's *Chair* (1974).

The musical work *For John Cage* by Morton Feldman (1926–1987) from which *Both Sitting Duet* is choreographed, also fits within this neo-avant-garde genealogy. In the early 1950s, John Cage (1912–1992) relied on the theatricality of the concert to break away from a modernist approach to composition. Following the famous *Untitled Event or Theatre Piece No.1* of 1952, considered the "first" happening, John Cage created several theatre pieces such as *Music Walk* (1958), in which musicians no longer simply played their instruments but moved from one sound source to another[21]. By staging the movement of the musicians, John Cage highlighted that "music is an excessive simplification of the [theatrical] situation" (Cage 1967:145). His pieces that "engaged both the eye and the ear" (Cage, Kirby and Schechner 1965:50), highlighted the limitations of the musical notation in organising the movement of musicians in space. The theatrical situation opened up musical composition to new practices of writing and reading, which were intensely discussed among members of the so-called New York School, including Morton Feldman. The concept of indeterminacy then referred to the possibility that a piece could be performed in substantially different ways, offering the performer a variety of unique possibilities to read and play the score[22]. Considering this historical reference, *Both Sitting Duet* could be described as an indeterminate interpretation of Morton Feldman's musical piece for violin and piano, emphasising the gesturing of the performers instead of the sound production of the instruments. This approach to the concert is shared by several choreographers and directors in the early 2000s, such as Xavier Le Roy in *Le Sacre du Printemps* (2007). However, Jonathan Burrows does not create a readymade from a concert situation, but rather focuses on the literacy event that lies at the heart of the concert, shifting the attention from sound to movement activities and theatricality. In this respect, the apparently exceptional reading situation staged in *Both Sitting Duet* is underpinned by a more general culture of reading and writing.

The literacy event of *Both Sitting Duet* reflects upon what constitutes a performance when it is organised through a prescribed choreography. In this piece, the score is literally placed in the middle of the stage, materialised by the two notebooks. During the rapid section, these artefacts focus performers' attention, while in between the parts of the musical work, their posture straightens and their gaze turns towards the audience. Relaxation follows concentration, the acknowledgement of the audience's co-presence replaces the intense absorption of the reading dancing; the public catches their breath, coughs, before refocusing together. In this respect, the literacy event modulates attention and dynamics. In the aphorisms collected in *A Choreographer's Handbook,* Jonathan Burrows emphasises how reading-dancing creates "a distraction from the self", a detachment from the situation of self-representation on stage and from oneself[23]. Reading becomes a way to exercise an attentional constraint, where the performer "only does what he is supposed to do, and [he] can't do any more than that" (Burrows 2010:104). Choreographers and performers achieve such a state of consciousness through various means, such as a counting complex rhythmic structure or rules of the game. These attentional exercises induce dancers to concentrate on the absent third party, which is choreography, materialised in *Both Sitting Duet* through the notebooks. The dynamic modulation at the core of Jonathan Burrows's piece exemplifies what psychologists describe as "joint attention" – the ability acquired by children from nine months old to shift from a dyadic situation focused on their parent (subject-object), to a triadic situation: observing or listening to what the parent observes, shows or looks at[24]. In *Both Sitting Duet,* the choreography appears as an attentional exercise where the audience watches two performers reading their notebooks that the audience cannot read. The written choreography appears as the third party that guides the group's and performers' joint exercise[25].

Document 5 — Performance of L'Innomée *(2003)*
by Myriam Gourfink at the Théâtre de l'Usine (Geneva) in 2008.
© Isabelle Meister, courtesy Myriam Gourfink

Fourth literacy event: choreography of reading

GENEVA, 2008. At the Théâtre de l'Usine, choreographer Myriam Gourfink performed the solo *L'Innomée* (2003), her first piece in which instructions are provided live to the dancer on stage. This literacy event in a performance situation encompasses many of the previous issues related to the modulation of attention in the piece of Borrow. Attention constitutes an important aspect of Myriam Gourfink's work; her pieces produce an extended temporality based on the organicity of movement, breath and music performed live by the composer Kasper T. Toeplitz. However, the scenography of *L'Innomée* reverses the installation of *Both Sitting Duet.* Throughout the performance, Myriam Gourfink shows her back to the audience and places the public in the position of reading the score.

Since 1999, Gourfink develops an idiosyncratic approach to Kinetography Laban. She studied this system of analysing movement with Jacqueline Challet-Haas (1934–2022). Instead of recording movement on paper, she uses the signs (Kinetograms) without adhering to their syntax to formalise instructions[26]. In *L'Innomée,* the score that the dancer discovers on stage is generated randomly. It provides indications regarding supports, body parts, paths, orientations and levels, while the duration and tempi are left to the discretion of the performer. Therefore, *L'Innomée* could be described as a form of structured improvisation in which the audience simultaneously discovers a dance and a score written in an alphabet they are unlikely to understand.

Throughout the piece, Gourfink moved in space, gradually shifting her gaze from one screen to another. The technical setup had been displayed to accommodate the different paths, orientations and levels of the dancer during the piece. Beyond the instructions themselves, the choreography of *L'Innomée* was structured by the reading posture, as the dancer never takes her eyes off the screens. She moves keeping her head fixed. Since the 1920s, numerous somatic practices have highlighted the significant role played by the neck and head in movement. For example, Frederick Alexander refers to this axis as the primary motor control (Alexander 1984 [1932]). It can be observed in the posture of an infant lying on his or her stomach with the head raised, a pattern also involved in daily activities of adults while transitioning from sitting to standing position. In *L'Innomée,* the literacy event structures the movement of the dancer based on this head-tail axis, which has been explored by Gourfink through the practice of Yoga[27]. In this respect, *L'Innomée* could be called the only choreography-of-reading among the four events described in this article since the reading posture serves as a support and motivation to the dance. However, Gourfink's piece also places the audience in a reading position. While the nature of the documents in this piece is exceptional, it is important to note that the exposed writing appears in a wide range of stage practices[28]. Surtitles, for example, placed above the stage frame constitute the most conventional form of text accompanying a performance. In the 1930s, Bertolt Brecht used placards (sign boards) as an integral element of his distancing effect, which subsequently influenced numerous theatre practices. Blackboards, flip charts and screens on which images or texts are projected, constitute another range of devices appearing in many lecture demonstrations supporting performers' activities. Finally, graphic artefacts are also posted or directly inscribed on the walls or on the floor of black boxes or constitute an element of stage sets. These varied examples attest to the considerable importance of exposed texts and images in performance. However, the written text of *L'Innomée* stands out in the sense that the audience cannot read it, only the dancer does, and the audience witnesses her reading. In this respect, for most of the spectators, the score does not fulfil a semantic function but a choreographic one. They assume the same posture and attitude as the performer who keeps her eyes fixed on the screens. *L'Innomée* creates a community or a group of readers who do not share the meaning produced by the choreographic score but rather the posture and attention induced by this activity.

In *L'Innomée,* reading is staged as a body technique. Beyond the various human written languages, literacy constitutes a technique that contributes to structure the posture and motor organisation of the human body. This thesis has been developed in the 1960s by the palæontologist André Leroi-Gourhan (1911–1986). In *Gesture and Speech,* he argues that the biological evolution of hominids, which allows bipedalism, is intrinsically linked to the development of technique as it frees the hands from locomotion[29]. This postural and functional change also transforms the face into an expressive organ that promotes the development of language. The emergence of graphic symbolism establishes new relationships between these two operative poles (hand–tools and face–language), which, according to the palæontologist, corresponds to the development of symbolic thought. Guided by the predominant role acquired by vision at the expense of smell, Homo sapiens developed two new functional pairs (face-reading and handwriting) that played a significant role in the cultural and technical evolution of humanity. Gourfink does not share this reference to palæontology. However, the way she choreographs reading engages the spectators of *L'Innomée* because their bodies and postures predispose them to reading. This activity no longer appears here as the mastery of a specific skill (reading and writing English or Labanotation), but as an organic and technical assemblage that articulates posture, muscle tone, focalization of vision and attention, which condition the very possibility of reading.

Conclusion

Through these four literacy events, I explore a set of interconnected issues involved with reading in dance. From movement analysis to coordinating actions on stage, from structuring an attentional situation to organising motor ability, reading emerges as a practice embodied in postures, gestures, spaces, habits and objects. The descriptions provided here intend to avoid dichotomies between subject and object, embodied and artificial memory, body learning and text learning that fuelled debates during the 1990s and 2000s[30]. These debates failed in shedding light on the challenges faced by dance practitioners in their daily work with graphic artefacts. The article aimed to capture the diversity and complexity of reading practices in choreography and dance and to understand what the art of dance can teach us about reading.

1. For further reading on the frame analysis refer to Goffman 1974.
2. The eighteenth-century witnesses what is often described as a reading revolution. On this matter refer to Chartier and Cavallo 2003 for further reading.
3. For an introduction to the new literacy studies, refer to Fraenkel and Mbodj-Pouye 2010.
4. The term "literacy event" is derived from the concept of "speech event" coined by linguist Dell Hymes (1927–2009). In the early 1960s, he sought to establish an "ethnography of speaking". Unlike Noam Chomsky, who describes the abilities of an "ideal speaker-listener", sociolinguistics advocates for the study of language within a context, based on the actual language use by social actors. Refer to Fraenkel 2018 for further reading.
5. *The Domestication of the Savage Mind* by Jack Goody serves as the reference upon which the new literacy studies are founded. Refer to Goody 1977 for further reading.
6. We can mention Arthur Saint-Léon's *sténochorégraphie* (1832) or Zorm's *grammar* (1887). The development of movement notation systems accelerated considerably during the 20th and 21st centuries. For further reading refer to Hutchinson Guest 1989.
7. For further reading on this historical change refer to Jarrasse 2018. For a conceptual approach of this question see Pouillaude 2009.
8. This methodology of reading a score was formalised as early as 1928 by Rudolf Laban in the journal *Schrifttanz* (Laban 1928).
9. In the 1940s, the American dance critic John Martin drew attention on this new figure of the dance world referred to as "scribes" (Martin 1940). The neologism "notator" or "professional notator" gradually gained prominence throughout the 1950s in various brochures published by the *Dance Notation Bureau*, the institution that developed the use of Labanotation in the United States.
10. Regarding this matter refer to Laemmli 2017 and Kraut 2016: 219–262 for further reading.
11. Regarding this matter refer to Launay 2017 and Klein 2020.

12 Regarding this matter refer to Baxmann 2000; Guilbert 2000; Locatelli 2019; Toepfer 1997.

13 Dancers are Lucinda Childs, Judith Dunn, Sally Gross, Deborah Hay, Tony Holder, Robert Morris, Steve Paxton, Yvonne Rainer, Robert Rauschenberg & Joseph Schlichter.

14 All the documents mentioned below are part of the archival collection of the Robert Rauschenberg Foundation. *Parts of Some Sextets* was recreated in 2019 in the frame of *Performa* (New York). For further reading on the piece refer to Rainer and Coates 2023.

15 The text in question is the *Diary of William Bentley, D.D.,* the journal of an Episcopal pastor from Salem (Massachusetts) written in the eighteenth century, which the choreographer reads in a monotonous voice. There is no meaningful connection between the dance and the recording (Rainer 1974: 55–63).

16 Robert Rauschenberg, however, replaces the metaphorical expressions with which Rainer refers to the dance material with imperative verbs. In the first sequence, "Sitting Figure" is replaced by "Sit"; "Looking figure" by "Look," and "Bird Run" by "Bend Walk". This rift reveals the different points of view of the choreographer and the performer, as well as the action that these documents enable them to perform – visualising the dramaturgy or memorising a role. The written artefacts create a form of ambiguity or language-game that allows for a shared, but not necessarily mutual, understanding of what they are collectively accomplishing.

17 *Parts of Some Sextets* created controversy due to this apparent coldness and systematicity. Refer to the review of Johnston 1965, for example.

18 For further discussion on this matter, refer to the analysis of the piece provided in Lambert-Beatty 2008: 75–126.

19 For further discussion on this matter, refer to Rot 2014; Hutchins 1995, 1996; Goodwin 1994, 2018; Latour and Woolgar 1979; Latour and Hermant 2006.

20 During rehearsals, Matteo Fargion and Jonathan Burrows worked with a metronome to meticulously adhere to the various tempos of the composition.

21 For further discussion on John Cage's theatre pieces refer to Fetterman 2010.

22 For further discussion on indeterminacy refer to Pritchett 1993: 105–110.

23 See also the interview with Jonathan Burrows in this volume. (Note by the editors)

24 For further discussion on joint attention refer to Lachaux 2011.

25 In his historical and sociological survey on attention, Yves Citton argues that joint attention counteracts the economy of attention implemented by capitalism since the 1920s to captivate consumers. For further reading refer to Citton 2017.

26 Myriam Gourfink's approach of Kinetography Laban could be compared with Motif Writing or Motif Description developed from the late 1960s onwards by Valerie Preston-Dunlop and Ann Hutchinson Guest to direct improvisations based on the signs and concepts of this system.

27 In the 2000s choreographers such as Maria Hassabi or Cindy van Acker explored similar postural mechanisms.

28 The concept of "exposed writing" is commonly used in epigraphy – the study of inscription. For further reading see Petrucci 1993.

29 For further discussion see Leroi-Gourhan 1993.

30 The relationship between live performance and the objects that mediate it has been discussed in the United States by Phelan 1993 and Auslander 1999; and in Europe by Pouillaude 2004 and Van Imschoot 2005. Hecquet and Prokhoris 2007 argued about the relations between the embodied memory of the dancers and the artificial memory of artefacts.

REFERENCES

Alexander, Frederick Matthias (1984 [1932]): The use of the self: its conscious direction in relation to diagnosis, functioning and the control of reaction. John Dewey (ed). Downey: Centerline Press.

Auslander, Philip (1999): Liveness: Performance in a Mediatized Culture. London & New York: Routledge.

Baxman, Inge (2000): Mythos: Gemeinschaft. Körper- und Tanzkulturen in der Moderne. Munich: Wilhelm Fink Verlag.

Brice Heath, Shirley (1982): What No Bedtime Story Means: Narrative Skills at Home and School. In: Language in Society 11(1), pp. 49–76.

Burrows, Jonathan (2010): A Choreographer's Handbook. London & New York: Routledge.

Cage, John (1967): A Year From Monday. Middletown: Wesleyan University Press.

Chartier, Roger and Gugliemo **Cavallo** (eds.) (2003 [1999]): A History of Reading in the West: Studies in Print Culture and the History of the Book. Amherst: University of Massachusetts Press.

Citton, Yves (2017 [2014]): The Ecology of Attention. New York: John Wiley & Sons.

Fabre, Jean-Henri (2009 [1912]): The Life of the Spider. Auckland: The Floating Press.

Fetterman, William (2010): John Cage's Theatre Pieces: Notations and Performances. London and New York: Routledge.

Frænkel, Béatrice and Aïssatou Mbodj-Pouye (eds.) (2010): New Literacy Studies, un courant majeur sur l'écrit (Langage et société 3 (133)). cairn.info/revue-langage-et-societe-2010-3.htm (26/12/2023).

Fraenkel, Béatrice (2018): La notion d'événement d'écriture. In: Communication & langage 3 (197), pp. 35–52. cairn.info/revue-communication-et-langages-2018-3-page-35.htm (23/07/2023).

Goffman, Erving (1974): Frame analysis: An essay on the organization of experience. London: Harper and Row.

Goodwin, Charles (1994): Professional Vision. In: American Anthropologist 96 (3), pp. 606–633.

Goodwin, Charles (2018): Co-Operative Action. Cambridge: Cambridge University Press.

Goody, Jack (1977): The Domestication of the Savage Mind. Cambridge: Cambridge University Press.

Guilbert, Laure (2011): Danser avec le IIIe Reich: les danseurs modernes sous le nazisme. Bruxelles: André Versaille éditeur.

Hecquet, Simon and Sabine **Prokhoris** (2007): Fabrique de la danse. Paris: Presses Universitaires de France.

Hutchins, Edwin (1995): How a Cockpit Remembers Its Speeds. In: Cognitive Science (19), pp. 265–288.

Hutchins, Edwin (1996): Cognition in the Wild. Cambridge: MIT Press.

Hutchinson Guest, Ann (1989): Choreo-graphics: A Comparison of Dance Notation Systems From the Fifteenth Century to the Present. New York: Gordon & Breach.

Jarrasse, Bénédicte (2018): Les Deux Corps de la danse. Imaginaires et représentations à l'âge romantique. Pantin: Centre national de la danse.

Johnston, Jill (1965): People and Mattresses. In: Marmalade Me. Hanover and London: Wesleyan University Press, pp. 51–53.

Kraut, Anthea (2016): Choreographing Copyright: Race, Gender, and Intellectual Property Rights in American Dance. Oxford: Oxford University Press.

Klein, Gabriele (2020): Pina Bausch's Dance Theater. Company, Artistic Practices and Reception. Bielefeld: transcript.

Laban, Rudolf (1928): Schrifttanz. Methodik, Orthographie, Erläuterung. Vienne: Universal Edition.

Lachaux, Jean-Philippe (2011): Le cerveau attentif: contrôle, maîtrise, lâcher-prise. Paris: Odile Jacob.

Laemmli, Whitney (2017): Paper Dancers: Art as Information in Twentieth-Century America. In: Information & Culture: A Journal of History 52(1), pp. 1–30.

Lambert-Beatty, Carrie (2008): Being Watched: Yvonne Rainer and the 1960's. Boston: MIT Press.

Latour, Bruno and Emilie **Hermant** (2006 [1998]): Paris: Invisible City. Paris: les empêcheurs de penser en rond and le Seuil.

Latour, Bruno and Steve **Woolgar** (1979): Laboratory Life: The Social Construction of Scientific Facts. Beverly Hills: Sage Publications.

Launay, Isabelle (2017): Poétiques et politiques des repertoires: les danses d'après. Pantin: Centre national de la danse.

Leroi-Gourhan, André (1993 [1964]): Gesture and Speech. Massachusetts and London: MIT Press.

Locatelli, Axelle (2019): Les chœurs de mouvements Laban: entre danses traditionnelles, gymnastique et expériences artistiques (Allemagne, 1923—1936). Étude à partir du fonds d'archives Albrecht Knust. Unpublished PhD dissertation, Paris: Université Paris VIII.

Martin, John (1940): The Dance: Scriveners; Notation Bureau Is Formed as National Center for Laban Script. In: The New York Times, 9 June 1940, p. 8.

Petrucci, Armando (1993 [1986]): Public Lettering: Script, Power, and Culture. Chicago: University of Chicago Press.

Phelan, Peggy (1993): Unmarked: The Politics of Performance. New York: Psychology Press.

Pouillaude, Frédéric (2004): D'une graphie qui ne dit rien. In: Poétique (137), pp. 99–123. *cairn.info/revue-poetique-2004-1-page-99.htm* (05/08/2023).

Pouillaude, Frédéric (2009): Le désœuvrement chorégraphique. Paris: Vrin.

Pouillaude, Frédéric (2017): Unworking Choreography: The Notion of the Work in Dance. Translated by Anna Pakes. New York: Oxford University Press 2017.

Pritchett, James (1993): The Music of John Cage. Cambridge: MIT Press.

Rainer, Yvonne (1974): Work 1961—1973. Halifax: The Press of the Nova Scotia College of Art and Design.

Rainer, Yvonne and Emily **Coates** (2023): Yvonne Rainer: Remembering a Dance. Parts of Some Sextets, 1965/2019. New York: Performa and Wadsworth Atheneum.

Rot, Gwenaëlle (2014): Noter pour ajuster. Le travail de la scripte sur un plateau de tournage. In: Sociologie du travail 56(1), pp. 16–39. *journals.openedition.org/sdt/4749* (05/08/2023).

Toepfer, Karl (1997): Empire of Ecstasy: Nudity and Movement in German Body Culture 1910—1935. Berkeley: University of California Press.

Van Imschoot, Myriam (2005): Rests in Pieces: On Scores, Notation and the Trace in Dance. In: Multitudes (21), pp. 107–116. *cairn.info/revue-multitudes-2005-2-page-107.htm* (08/09/2023).

Choreographic Wr
Material Practice
Artistic Productio
Gabriele Klein
Franz Anton Cra

Introduction Writing has been an important object of research in dance studies since the 1980s. So far, two lines of research have emerged: firstly, research on dance notations, and with it an approach that examines systems of symbolic or sign-like representations of steps, movement patterns, dance figures and spatial arrangements that were and are recorded on paper. These dance notations were first developed in Europe in the sixteenth century in court dance and have been modified and used many times since then (Jeschke 1983, 1999, 2010; Louppe 1993; Hutchinson-Guest 1998; Brandstetter 2010).

These kinds of dance notation have different meanings and functions: on the one hand, they aim to document movement elements or entire dances; they usually refer to an existing dance practice. On the other hand, especially in the French classical tradition, for example in the *Beauchamp Feuillet notation* (Feuillet 1979), writing practices were used in the (literal) sense of "scripting dance": the scripts should help to develop new characteristics of dance and to record movement sequences – as "choreo-graphy" – that were then performed by the dancers. These dance notations were pre-scriptions and as such normative. They were based on clear aesthetic and political intentions: They served to establish dance techniques and standardised movement figures as well as to represent a hierarchical order of power. In the performative act, this representation of social order was and is corporeally practised and habitualised.

The second line of research looks at the relationship between dance and writing from a literary studies perspective. This approach is based on metonymic ideas that identify analogies in the corporeal act of writing and dancing. Here, dance movement is seen as analogous to textual processes and thus understood as a process of meaning. Both writing and script are analysed as bodily practice (Hahn et al. 2019; Wortelkamp 2021). Writing and dancing are understood as ongoing signifying practices. In the tradition of Stéphane Mallarmé, the forms created by the body and as bodily practice are perceived as "écriture corporelle", as a writing in space by the moving body without, however, producing semantic meaning.[1] Whereas the more documentary or affective practice of writing on dance can be interpreted as an act of "performative writing" (Wortelkamp 2015).

In contrast to these two research traditions, the artistic practice of contemporary dance has developed a different relationship to and a different practice of writing. This is because there are only a few choreographers who have mastered dance notation systems such as *Labanotation, Benesh Movement Notation* or *Écriture du mouvement* by Pierre Conté and use them consistently in their artistic practice. Nevertheless, contemporary choreographers in particular have recently been exploring the analogies between writing and dance in their artistic work. Writing in contemporary dance is a central practice of artistic work and at the same time an aesthetic tool in contemporary performances. In their artistic work, contemporary choreographers use different and individual writing practices, so that there is now a broad spectrum of highly individual written artefacts. Although they are an important part of the working process, these written documents are sometimes difficult to comprehend intersubjectively and pose a great challenge for reconstructions, revivals and also research processes.

As a conceptual aesthetic tool and as a genuine component of artistic practices and production, written artefacts – not only in dance – have been recognised since the 1990s (Louppe 1993; Rajchman 2008; Kelter and Skrandies 2016; Sermon and Chapuis 2016). What is striking about these artistic artefacts is that the preparatory writing, i.e. the writing that serves the conception and design of the choreography, moves between systems of movement notation and practices of writing. In other words, writing in the choreographic working process has more to do with noting down and designing as part of the creative process than with fixing the results of choreographic trial-and-error experiences, such as are common in rehearsals. These conceptual written artefacts of choreographic practice (Klein 2023) have been investigated in our research project "Choreographies of Archiving"[2], focusing on the relationship between writing techniques and choreographic processes. In doing so, we did not focus on those dance notations that circumscribe the performed movement by attempting to record it in writing. Neither were we interested in the movement specifications of choreographers who pre-scribe a movement sequence on paper and then transfer it to the dancers.

Rather, we understand choreographic writing practice as a process that gives materiality to a yet-to-be-developed (choreographic) artefact (Amelunxen et al. 2008; Hoffmann 2008; Krauthausen 2010). From our analysis of the material, we were able to derive three theses, which we elaborate on in this text.

Writing, according to our first thesis, can itself be understood as a performance practice that is closely interwoven with the practice of stage performance.

The written artefacts that are created in the run-up to the performance form an important basis for the transmission of choreographic works, according to our second thesis.

Written artefacts in dance production, according to our third thesis, have their own efficacy. They are not prior or subordinate to the artistic process, but are themselves agents and thus also producing and generating; they are not just a trace, but constitutive of reality in that they are directly involved in the emergence and shaping of the choreographic production in their materiality. As such, they document what is to come before it becomes tangible.

To support our findings, we will first present three choreographic examples of writing practices, then explore the materiality of choreographic writing, and finally identify patterns in choreographic writing practices.

Writing practices: three choreographic examples

We have examined the written material of eight choreographers, whose creative period ranges from around 1970 to 2020:

Lucinda Childs NEW YORK
Andy De Groat PARIS
Kattrin Deufert & Thomas Plischke
(deufert+plischke) SCHWELM
Jutta Hell & Dieter Baumann
(Tanzcompagnie Rubato) BERLIN
Reinhild Hoffmann BERLIN
Carlotta Ikeda PARIS
François Raffinot PARIS
Hideyuki Yano PARIS

For this chapter, we have chosen three choreographers – Lucinda Childs, Hideyuki Yano and François Raffinot – whose archives we were able to access at the French National Dance Centre (Centre national de la danse, Pantin). The three have different aesthetic backgrounds (Baroque dance; classical dance; post-modern dance; Butoh; theatre) and are from different countries (USA; Japan; France).

They have worked either as freelancers or at institutions (Centre chorégraphique national). The US choreographer Lucinda Childs is an exception: she lived and worked in New York, but she also worked regularly in France.

The archival holdings of the choreographers in question are organised by pieces, which corresponds to common archival practice and the indexing systems used. From this material available, we made a selection in ten-year intervals in order to observe possible developments and changes in writing behaviour and writing practices over time. We have not looked at personal documents, photo collections, accounting, administrative records, etc., although writing practices are used here as well.

Lucinda Childs: transformations of the scriptural

In the archival corpus of Lucinda Childs[3], we can observe what we describe as "the artisanal": a workshop of writing where manuscripts are produced in various processes and mixed techniques. Here is an example: *Melody Excerpt,* premiered in 1977, was part of a series of choreographic works in which the artist experimented with a diagrammatic way of setting spatial pathways for the dancers. These pathways and the movement material of the dancers were written down on index cards, covered with paper and reinforced with adhesive tape. Childs uses cipher-like signs and abbreviations *(fig. 1)*, which are based on the detailed drawings in earlier stages of development *(fig. 2)*. These cards are a condensation of the previous work. However, they are hardly comprehensible to outsiders. The processual nature of the rehearsal and the choreographic sequence become visible here, while also addressing the stage performance as a corporeal realisation of what is written. The type of writing alternates between descriptive – using script and sequences of alphabetic characters – and illustrative, i.e. using directional signs such as arrows, dashes, or lines. Colouring is also an important structuring element and illustrates choreographic sequencing.

Fig. 1 — Performer's card nr. 1, recto, for Melody Excerpt *by Lucinda Childs.* CHIL *120-147. © Médiathèque du Centre national de la danse, fonds Lucinda Childs*

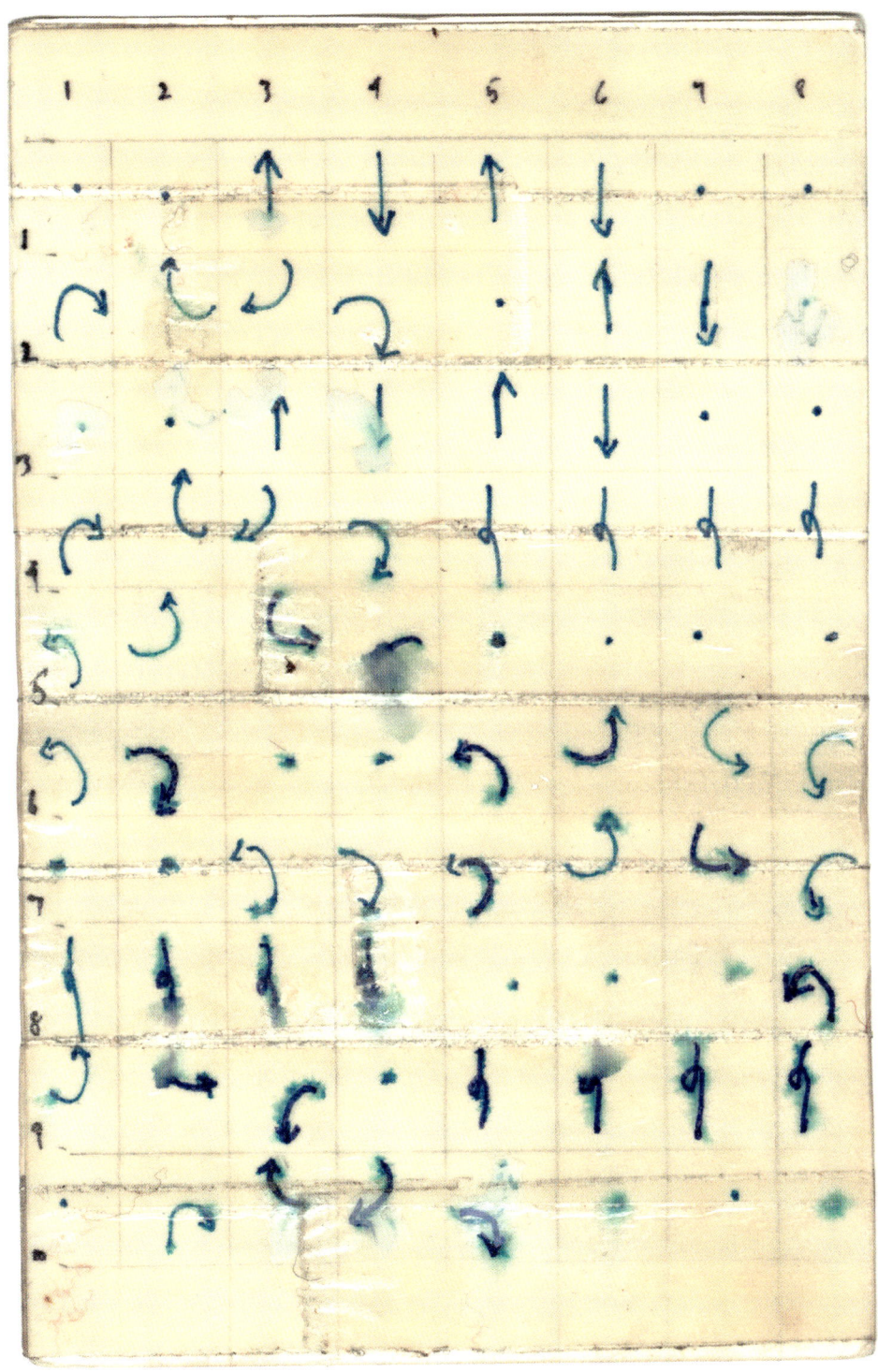

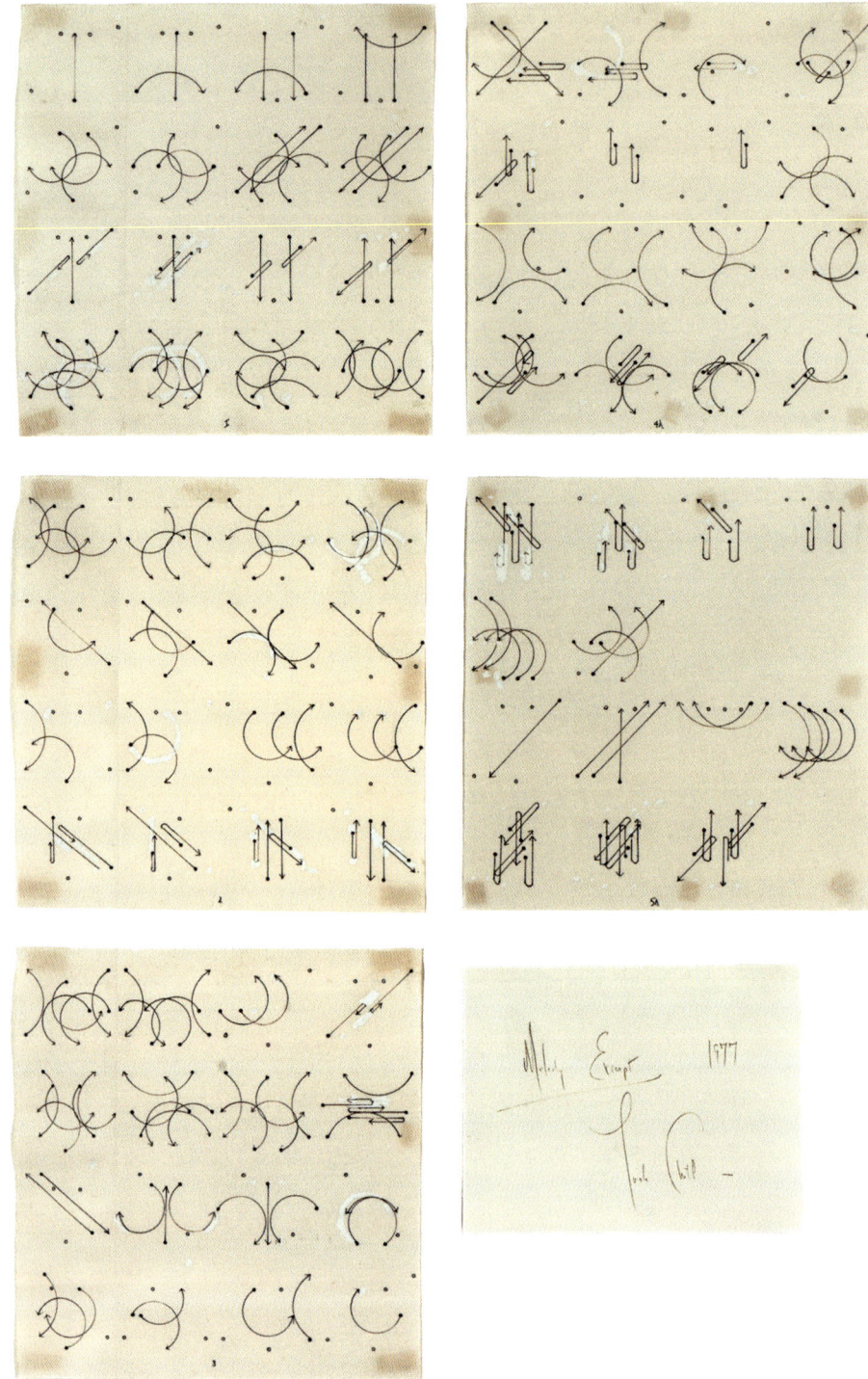

*Fig. 2 — Handwritten full score, glued on cardboard,
for* Melody Excerpt *by Lucinda Childs.* CHIL *120-150.
© Médiathèque du Centre national de la danse,
fonds Lucinda Childs*

Overall, Childs's notes are formal, mathematical and organised in numbers and blocks, often arranged in a sequential layout. The writing remains abstract, without explanatory gesture. It does not aim to help understand the piece or reflect on the working process. Childs is also not concerned with supporting future reconstructions by third parties based on the records. Rather, the conceptual and formal demands of her art, her choreographic style, become visible in the material procedures of noting down. The artistic idea is processed in writing, it gains its own, material, writing-based and paper-based form. And this is first of all independent of the physical performance or the choreographic shape on stage. However, the names of the dancers are often noted down – indeed the cards themselves are personalised –, thereby integrating the performance of the piece to come into the formative writing. In this mark, the materiality of the written manuscripts meets the corporeality of the stage performance.

Hideyuki Yano: designing, reflecting and memorising
Hideyuki Yano[1] consistently uses bound notebooks for his production notes. He has numbered them consecutively. As an example, we chose the notebook for the production *Ciné-Fictions 1: épilogue pour Salomé* (1982–1984). It was a hybrid piece mixing dance, spoken word and music, based on Oscar Wilde's dramatic text *Salomé* (1893; first performed as a ballet version on stage by Loïe Fuller in 1907). Yano had worked on different versions of the piece since 1982, and two more parts were premiered in 1985 and 1986, making it trilogy.

The notebook is bound in black and has lined paper in DIN A4 format. In the notebook we see a kind of cut and paste technique: sheets of other paper quality and format are slipped in, some of them typewritten and annotated with pens. Also, small note tags with telephone numbers and addresses have been inserted. The text itself is written in several colours, with pen, coloured pencil and fountain pen *(fig. 3)*. And it is designed with framing and underlining of words and sentences. Unlike Lucinda

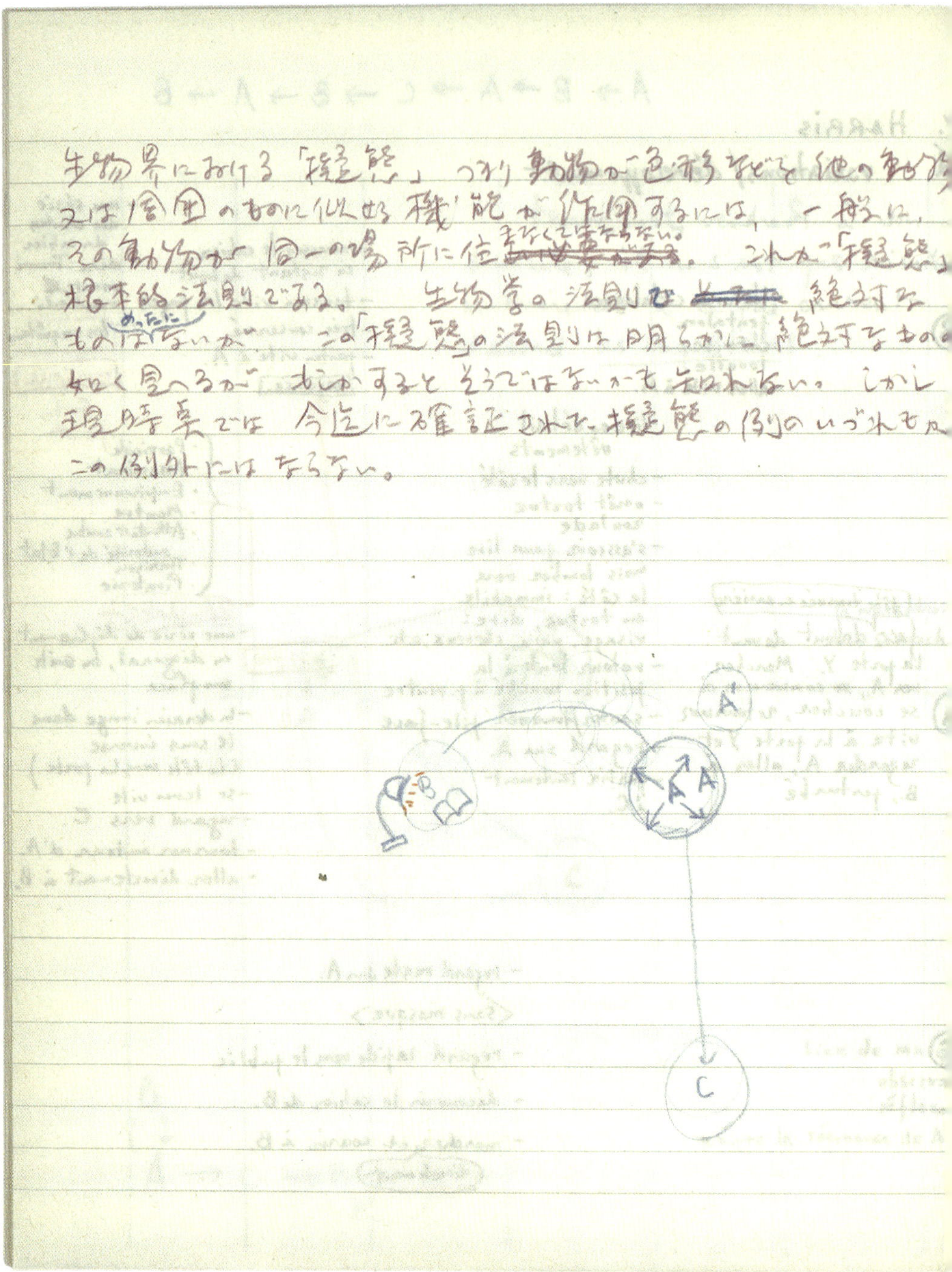

生物界における「擬態」、つまり動物が色彩などを他の動物又は周囲のものに似せる機能が作用するには、一般に、その動物が同一の場所に住まなくてはならない。これが「擬態」の根本的法則である。生物学の法則は絶対なものではないが、この「擬態の法則は明らかに絶対なものの如く見えるが、もしかするとそうではないかも知れない。しかし現時点では今迄に確認された擬態の例のいづれもがこの例外にはならない。

Fig. 3 — Double page from Hideyuki Yano's notebook for Ciné-fictions 1. © *Médiathèque du centre national de la danse, fonds Hideyuki Yano, YAN 119.*

B → A → C → A' ↑B

YANO
variations / développement

- dans la même position que Colin
- reprendre le cahier
- 2 chutes
- aller assez lentement à A
- (vieillard)
- sur le chemin avant d'arriver à A, dire : un soir, tard...

- une chute abrupte
- une série de déplacements latéraux d'abord rapides ensuite lents (extrêmement) (à 4 pattes)
- se mettre verso
- repartir vite
- aller à C.

- s'asseoir pour lire
- chute vers le côté
- roulade lente ralentie
- une série de déplacements / chutes (au moins 5 fois) sur place dans les sens X (mitraillés) et sortie à A' assis, dos vers le public
- retourner à A, se coucher sur le côté, et puis sur le dos
- partir à B, perturbé
  → il sort de sa poche le bandeau noir, commence à le mettre en marchant vers B.

- regard reste sur A
- 1er masque centripète
- tourner
- 2ème masque : cri
- regard vers le public (oblique)
- marcher vers A.

mettre **le bracelet noir**
- regard sur A.
- dire : cet ouvrage a été achevé d'imprimer le 31 décembre 1943....
  ...sous le numéro 22563.

reproduit par procédé photomécanique

Colin sorte de la porte Y., la main droite dans sa poche, se coucher à A.

→ noir — sortie - Yano

CINÉ-FICTION NO 1.

I. deux ombres d'hommes / magnétophone / flash-lights

II. Hideyuki seul (B) < lampe de chevet   "le 31 déc.
                      livre   tard, neige"

  ✱ couché - allongé à (A.) [se lever vite
                              aller à A'
  Colin, à côté, le regarde   reculer coucher sur le dos
                              retourner] nouvelle version

III. Colin seul
  (B) chute de livre / s'asseoir / lire: "un soir, tard"
  (A) s'asseoir et lire: "assis à la table, vieil homme, neige."
      chute vers le côté → musique F.I
      continuer à rouler vers la droite / retourner à A
      rester couché pendant le passage ~~vers le~~ de Hidé
  musique C.O. → se lever vite, aller à (A') derrière Hidé, puis s'en va
      entrer de biais (2 répétition rapide)
      sortir vite pour aller à (C.)
  (C) masque
      aller en contournant (A) à (B)
  (B) prendre le livre et lire: "Pour qu'un mimétisme s'instaure
      jeter le cahier con furioso

IV. Hideyuki à la place de Colin   lire en japonais 積雲ドリフ...
  ⎡ (B) jeter le cahier con furioso
  ⎢   aller vers (A) en disant "un soir, tard"
  ⎢   continuer à aller jusqu'à (C.)
  ⎣ (A) Colin entre, se coucher à (A)
        (laisser passer Hidé qui va directement à (C.))

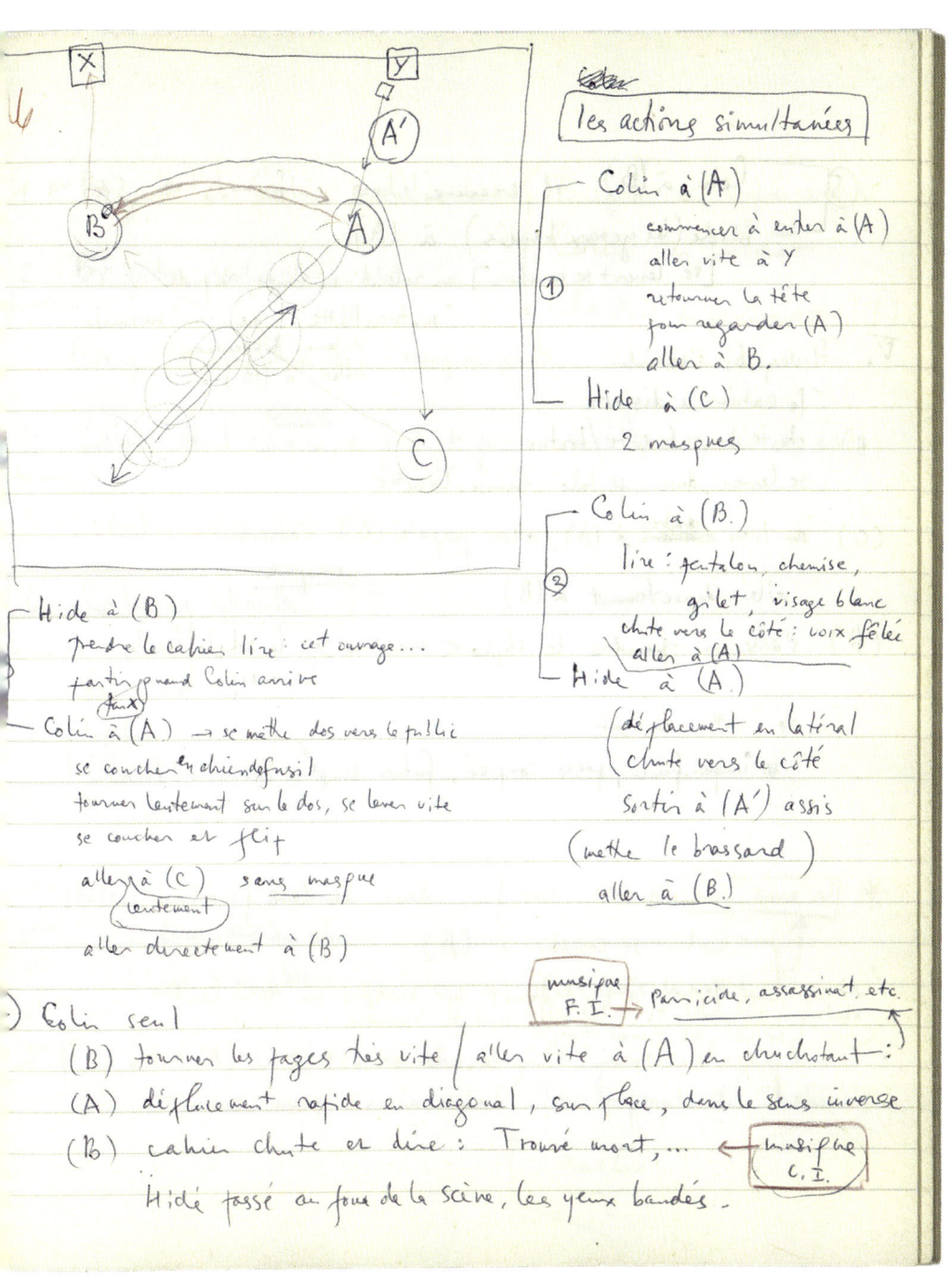

Fig. 4 — Double page from Hideyuki Yano's notebook for Ciné-fictions 1. © *Médiathèque du centre national de la danse, fonds Hideyuki Yano, YAN 119.*

Childs's notes, Yano's notebooks contain different types of text:
- The systematic and structured exposition of what the piece is about – i.e. dramaturgical explanations, often with corrections and additions
- Drawings and sketches of the stage and thus the spatial configuration of the piece's action, plus a list of time units (dancers'/performers' appearances) *(fig. 4)*
- Descriptions of individual scenes, i.e. what the individual performers do, what their motivations are, along with sketches of movements in space and details of individual scenes' duration – partly in keywords, partly formulated in sentences
- Sketches of characters/costumes
- Lists for the timing of rehearsal days
- Sketches of stage spaces of performing venues (Besançon, Maastricht)

Overall, this notebook is characterised by great accuracy and care. Much seems to be fixed in advance so that there is little searching movement, improvisation, or discarding in the graphic work. The decisive feature of Yano's notebooks is the clear sequence, provided by the thread-stitched notebook, and the dramaturgical and expositional order, also favoured by the template of Oscar Wilde's dramatic text. We do not see a chaotic collection of ideas, but rather the careful documentation of the creative process or the definition of a scenic progression. Yano's records give the impression of a structured, systematic elaboration: he writes down continuously and carefully, from page to page, in constant development of a theme.

François Raffinot: analogue and digital
François Raffinot (born 1953) came to choreography through baroque dance, which was a major trend in French stage dance of the 1970s and 1980s (see Franko 2020). In 1980, he became a member of Francine Lancelot's Compagnie Ris et danseries in Paris. From 1983 onwards, he directed artistic ensembles himself. From 1993 to 1998, he was director of the National Choreographic Centre of Le Havre in the North of France, and from 1999 to 2001 was an associated artist at Ircam (Institut de recherche et coordination acoustique/musique) in Paris. His quite compositional as well as technology-savvy style is evident in his choreographic notes.

This can be seen, for instance, in the notes on the production *Al Segno,* dating from 2000, when Raffinot was working at the IRCAM. It was a collaboration with the Tanzhaus NRW in Düsseldorf, Germany and was meant to celebrate the new millennium.

For *Al Segno,* François Raffinot used spiral-bound notebooks and loose sheets of paper inserted in them. The pages contain detailed graphic representations of individual scenes, sequences, reflections and personal notes in the first person. Scenic setups and especially technical settings are also depicted *(fig. 5).* However, the lack of dates is a conspicuous feature. Although the temporal sequences of the future piece are noted very precisely, nothing can be deduced from the notebooks about the duration of the rehearsal process or the developmental phase of the piece.

In his notes, Raffinot also uses electronic writing methods, especially word processing and spreadsheet programmes (see archival compound RAF 751) – sometimes even in colour print. These are used to create the sequence of scenes and the dancers' movements. At the same time, they supplement and imitate the handwritten notes, which were painted, written on, drawn on, torn, and thus materially altered in many ways. Email printouts are also included in this collection for the first time as part of the written record (see archival compound RAF 749). We can observe digital and analogue writing processes used in simultaneous and complementary ways.

This parallel use of typewritten and handwritten manuscripts is, however, already evident in the notebooks of an earlier production of Raffinot's, namely his contribution to the choreographic project *Suitte d'un goût étranger* (1985). The first sheet of the archival compound RAF 254 shows the typescript version of a form that is used for structuring the piece and its scenes, roles and individual actions. Directly after that is the handwritten version that served as model for the typewritten version. The conceptual part was handwritten, the functional version in turn was typescript. This hints towards a shift in writing practices and their technical apparatuses.

There is another example for the simultaneous production of typewritten and handwritten text. A handwritten table with the rehearsal schedule from Monday, 22 April to Tuesday, 30 April (1984) is also a hybrid form. Although it is a

			8 MONITEURS DU FOND	FOND DE SCÈNE PROJECTEUR 1	SURFACE 1.2. PROJECTEUR 2
1 2 3 4 5 6 7	SOLO EVD Jean Michel		↑ BOUE ↓ ASCENSEURS RUE CRESPIN DU GAST ÉTEINTE (BOUGIES BRULÉES)		
8 9 10 11 12 13 14	DUO SEXTUOR EVD		et comparaison de la longueur des mémoires → TRAVELLING SOL BOUE		SOL EMPREINTE
15 16 17 18 19 20 21	TRIO FR	H A R P E		BOUCLE 1 OREILLE → ÉCRAN ORDINATEUR → SOURDS → MANTEGNA PLI TISSUS → SABLE → FIGURE DU PANIER → OREILLE	
22 23 24 25 26 27 28	TRIO FR	P E R C U S S I O N	↑ LAVE ↓ ÉTREINTE		
29 30 31 32 33 34 35	SOLO FR (REPAS SCÈNE RITUEL DES CENDRIERS)		LE JOUEUR DE LA TAIRE. SALIÈRE CENDRIERS TERRE	et comparaison de la longueur des mémoires	PLONGÉ FIXE REPAS, NAPPE BLANCHE etc.
36 37 38 39 40 41 42	DUO EVD	P E R C U S S I O N		BOUCLE 2 ○	
43 44 45 46 47 48 49	DUO FR EVD		DÉBUT PIÈCE SOLISTE SABLE ÉTREINTE		
50 51 52 53 54 55 56	TRIO EVD	HARPE PERCUSSION + 3ème Instrument	MURMURES À L'OREILLE		SOL PIEDS DÉVALANT DES ESCALIERS Rue Crespin du Gast ?
57 58 59 60	SOLO EVD/FR			BOUCLE 3 OEIL → OBJECTIF PIED CAMERA → ÉCRAN → CORPS → OEIL	

Fig. 5 – Double page from a production notebook by François Raffinot for Al Segno. *© Médiathèque du Centre national de la danse, fonds François Raffinot, RAF 750.*

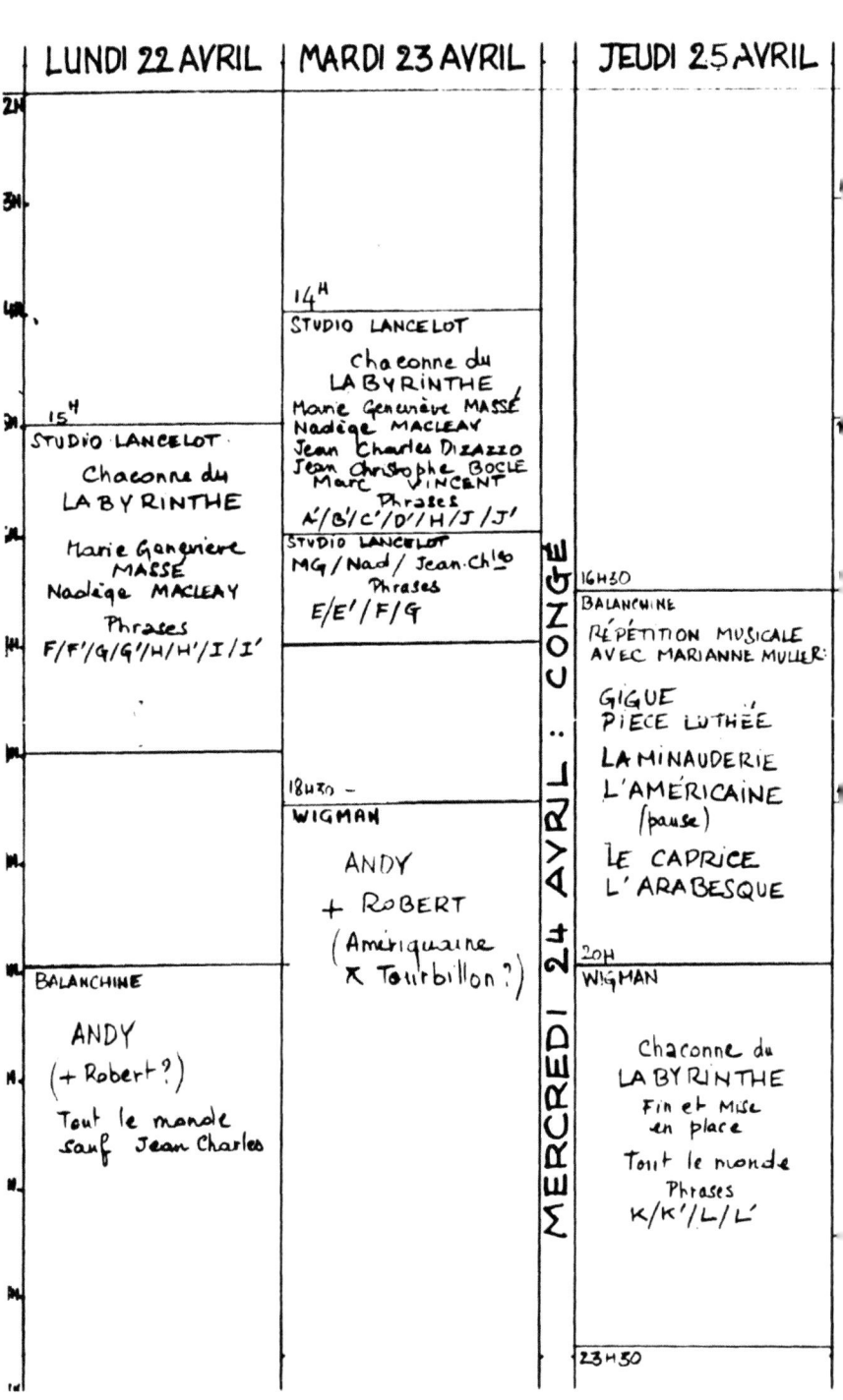

Fig. 6 — Handwritten rehearsal schedule for Suitte d'un goût étranger *by François Raffinot.* © *Médiathèque du Centre national de la danse, fonds François Raffinot, RAF 258.*

REDI 26 AVRIL	SAMEDI 27 AVRIL	DIMANCHE 28 AVRIL		MARDI 30 AVRIL
		12H WIGMAN NETTOYAGE CAPRICE LABYRINTHE ARABESQUE SAUTERELLE GAVOTTE MUZETTE		
LANCELOT TERELLE R VOTTE en place Nettoyage pour marques (sol).				
TE EN MUSICALE ARIANNE MULLER E ZYLBERAJCH TERELLE VOTTE		LA TOURNEUSE raccord avec fin pièce luthier Jean-charles Jean-Christophe Nadège Marc		16H30 WIGMAN RACCORDS Allemande + RACCORD GÉNÉRAL
UZETTE Geneviève MASSÉ harles DIZAZZO RICHARD MACLEAY	18H WIGMAN REPETITION MUSICALE AVEC MARIANNE MULLER ALINE ZYLBERAJCH ISUNORI IMAMURA FÊTES CHAMPÊTRES SARABANDE (avec tambourin et castagnettes) + FILAGE	18H	LUNDI 29 AVRIL : CONGE	19H30 WIGMAN À DETERMINER ?

handwritten document, it is almost calligraphic and looks as if it was type-set *(fig.6)*. One might say: handwriting has made an effort to be a simile of typewriting. Sheet number 6 from this notebook again uses a typewritten or here presumably photocopied version of a typewritten form and supplements it by scripted details and corrections *(fig. 7)*. The simultaneity of typed and handwritten manuscripts is thus already inherent in Raffinot's writing practice even before the introduction of PCs and digital word processing programmes. This might suggest that the directness of handwriting is of great importance in the artistic process, while the transfer into typewriting serves clarity and intersubjective understanding.

Summarising our three examples, we can state the following: The written artefacts are not dance notations – in the sense of prefabricated writing and use of notational sign systems – but individual notes. They are often crafted and manufactured and aim at a piece that does not yet exist. Therefore, the piece cannot be deduced from the written documents alone. Nevertheless, the written artefacts that were created in the run-up to the performance provide an important basis for the passing-on of choreographic works. They expand the knowledge of all stakeholders involved in the performance-making and link it to the knowledge of those who want to reconstruct the piece subsequently or otherwise investigate its genesis. Written artefacts inform about the formative processes that were important for the choreographer in the development of the piece – those processes in which they imagined the piece to come and that occurred before the performance was ever shown. These artefacts are therefore telling about the intentions and artistic / creative context in which they emerged.

While differentiated descriptions of dance movements or statements about the relationship between music and dance, choreography and composition can hardly be found in all three examples, there are different types of choreographic sketches, such as stage layouts, movement patterns, instructions on gestures or placement in space. In many of the documents we have examined, the precise minute markings are particularly striking – this in contrast to the often confused and seemingly chaotic or cryptic exposition of the scenic or visual material. The choreographic form of a piece in spatial directions, arrangement

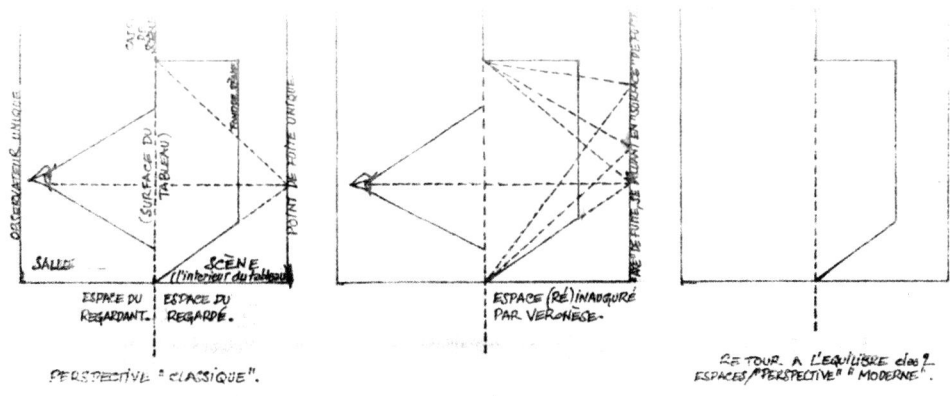

PROLOGUE			
la rêveuse ~~ENTRACTE~~	De Groat	?	8'15"
ACTE I (physique I)			
L'arabesque	Raffinot	7 danseurs	5'55"
gigue en fa dièse	Kovich	{Ségo/Naoλège/Mare/Sylvain} (1)	1'20"
Pièce luthée	Kovich	Ségo/Naoλège / Jean Charles	1'40"
La tourneuse	Raffinot	Sylvain + Marie Nad. St. JC.	0'35"
L'allemande ~~ENTRACTE~~	Kovich=gigue/Raffinot=allemande M.G/JeanChristophe/J.Ch⁴⁶ +(1)		2'15"
ACTE II (métaphysique)			
Caprice	Bagouet/De Groat/kovich/Raffinot	7	5'16"
Le labyrinthe	De groat/Kovich/Raffinot	7	12'16"
~~Le tourbillon (première version transposée)~~ ENTRACTE (sans comédiens)			3'15"
ACTE III (pastorale)			
~~Musette~~	Bagouet/Raffinot	6 danseurs + Pas de quatre	1'38"
La Maraudarie	Kovich	Ségolène/et les garçons	2'09"
La Fougade	Raffinot	Ségolène/Mare (duo)	1'33"
Gavotte en mi bémol	Raffinot	6 ou 4 (?)	4'20"
Les Fêtes Champêtres ENTRACTE	Bagouet	7 danseurs	
ACTE IV (physique II)			
Le tourbillon (version 2)	De Groat/Kovich	?	1'30"
l'Américaine	De Groat:Kovich	?	2'46"
La sauterelle	Raffinot	= chorégraphie de la Gavotte	1'21"
Tartarine et ses doubles	De groat/Raffinot	5 danseurs + duo Sego./Nad.	2'14"
Sarabande	Raffinot	Marie-Geneviève (unique solo)	3'45"
ACTE V (Postlogue)			
~~Le tourbillon (reprise)~~			
Marche tartare	Kovich	au + 6 ? (sf Marie)	2'02"
Le badinage	Kovich/Raffinot	au + 6 ? (sf Marie)	5'43"

Fig. 7 – Spatial layout and order of scenes for Suitte d'un goût étranger *by François Raffinot. © Médiathèque du Centre national de la danse, fonds François Raffinot, RAF 258.*

of people or group formations, appears only in ciphers, markers and abbreviations. The duration of the performance as a sequential process, on the contrary, is more clearly materialised in the writing.

In addition, the widespread lack of dating, i.e. on what days the notes were written, points to their peculiar status: the notes do have a mnemonic character, but this apparently does not require a chronology in the written record. This a-temporality creates hurdles for research. While we can assume that in cases where bound notebooks or pads are used, chronology is inherent in the writing support, we cannot see how much was noted down on one (rehearsal) day, or how long the intervals were between the individual entries. Also, we cannot know whether a bound notebook was actually written continuously from front to back. These ambiguities make it difficult to trace a generic and temporal coherence of the piece under development. Thus, the written artefact has its own testimonial agency. It can be seen as agential rather than subordinate to the artistic process; it is not just a trace, but directly involved in the making and designing of choreographic production.

The materiality of choreographic writing

From the analysis of the choreographic written artefacts of the eight choreographers studied, we can summarise the following findings:

Written artefacts in dance and choreography are a materialisation of what has not yet been created. It is not about recording, about capturing a so-called ephemeral art, but about the conceptual development of a choreography. Since choreography is also based on writing and is created in written form even before a piece is performed on stage or in the studio, the choreographic writing anticipates the stage performance. The writing is a condition or a pre-form of the dance piece, it is not subordinate or secondary. At the same time, the materiality of the manuscript faces the materiality of the stage performance and is overcome in the latter.

Choreographic writing translates possible, imagined or intended space and body formations into writing and makes them conceptually visible. Choreographic writing can therefore be described as a kind of thought experiment; as such, it is contingent and hypothetical.

In writing, uses of space are set out and temporal sequencing is established (rhythm, dynamics, volume, form, synchronicity, etc.). In many cases, the mode of presentation is diagrammatic. Thus, a simultaneity appears in the written form that cannot be realised in the stage performance, the latter being essentially linear and sequential. In this respect, writing creates a spatio-temporal materiality of the choreography it cannot have on the stage.

Written choreographic artefacts are directed towards the dance piece to be created. But writing is also and above all an independent process that has its own agency: As a formative action, writing establishes a material relationship to the immaterial as well as material processes that lead to creation: thinking, imagining, rehearsing, trying out, discarding.

Patterns in choreographic writing practices The choreographic written artefacts which we have studied are highly individual and thus highly diverse.
According to our observations, these differences are not only manifested in what is actually written down. What is even more significant is how writing is done, i.e. the material characteristics of the scripting craft. This includes aspects such as arrangement on the pages or writing support, legibility, use of colours and different pens, subsequent editing, collation, binding and many more. In order to more fully understand the nature of these differences in writing styles and individual characteristics, we were able to identify some criteria that are common to the writing practices and according to which the choreographic written artefacts can be examined:

DYNAMICS AND ENERGETICS OF WRITING: characteristics here are fast and improvised writing as opposed to posed, structured, ordered and planned record-keeping. The use of templates such as geometric shapes, grids on paper, tables or linear structures also has relevance. The firmness of the writing, the pressure of the writing tool on the paper, a narrow or wide run of the script can also provide important clues.

IN/ACCURACY OF WRITING: It is a matter of either formulating and recording ideas that do not yet have a clear outline, or a matter of hinting at formal elements. Writing here has the role of commentary, explanation or instruction and thus refers to itself as much as it refers to its object.

TYPEFACE: Text blocks run straight or change as they progress. The writing can be legible or rather clumped and sketchy. Furthermore, the presence of abbreviations and acronyms can be canvassed for specific functions.

DIAGRAMMATICS: In addition to the use of writing in the lexical and grammatical sense, in the vast majority of cases numerous other signs appear that are graphic, iconic or alphabetic; there are, for example, sketches, stick figures, geometric outlines or perspectival representations. Thus, we observe a recording practice that goes far beyond writing and approaches drawing and other visualisation procedures.

WRITING SUPPORT: The writing materials are generally standardised and commercially available: spiral pads, loose sheets in the standard format, ring binders, bound notebooks, exercise books, and writing pads (DINA4; DINA5; legal letter; post-it tags). In addition, we find material processes such as collages, writing in several layers and colours, cut-outs, gluing, folds and rips.

These criteria draw attention to specific relations between writing and performance: how writing relates to the performance situation and how the performance, conversely, is conducive of writing. Writing, especially handwriting, is a necessarily linear process. It can only represent certain situations successively, in sequence, even though what is written relates to a single scene or moment in the performance. At this point where imagination turns into writing and writing becomes visual, choreographers find different but always very precise and idiosyncratic forms of representing this creative interaction – often especially in writing's very materiality.

Disruption: The archival materiality of writing and performing

The choreographers who we studied were active at a time when fundamental changes in recent media history occurred. In 1981 the PC was introduced; in 1997, there was the first social media platform (Six Degrees); in 2007 the introduction of iPhones changed digital communication and three years later the iPad as well as voice recognition and dictation software for computers or smartphones, followed by current social media. This version of iPad in turn was replaced by the iPad with hand-lettering and specialised software (Mindmap; Padlet; ...) in 2015. Finally, in 2023, a novel form of AI appears on the market with Chat GPT.

However, these new media possibilities have not fundamentally changed the handwritten choreographic writing practice. Despite the smart media, which make hand lettering with a finger or pen on the screen possible, handwriting on paper is the almost exclusive form of written tradition in choreography. This can be seen in the testimonies of the choreographers we have selected and is also confirmed in literature (Hoffmann 2008; Krauthausen 2010; Hahn 2019; Wortelkamp 2021).

Even now obsolete document types such as printed emails, fax sheets or computer-based texts (as printouts on paper) are included with the choreographic records only in very few cases. This raises relevant questions for research: Were these documents not included in the material handed over to archives? Do the personal archives include digital writing media at all? Was there a special status accorded to written artefacts as opposed to technological writing, especially typewriting? It is not yet possible to affirm whether the "culture of digitality" (Stalder 2016) will lead to a change in the function of handwriting in choreography. What we can say, however, is that dance archives only start to think about collecting hard drives or similar electronic data storage items for email, padlets, mind maps, chats etc., and how to treat them archivally.[5]

Writing practices in the field of dance and choreography do not follow a uniform rule, and they are highly self-referential. Therefore, their documentary claim cannot be applied from the outside. The fact that, for example, detailed descriptions of movement execution, as are central to established notation systems, rarely occur in the instances that we have studied is not necessarily a deficit. For this, we are usually dealing with preliminary materials in the choreographic notes that serve the ordering of ideas, views, possibilities, meanings, etc. The choreographic writings are steps towards the creation of a movement, steps towards a choreographic form that does not yet exist. We can therefore state that writing as part of the choreographic process is not dialogical and communicative, but rather functions as a kind of soliloquy.

From this point of view, the category of completeness of the writing would not be as relevant as how the writing process relates to the interaction with the dancers, dramaturges, producers etc. Likewise, we should rather ask what relevance the writing process, once transformed into the stage performance, has for documenting in the eyes of the artists themselves. As researchers, we presuppose a consistent, linear process. And we would like it to be so as this facilitates research as well as the reconstruction of artistic working processes and choreographies.

In terms of passing-on and archiving, of artistic and scholarly reconstruction, choreographic manuscripts have a lasting and sustainable value. Through the materiality of the writing practices, information can be gained about the choreographic style and the artistic working process. Therefore, it is neither the notational procedures nor the metonymic constrictions of physicality as writing in which the relationship between writing and dancing becomes productive. Handwriting is a part of the choreographic craft. But the relationship between performance in writing and on stage is characterised above all by ruptures, discontinuities and voids. They show up in the materiality of the written word.

---

1   On Mallarmé's poetic of movement, dance and writing see also Schwan 2022; Brandstetter 1998; Massias 1998; Louppe 1997; Brandstetter and Ochaim 1989. Mark Franko (1993) has analysed the late Renaissance and early Baroque French dance spectacle as a constant negotiation between textual and physical parameters.

2   The project, whose full title was "Choreographies of Archiving. A Cross-Cultural Study of Archiving Practices in Contemporary Dance", started in April 2020 and ran until October 2023. It was part of the Cluster of Excellence "Understanding Written Artefacts" at Universität Hamburg, realised within the Centre for the Study of Manuscript Cultures (CSMC).

3   Lucinda Childs (born in 1940) is one of the pioneers of so-called postmodern dance, a movement that renounced everything theatrical and treated dance as a purely physical event in space. She founded her own company in 1973. As a choreographer and dancer, she worked with renowned artists from various disciplines, such as John Cage, Robert Wilson and Sol LeWitt.

4   The Japanese choreographer Hideyuki Yano (1943–1988) started his artistic education in the US in 1961, then returned to Japan in 1968 and migrated to France in 1973 to continue his artistic work there. In 1986, he became Director of the National Choreographic Centre of Besançon (France). His early works are deeply indebted to the Japanese Noh theatre. However, Yano turned away from this aesthetic and developed a cross-disciplinary, theatrically influenced, image-based mode of expression.

5   A brief survey among dance archival institutions (Archiv Darstellende Kunst der Akademie der Künste, Berlin; Tanzarchiv Köln; Centre national de la danse, Pantin) has confirmed this view (email correspondence October 2022).

REFERENCES

Amelunxen, Hubertus von, Dieter **Appelt**, Peter **Weibel** and Angela **Lammert** (eds.) (2008): Notation. Kalkül und Form in den Künsten. Berlin and Karlsruhe: Akademie der Künste, Zentrum für Kunst und Medientechnologie.

Brandstetter, Gabriele (1995): Tanz-Lektüren. Körperbilder und Raumfiguren der Avantgarde. Frankfurt: Fischer.

Brandstetter, Gabriele, Franck **Hofmann**, Kirsten **Maar** (eds.) (2010): Notationen und choreographisches Denken. Freiburg: Rombach.

Feuillet, Raoul Auger (1979): Chorégraphie, ou L'art de decrire la dance, par caracteres, figures et signes demonstratifs. Hildesheim: Olms (facsimile of the original 1700 edition, Paris: Michel Brunet).

Franko, Mark (1993): Dance as Text. Ideologies of the Baroque Body. Cambridge: Cambridge University Press.

Franko, Mark (2020): The Fascist Turn in the Dance of Serge Lifar: Interwar French Ballet and the German Occupation. New York: Oxford University Press.

Hahn, Daniela et al. (eds.) (2019): Expanded Writing. Inscriptions of Movement between Art and Science / Expanded Writing. Bewegung (ein)schreiben zwischen Kunst und Wissenschaft. Berlin: Revolver Publishing.

Hoffmann, Christoph (2008): Festhalten, Bereitstellen. Verfahren der Aufzeichnung. In: Christoph Hoffmann (ed.), Daten sichern. Schreiben und Zeichnen als Verfahren des Entwurfs. Zürich: diaphanes, pp. 7–20.

Hutchinson Guest, Ann (1998): Choreo-Graphics. A Comparison of Dance Notation Systems from the Fifteenth Century to the Present. Amsterdam: Harwood Academic.

Jeschke, Claudia (1983): Tanzschriften. Ihre Geschichte und Methode. Die illustrierte Darstellung eines Phänomens von den Anfängen bis zur Gegenwart (= Tanzforschungen. 2). Bad Reichenhall: Comes.

Jeschke, Claudia (1999): Tanz als BewegungsText. Analysen zum Verhältnis von Tanztheater und Gesellschaftstanz (1910—1965). Tübingen: Niemeyer.

Jeschke, Claudia (2010): Tanz-Notate: Bilder. Texte. Wissen. In: Gabriele Brandstetter, Franck Hofmann, Kirsten Maar (eds.), Notation und choreographisches Denken. Freiburg: Rombach, pp. 47–65.

Jeschke, Claudia (2023): Gedächtnistransfers, Spurensuchen – und Nijinsky. In: Irene Brandenburg and Claudia Jeschke (eds.), Tanz schreiben: Artefakte, Hypertexte – und Nijinsky. In: Tanz&Archiv, ForschungsReisen, nr. 10. Munich: epodium, pp. 56–90.

Kelter, Katharina and Timo **Skrandies** (eds.) (2016): Bewegungsmaterial. Produktion und Materialität in Tanz und Performance. Bielefeld: transcript.

Klein, Gabriele (2023): Artefakte übersetzen. Methodologische Aspekte einer praxeologischen Tanzforschung. In: Irene Brandenburg and Claudia Jeschke (eds.), Tanz schreiben: Artefakte, Hypertexte – und Nijinsky. In: Tanz&Archiv, ForschungsReisen, nr. 10, Munich: epodium, pp. 110–125.

Krauthausen, Karin (2010): Vom Nutzen des Notierens. Verfahren des Entwurfs. In: Karin Krauthausen and Omar W. Nasim (eds.), Notieren, Skizzieren. Schreiben und Zeichnen als Verfahren des Entwurfs. Zürich: diaphanes, pp. 7–27.

Louppe, Laurence et al. (eds.) (1994): Danses tracées. Dessins et notation des chorégraphes. Paris: Dis voir.

Louppe, Laurence (1997): Poétique de la danse contemporaine. Brussels: contredanse.

Massias, Sylvia (1998): Mallarmé et la danse. In: Yves Peyré (ed.), Mallarmé 1842—1898. Un destin d'écriture. Paris: Gallimard and Réunion des Musées nationaux, pp. 137–143.

Rajchman, John (2008): Die Kunst der Notation. In: Amelunxen et al. (eds.), pp. 68–76.

Sermon, Julie and Yvane **Chapuis** (eds.) (no year [2016]): Partition(s). Objet et concept des pratiques scéniques (20e et 21e siècle). Dijon: Les presses du réel.

Stalder, Felix (2016): Kultur der Digitalität. Berlin: Suhrkamp.

Wortelkamp, Isa (2015): Performative Writing – Schreiben als Kunst der Aufzeichnung. In: MAP #6 Aufzeichnen. Verzeichnen. *nbn-resolving.org/urn:nbn:de:bsz:14-qucosa2-75015* (1/12/2022).

Wortelkamp, Isa (2021): Notieren im Tanz. Zu einer choreographischen Schreibpraxis als Instrument der Reflexion. In: Rita Rieger (ed.), Bewegungsszenarien der Moderne. Theorien und Schreibpraktiken physischer und emotionaler Bewegung. Heidelberg: Winter, pp. 111–125.

Passing on the Legacy of Collaboration: Material Goods and Marginalia

Bojana Kunst

Legacy waiting to be found again

A book to be

In May 2016, I received an invitation from choreographer and author Ivana Müller to participate in her work *Notes.* Inspired by the nineteenth-century practice of marginalia, which cultivated the gesture of personalising a book by writing notes in the margins before offering it to a friend or lover, Ivana invited seven readers, all of whom were related to her in one way or another, either through a previous collaboration, a history of friendship or simply as allies and fellow travellers; we were the group of con-temporaries. To paraphrase lightly Agamben's writing on temporality: we all experienced the shared state of proximity to our own temporality (Agamben 2019). David Weber Krebs, Paola Caspão, Jonas Rutgeerts, Ant Hampton, Ivana Müller, Paz Rojo and I came first together on October 2016 in Freiburg to participate in the work *Notes,* which consisted of reading the book together and writing notes in the margins. The work was a response to the invitation of Anne Kersting, at the time dramaturge in Freiburg, to Ivana Müller to propose a work for *Heritage Depot,* a joint project of the Freiburg Municipal Theatre (Theater Freiburg) and the Museum for New Art (Museum für Neue Kunst) Freiburg. *Heritage Depot* was part of the larger project *Tanzfonds Erbe.* It was an exhibition in March 2017 that focused on the processes of transmission and the examination of the role of heritage.[1]

We chose the philosopher Daniel Heller-Roazen's *Echolalias: On the Forgetting of Language* (2008) in which he reflects on the many forms that linguistic forgetting can take and writes about various ways in which the destruction and making of language are inseparable. The book travelled by post for five months from one annotator to another, each of us commenting on the book as we read it, leaving the notes, traces and remnants of our reading for another reader to continue. The annotated book slowly became an archive of the long process of collective reading and writing, a hybrid parallel manuscript created by seven readers. At the end of the five-month period, we also had to decide how to share our reading process, and we agreed that the book would be available in the exhibition but would also continue to circulate after the exhibition was over.

In the exhibition, we were given a large room painted light blue to display the 291 facsimile pages of the annotated book, page by page, on the wall. In the same order as they appear in the book, we created a kind of 'dissected map' for the visitor to wander through, either alone or in a group with others. As well as looking at the pages on the wall, visitors to the exhibition could listen to an 11-hour audio document in which seven annotators read the book chapter by chapter. At the same time, the annotated book was on display at the opening of the exhibition, available for visitors to skim through and read if they wished. *(fig.1 & fig.2)*

After the exhibition, the book was passed on to readers, with the rule that each reader could have the book for a certain amount of time, then they had to pass it on to another reader. In this way, we hoped we could follow the book for the next ten years. We even created a blog entry to which people could send a description of the very act of passing the book on. These entries are still on the Notes website, but there are not many to read.[2] After a few readers and a few entries, there was suddenly silence. The trace of the book disappeared much more rapidly than we had hoped. After a few months of circulation, the book got stuck and stopped circulating. Some of us even guessed who the person was who had stored it, but there was no response to our queries. So maybe the book is really hidden in the private possession of this half-known person, or maybe it has been destroyed, lost forever; nobody knows. At the moment, we are not sure that the book will ever be found.

I vividly remember how we, the first group of annotators, came together in 2016 to think about how the book should be passed on, discussing whether it should be left to the local library, the museum, the artists. From the beginning, we wanted the book to move and to belong; what we did not want was to create an object; even if in the end we created a very beautiful book and something that it would be tempting to protect. Therefore, we came up with the plan of choreographing forward in time, imagining the circulation of the book and its readers, many worlds that would be created around it, and perhaps new annotations that would appear, not knowing that the book would be lost so quickly and that what would probably remain would only be a facsimile of pages from our exhibition.

Unfortunately, even the facsimile pages didn't survive, and all we have left are a few photographs and a story that I'm writing down here. Because the printed pages did not want to stay on the smooth wall of the gallery, we had to use strong glue (with a very unhealthy smell) to force them to stick to the wall. In this way, the glue slowly destroyed all the copies of the pages from the book.

The exhibition *Heritage Depot,* curated by Anne Kersting, investigated the culture of remembrance as a future practice; it called into question existing logics of descent and inheritance. Instead of curating an exhibition of an archive or of inventing and imagining other ways of collecting performances, the aim of the exhibition was to develop artistic proposals on how to actively deal with the handing down and passing on of cultural heritage. The exhibition aimed to examine the role that artists and art can play in the act of handing down, thus critically exploring who owns cultural heritage and challenging the usual flows of cultural ownership.

Ivana Müller's work is known for its exploration of choreographic imagination. In her performances, she asks how new worlds are constructed by establishing a web of relationships between bodies, language and things. In her work *Notes,* the exploration of choreographic imagination is focused on the book, which is a kind of torch passed between the times of the past and the future. The book is considered to be a hinge between the shared past and the future legacy. At the same time, the book connects communities of readers; it is clearly oriented towards common practice, sharing and weaving the experience of reading around the texture of the book. The process of reading and noting marginalia on the margins of the pages created a caring responsibility between readers and annotators, but also a connection to the future of memory in this process. We have created something together, a dense network of entanglements around this book. So how do we transport this togetherness in time, how do we pass it on? Do we have to pass it on at all? Can we pass it on and avoid turning it into an object, a cultural asset? Wouldn't it be better to leave the book in the public library? Or perhaps give it to the guardians, as if it were part of a museum collection? What does it mean for our common annotation and reading to continue? How can we pass it on to among its readers?

During the five months in 2016, we developed a common practice of reading and annotating that we wanted to pass on. But at the same time, we created a beautiful object, a layered, decorated book that folded and unfolded through many

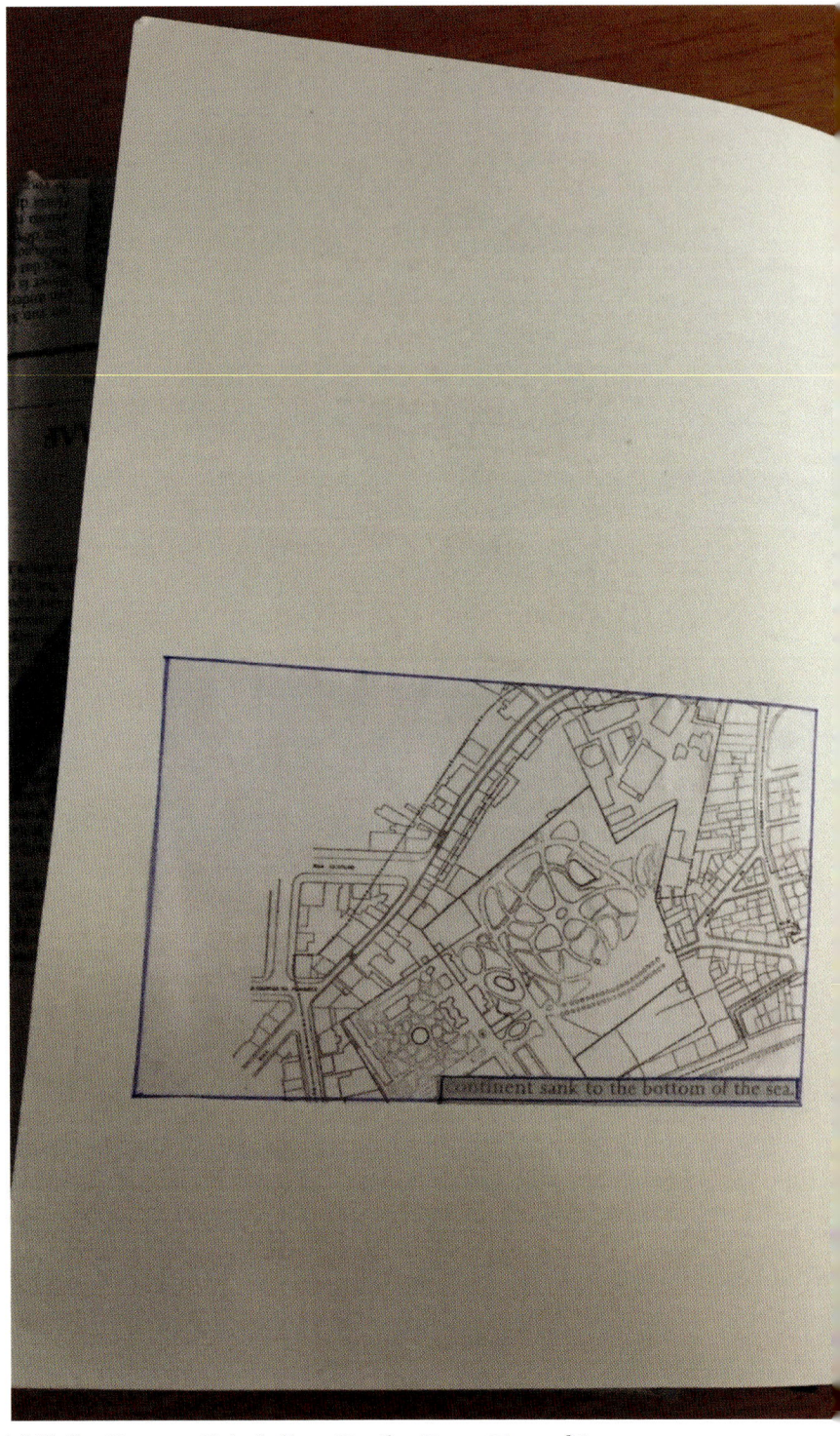

Fig. 1 — Daniel Heller-Roazen: Echolalias: On the Forgetting of Language. *Annotated by: Bojana Kunst, Paola Caspão, David Weber Krebs, Ant Hampton, Paz Rojo, Jonas Rutgeerts and Ivana Müller; hosted by Theater Freiburg & Museum für neue Kunst, Freiburg, Germany 2017. Photo © Ivana Müller*

Chapter Nine

Strata

— a layer of rock or soil with characteristics that distinguish it from other layers

sedimentation ↑

In the passage from one language to another, something always remains, even if no one is left to recall it. For a tongue retains more than its speakers and, like a mineral slate marked by the layers of a history older than that of living beings, it inevitably bears the imprints of the ages through which it has passed. If "language is the archives of history," as Ralph Waldo Emerson wrote, it does, in this sense, without keepers and catalogs.[1] Its holdings can only ever be consulted in part, and it furnishes the researcher with elements less of a biography than of a geological study of a sedimentation accomplished over a period with no clear beginning or end. Like the multiple memories of indistinct and immemorial origins invoked by the nearly nameless narrator of *Remembrance of Things Past*, the remains of the past are superimposed on one another in speech with an often-impenetrable density and complexity. In language, as in the mind of the novel's protagonist, the present invariably contains the stratified residues of a past that, when examined, retreats beyond the memory of the individual who uncovers it. "All these recollections, superimposed upon one another, formed only a mass," he recalls, "but it was still possible to distinguish between them, between the oldest ones and the more recent ones born from a scent, and still again from those

yes, because poetry is historical TRACE 2

be left open for poetry — silent e?

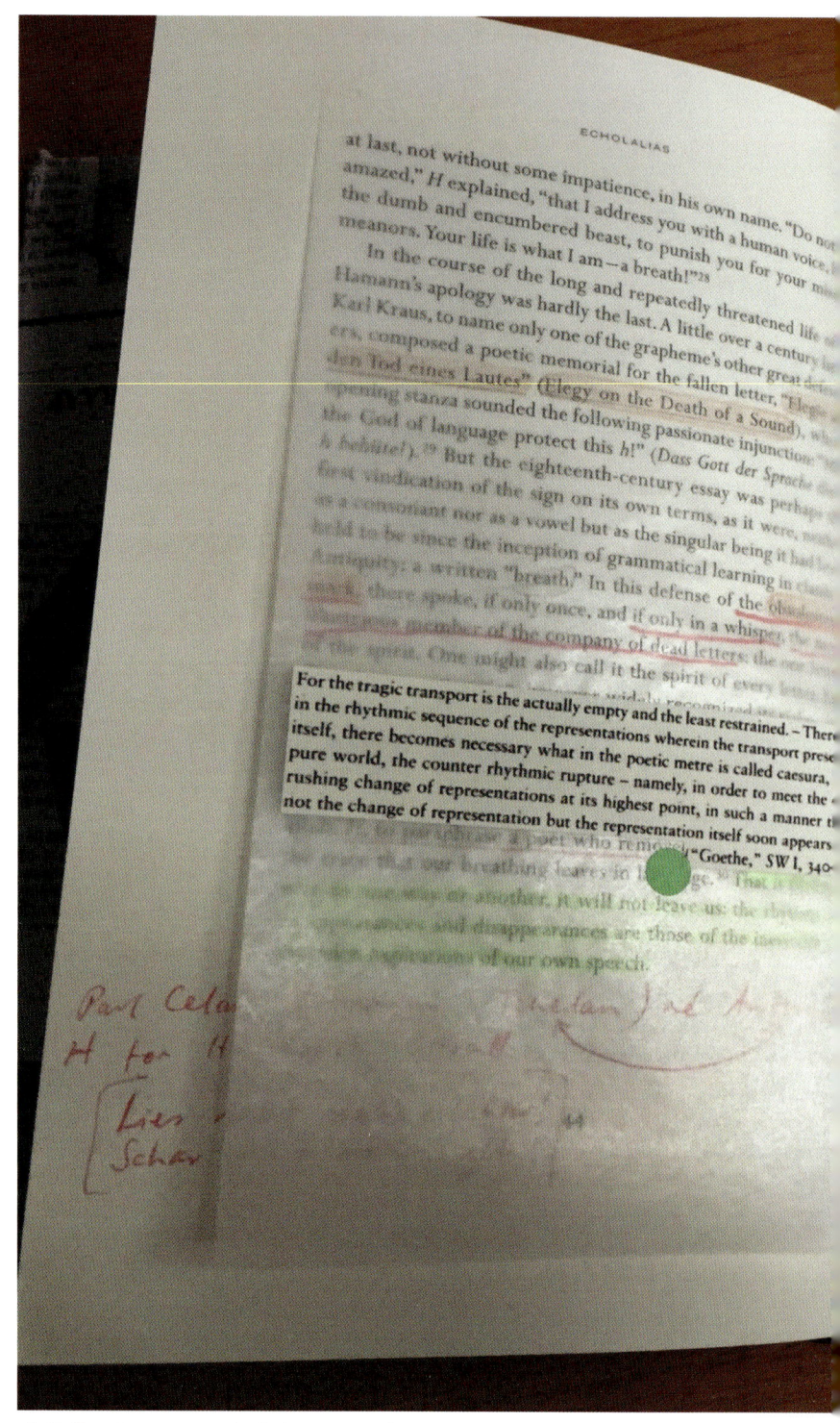

Fig. 2 — Daniel Heller-Roazen: Echolalias: On the Forgetting of Language. *Annotated by: Bojana Kunst, Paola Caspão, David Weber Krebs, Ant Hampton, Paz Rojo, Jonas Rutgeerts and Ivana Müller; hosted by Theater Freiburg & Museum für neue Kunst, Freiburg, Germany 2017. Photo © Ivana Müller*

Chapter Six

Exiles

A group of speakers can lose the capacity to produce not only some but even all the sounds and letters of its language as an entire idiom falls, for one reason or another, into oblivion. One then says that the language is dead or, more precisely, that a new language has begun to be spoken. Such terms belong to historical linguistics, a discipline that approaches its obsolescent objects with the benefit of hindsight. In the moment a people begins to forget what was once its language, of course, things are rarely so clear. The possibilities are many. A tongue can vanish without its ever being noticed; it can also be recalled by those who once spoke it at the moment it becomes for them only a memory. But no language, even one considered holy, can escape the time of its transience. It was thus that the language of the five books of Moses, for example, progressively gave way, within the single yet diverse collection of texts that form the Hebrew Bible, to the later forms of speech that supplanted it, ultimately ending with the "Syriack" in which the Chaldeans in the Book of Daniel are said to communicate, which modern philologists identify with a different yet related language, Aramaic. And it was thus that this second Semitic language, which in truth belonged not only to the advisers of Nebuchadnezzar but also to those who claimed to be descended

45

different readings. There was this solid "material good", an object in the form of an annotated book, which through the process of sharing became incredibly tangible, sensual, overwhelming, but at the same time immaterial, almost auratic. We somehow put it into circulation to get rid of its monumentality, but we could not completely take away its allure. Perhaps it was this attraction that triggered the unknown reader in whose room the book ended its circulation for the time being; perhaps this unknown reader simply wanted to be the sole guardian of its future, to protect it from the caprices and unknowns of sharing something, from the storms that can occur in the circulation of material goods.

Collaborative engagements and their marginalia

The act of passing on a legacy is part of any collaborative engagement, especially when new political, artistic, and social alliances and entanglements are created in these processes. Walter Benjamin's writings (Benjamin 2016) offer an insight into the emancipatory potential of past political practices, while black feminist writers have shown how it is precisely through acts of archiving that violence is done to imaginative processes of emancipation (see Love 2009; Hartman 2021, Hartman 2008). The archiving and transmission of emancipatory voices challenges the very process of relating to the past and disrupts the ways we remember and experience the present. Artistic collective experiments and processes are bound to the present, but at the same time, they are deeply intertwined with the possibilities of transmission between the emancipatory past and its utopian future. However, there is also a temporal dynamic in performance and dance that causes its rapid forgetting: a temporal rhythm of its production that is closely linked to the economy of accelerated cultural consumption.

This temporal rhythm is particularly destructive when thinking about collaborative processes, which tend to take time and are closely linked not only to artistic, but also to institutional, social and political experimentations. In recent decades, performance and dance practices in Europe have developed through experimentation with collaboration and working processes, challenging the ways in which they are institutionally present. Thus, the temporality of production demands, on the one hand, the continuous accumulation of projects. On the other hand, there is also a desire for continuous experimentation with procedures, means and conditions within this very project logic. Therefore, performance and dance, especially when not really supported by a stable institutional structure, do not have much temporal freedom to endure and build their own institutional, political and spatial legacy. In fact, most of the production frameworks in which current performance and dance works are made are temporally unstable, dependent on the whims of the present. They can quickly disappear when, for example, there is a cut in funding or a sudden shift in cultural policy; or when there is a loss of working space due to gentrification and rising prices; or when, with the acceleration of working time, exhaustion simply cannot cope with following one project after another. Entire artistic environments can disappear due to the privatisation of spaces, the closing of borders or difficulties in travelling. At the same time, in this competition of projects, it can easily happen that some creative processes with a stronger economic and institutional background become monuments in themselves, becoming obsessed with an eternal repetition, directed by a melancholic desire not to allow their loss of the present, while others who are made in much more precarious and unstable economic circumstances disappear much faster and without any traces.

  What might be other ways of passing on a legacy of collaborative work that do not succumb to the temptation of eternity? A work of art that rather creates an imaginative temporal kinship between the past and the future that is alive, open to change and to constant rewriting or redoing? I don't have to go very far to answer these questions but can start looking for the answers in my own home. Around my desk and among my books, there are many marginalia that come from the legacy of collaborative work. They are side-witnesses of various collaborative processes and they come from the invention of shared working processes. Many of them have been given to me or come from various processes in which I have been involved. When I received the invitation to the conference "Material Goods", for which this essay was first written, I couldn't resist the temptation to go through some of the material goods that inhabit my room, the things that come out of collaborative or collective working processes that I still often work with when teaching or researching. On my desk, there is often a small white booklet called

Vocabulaboratories, in which the choreographer Paz Rojo together with her collaborators Manuela Zechner and Anja Kanngieser collected and meticulously linked the voices of many dancers, choreographers and writers into a tangled composition of practices around 2003 (Rojo et al. 2003). Then there are several colourful notebooks belonging to *Everybodys,* a group of dancers and choreographers who, in a manner of open-source technology, shared the games, dance and choreographic scores as well as self-interviews in the period around 2009 (Ingvartsen and Chauchat 2009).

There is also a booklet that came out of the decelerated time of *6 Months 1 Location* in Montpellier, which tried to experiment with the possibilities that arise when artists have time to work and collaborate in one place for an extended period of time (Ingvartsen 2009). I often open a small beige box made of rough cardboard in which the scores on the grey cards are kept. If I open it now, at the moment, I am writing this sentence, I can read on the first card: *"…the smallest common denominator: At each moment, make sure you share one and only one element of your dance with the others."* This is the collection of scores by the dancer Alice Chauchat, and the title on the box is *Companions, Telepaths and Other Doubles* (Chauchat 2015). There is also a chaotic collective booklet, *Collect-if,* in which it is difficult to meander through the overflowing material produced in a chaotic process. And an issue of the Spanish theatre review, which took a long time to come about, as ten writers and artists completed it in a chain, one after the other. But they did not always respect the time given to finish their contribution. It is a voluminous publication from which something always falls out, something always has to be put back or rearranged. It lies next to the thick but light silver book on choreography, without a table of contents or pages. And there is a computer stick, dipped in a pink mass, lying in a box on a soft pink feather, on which the online performance was sent around to be watched. I should also mention a white T-shirt with notes on artwork and care, from Frankfurt's AdA KANTINE, the collective kitchen for the homeless, where I recently gave a talk and cooked the meal. *(fig. 3)*

All these material things from my room are just a tiny part of an impressive body of production in dance and performance art over the last few decades, which shows how artistic production cannot be thought of separately from the growing

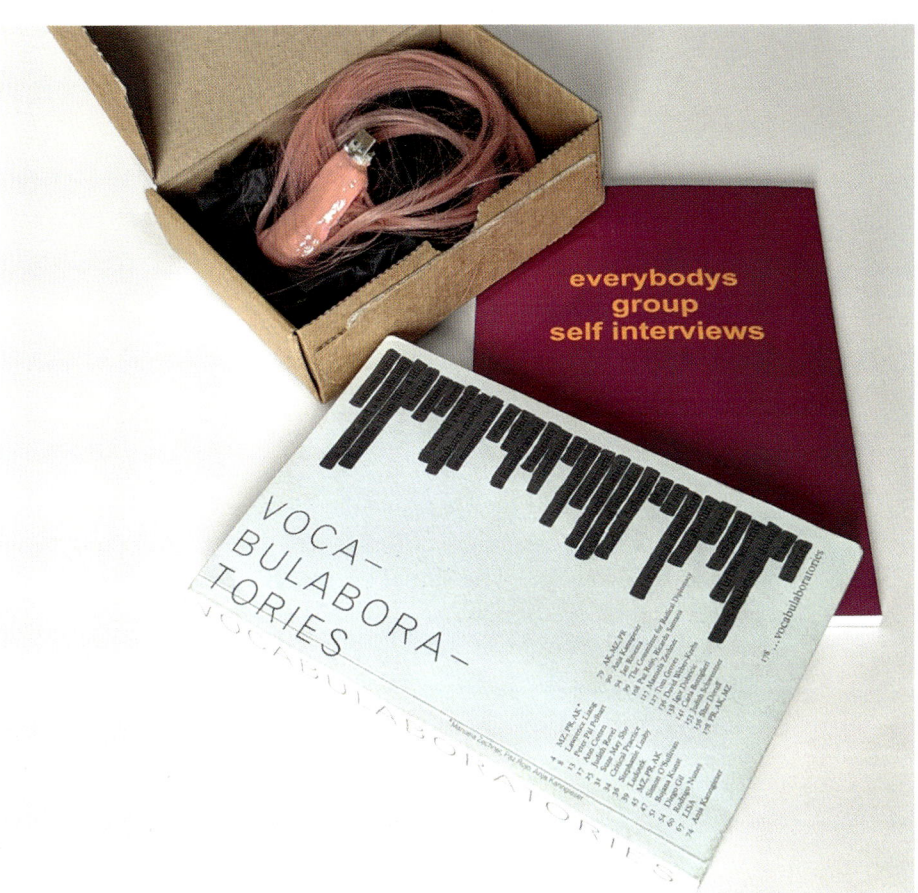

Fig. 3 — Paz Rojo, Manuela Zechner and Anja Kanngieser: Vocabulaboratories, *2003. Alice Chauchat and Mette Ingvartsen (eds.):* Everybodys self-interwievs, everybodys publications, *2009. Filomena Krauße:* verstand&Gefühl *(sense&Sensibility), 2020. Photo © Igor Štromajer*

accumulation of things, the accumulation of material goods. I would not say that these various things are documents staying after the performance was finished. They are more like vessels for methods of working and imagining different ways of working together. They are fictional and imaginary apparatuses, thingy inventions and spaceships for different politics and art making. And at the same time, they are all marginalia, notes on the edge of performances. They have a choreographic and embodied quality because they have somehow emerged within relationships and their entanglements, they arise from the sharing and circulation of practices, experiments as well as artistic and social inventions.

It is true that most of these things are in the form of books, which can also contribute to the fact that these material goods are part of the rise of linguistic and communicative work in the arts created within the post-Fordist economy. Thus, they can also be seen as witnesses of the change of values in the economy and show how the transfer of knowledge, and the production of knowledge in general, became part of the way dance and performance were made in the last decades. Dancers and choreographers are now equipped with linguistic skills in creation and production, and in experimenting with their own modes of production, contributing to the production of communication in general. In this sense, this material can also direct the distribution and production of dance practice. So many of these material goods have contributed to the expanded notion of dance and its linguistic and conceptual circulation, where dance is shared not only as an aesthetic but also social practice. Dance is not only distributed through performances but as specific collaborative, social and community practice.

But such a socio-economic explanation does not explain the allure, the sensual, ticklish and sometimes even excessive quality that all of these objects have in themselves. Even though many of them are books, they are often abundant books, off the scale, off the format, inflated, untidy and asymmetrical. They are somehow things beyond themselves, inviting us to enter into a concrete embodied relationship with them, but also to reuse and recycle them; at least that is how I perceive them and use them in my daily work as a teacher and writer. Their appeal has something to do with their specific temporality. They are not witnesses to something that is no longer there, because they always fail to retell the past. However, they are witnesses to the future, to potential histories of collaborative, collective, politically engaged ways of working. In this way, they unsettle institutional hierarchies and authorial authorities. In them lies the legacy of potential histories that at one point in time brought people together to imagine and experiment with artistic, political or social relationships.

This sense of future possibility is what is so magical about these boxes of scores, these books wrapped in cloth, these messy and chaotic collections of past experiments. There is something in their materiality that also resists their reproduction, but it also invites us to continue their practice. They are stubborn and persistent, challenging the very economy of circulation to which they belong. In fact, most of these material goods originate from specific collaborative ethics. However, they do not just make public the politics of this ethics, they express it in the form of things, imagining a way of sharing, continuing and remembering this collaborative politics. Their role is not only to expand our understanding of dance and choreography but also to change the way dance and performance works are shared and passed on. In this way, they became material goods, with an almost magical value. They continue to challenge me as a teacher as to how I can circulate and offer them as material in common, helping me also to retell the stories of communities that have already been lost. Many of these material goods are in fact a direct result of challenging the hierarchies of work in choreography and dance because they were created to unsettle notions of originality, authenticity, very often to dismantle authorship. They become things in which we can see a weakening of the rupture between process and product. It is an attempt to open up collective, collaborative and more transindividual practices through which a continuous transmission of knowledge can take place; they are charged with a choreographic imagination of their own continuation and circulation. They are annotations of love and friendship written on the margins of performances that have already disappeared, but also of failures and difficulties in collaborative processes. Through them, we can hear the voices of communities murmuring, even if their practices have disappeared.

In recent decades, there has been a great deal of work (in practice as well as in academia) on the temporality of performance, particularly in unsettling its ontological fixation on disappearance and liveness (Schneider 2022; Taylor 2003). Dance and performance art have discovered their own past, developing practices of return, looping, repetition and replay to challenge the exclusivity of contemporaneity and its grounding in the colonial history of the West. This return to the past also opens up the freedom of reinventing performance and unsettling its canonisation, opening up other invisible practices and histories (feminist, queer, underground, etc.). The material goods produced by these processes are thus an inseparable part of the working ethos, resisting the historical hierarchies present in the way the work of performance is (or should be) produced and organised. Performance emerges here as the result of specific biospheres of work and co-habitation, a series of collaborative processes or practices, temporalities of rehearsal and economies of distribution. Through these collaborative marginalia, we can also see how the continual rearrangement and attention to the micro-political acts of bodies and their relations, objects and atmospheres are an integral part of the experimentation of performance: performance creates an environment, belongs to the relations of which it is made. In this sense, the material goods are a kind of legacy of this belonging, a transmission of practices and lives in common, and it is from there that their magical allure shines and sometimes really works like a spell. *(fig. 4, fig. 5)*

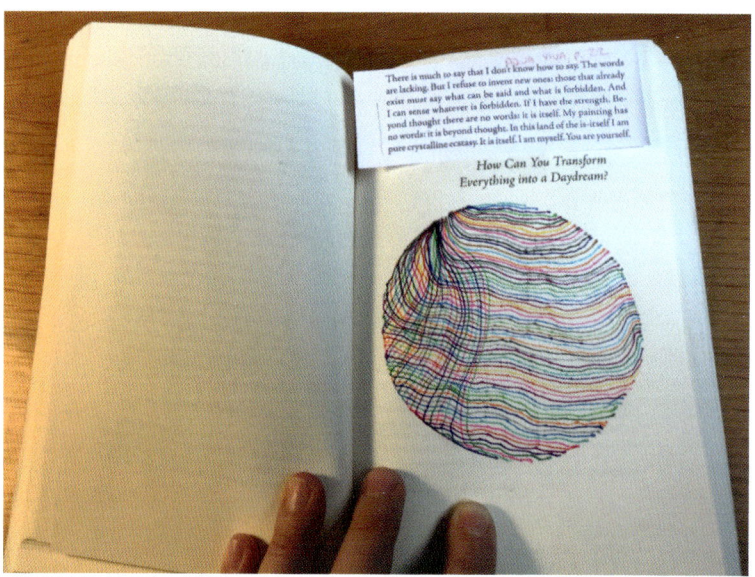

Fig. 4 — Clarice Lispector, A Breath of Life. *Annotated by: Andrea Bozic, Lisa Skwirblies, Erin Hill and Jasiek Mischke; hosted by Veem, House of Performance, Amsterdam, The Netherlands, 2018. Photo © Ivana Müller*

Fig. 5 — Wanda Coleman: strände warum sie mich kaltlassen *(original title: wicked enchantments). Annotated by: Martina Hefter, Lina Majdalanie, Caroline Kapp and Stefanie Wenner; hosted by Breaking the Spell, Schauspiel Leipzig, Germany, 2022. Photo © Ivana Müller*

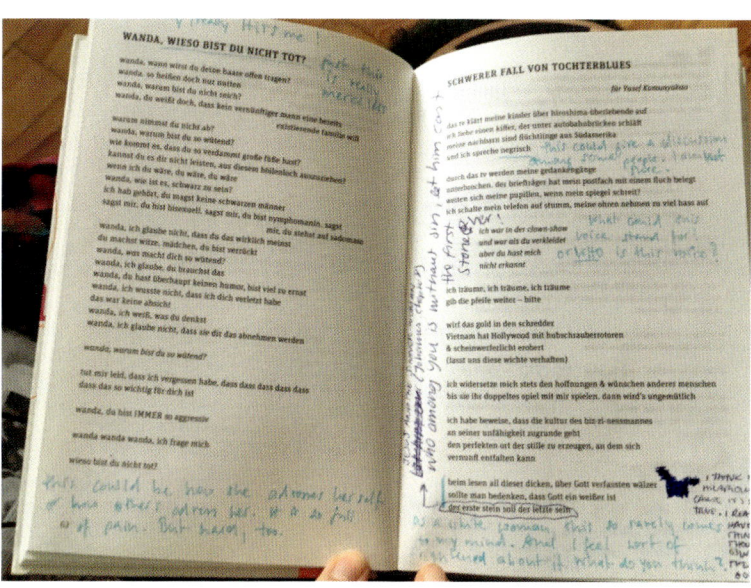

Postscript   At the end of July 2023, the first annotated book we created together in the work *Notes* is still lost. But Ivana Müller decided not to give in to melancholic mourning. In the summer of 2017, she invited new groups of annotators to read together and to continue the exchange and circulation of more books. There are currently eleven books annotated, but there are probably many more, as a reading group in a small Italian town has adopted this practice as its regular reading practice and has been doing so for several years. Some books are still in circulation – at the moment the artist knows the approximate whereabouts of four books. Another book has even been imprisoned, because someone gave it to a reader in prison, not knowing that it is impossible to take anything out once it has landed there. There are already many annotators, and with them the books are taking on different forms, becoming exuberant, their pages are embroidered, some are more like herbariums, with food and many other additions, almost half alive. Moreover, they continue to exist in common, not only through the sharing but through the continuation of the practice. Like the material goods described earlier, books do not belong to the past (they are not documents, witnesses of the past), nor to the future (they are not the result of an archival consciousness, a narcissistic caprice that we think will control the future). Rather, these material goods are a temporal hinge between the past and the future that we can continually open and close by returning, re-touching and re-opening, by sharing the materials again and again. These material goods are the

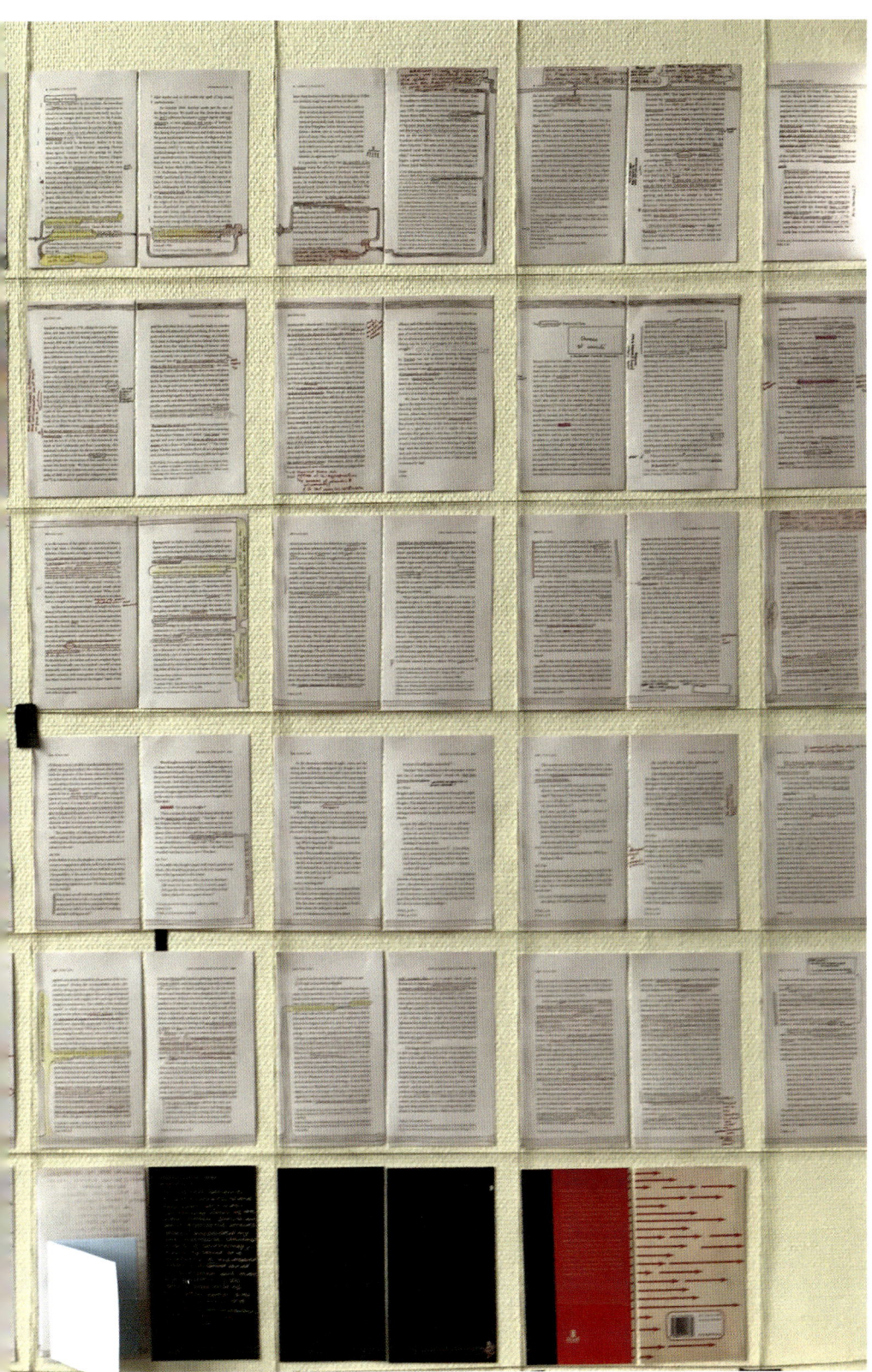

Fig. 6 (previous page) — Furio Jesi: Spartakus: The Symbology of Revolt. *Annotated by: Laurence Rassel, Christel Stalpaert, Roise Goan, Andrea Livia Piazza, Michiel Vandevelde, Maxime Arnould; hosted by KunstenfestivaldesArts, Brussels, and Vooruit, Ghent, Belgium, 2018. Photo © Ivana Müller*

legacy of the worlds of people who establish the relationships, and the only way we can return to them is not to separate them from these relationships. Speaking from a broader perspective: this is also a crucial way if we want to decolonize the practices of how to return to the objects we have from the past. In this return the objects should not be a vessel for another violent separation from the relations that established them.

At the same time, the expansion of material goods affirms that performance or dance pieces are not a sum of individual initiatives, but rather a specific biosphere of enmeshed environments and bodies. This also changes the way we think about archives and legacy, admitting that works of art always belong to sharing and circulation, not to the possession of their guardians. From this perspective, the work of art belongs to the many who will perhaps disappear but reappear through new communities and their yet unknown relationships in the future. *(fig. 6)*

---

1   More information on: *tanzfonds.de/en/project/documentation-12-2015/depot-erbe/* (27/07/2023).

2   More information on: *ivanamuller.com/works/notes/* (22/10/2023).

REFERENCES

Agamben, Giorgio (2009): What is the Contemporary. In: What Is an Apparatus? and Other Essays. Translated by David Kishik and Stefan Pedatella. Stanford: Stanford University Press, pp. 39–54

Benjamin, Walter (2016): On the concept of history. *sfu.ca/~andrewf/CONCEPT2.html* (12/09/2023). Original German publication in: Die Neue Rundschau, vol. 61. Frankfurt: S. Fischer 1950, p. 560.

Chauchat, Alice (2015): Companions, Telepaths and Other Doubles. No place: Samizdat.

Chauchat, Alice and Mette **Ingvartsen** (2009): Everybodys Group Self-interviews. No place: Lulu.com. *metteingvartsen.net/wp-content/uploads/2016/12/2009--everybodys--publiction--group-self-interviews-copy.pdf* (12/09/2023).

Hartman, Saidya (2008): Venus in Two Acts. In: Small Axe, Number 26 (Volume 12, Number 2), pp. 1–14.

Hartman, Saidya (2021): Lose your Mother. A Journey along the Atlantic Slave Route. London: Serpent's Tail.

Heller-Roazen, Daniel (2008): Echolallas: On the Forgetting of Language. New York: Zone Books and Princeton University Press.

Ingvartsen, Mette (2009): Everybodys Six Months One Location. *metteingvartsen.net/wp-content/uploads/2016/12/2009--everybodys--publication--6-months-1-location-copy.pdf* (12/09/2023).

Love, Heather (2009): Loss and the Politics of Queer History. Cambridge, Massachusetts: Harvard University Press.

Rojo, Paz, Manuela **Zechner** and Anja **Kanngieser** (2003): Vocabulaboratories. Amsterdam: Lisa. *annas-archive.org/md5/f2e060179fb986a0b8e608ca3bd61fdf* (12/09/2023).

Schneider, Rebecca (2011): Performing Remains. Art and War in Times of Theatrical Reenactment. London: Routledge.

Taylor, Diana (2003): The Archive and the Repertoire. Performing Cultural Memory in the Americas. Durham, North Carolina: Duke University Press.

Docum
as Kno
Produc

enting
wledge
tion

"I want to continue working on the body"
Gabriele Klein and Sasha Waltz in Conversation

GABRIELE KLEIN *In C* **was created during the Covid 19 pandemic. A different way of working was necessary because of the contact restrictions. In this piece, you transferred the 53 musical figures that Terry Riley had developed for musical composition to movement figures. How did you proceed?**

SASHA WALTZ Our work started as research because we were so desperate in the second lockdown. It was important for me that we could come together and create something again. I listened to a lot of music and really planned to try different pieces of music and then check what I wanted to work on. And then I was so caught up in *In C* that I actually just worked on that.

At first, I approached it very playfully, perhaps also because I had no deadline pressure. I gave the dancers small tasks – movement tasks that had very little content because it is an abstract piece. I had read articles about how micro-robots have been developed that are oriented towards movements from nature, for example: caterpillars, insects, or sea animals.
I found this transformation of movements from nature into the mechanical body intriguing and exciting as an approach to movement figures.

I created small fragments of movement with the dancers and followed Terry Riley's score and the musical notation stringently. And I thought, we dancers should treat ourselves like musicians, work with the body like musicians work with their instrument. Then I built smaller blocks and saw how that worked – in time and space. I wanted a wide range of moving and static, small gestural and large dynamic figures to emerge.

You said: "I created fragments of movements." How did you do that? Did you do it with your body? Did you write it down? Did you take notes? Did you make sketches? Did you develop it alone or in dialogue with the dancers?

It's actually always a group process, a dialogue. We were ten dancers and we did it together. Actually, I tend to be observant in bigger productions, but with *In C,* I took part and danced along. Of course, I usually take a lot of notes. In *In C,* the movement figures were not so long, the sequences and scenes were not so complex, as the complexity rather emerges in the composition, in the superposition of the figures and the spatial design. Scenes often go through big transformations when I develop a

Fig. 1 — In C, *Sasha Waltz & Guests, Terry Riley, Ensemble* © *Yanina Isla*

choreography. Here it was different. That's why I have much fewer notes from *In C* than from other pieces.

I worked a lot with a kind of blackboard, and I wrote down all the figures – there are 53 in total – with chalk on the wall, wiped out the changes to the score constantly and rewrote over. It was very important that we sort of developed a vocabulary, labelled the figures, and made them obvious to us because the work was so abstract. In other rehearsal processes, I gave the scenes titles – sometimes these were movement qualities, sometimes associative images. Sometimes the title came from the music or the libretto. That is our common linguistic level. In *In C,* I started naming the individual choreographic figures very early on, and so all 53 have a name. For example: *Shoulder – Yellow – New York – Hug – Hang – Ging – Hippie – Tango – Fall – Bird – Ling – Baby – Chin – Insect – Orange – Dog – Wind – Pencil – Earth – Banana – Catch Apple – Ed – Angry Apple – Puppy – Sleeping – Blue – Eleven – Band – Flamingos – Spy – Don't talk to me!* The names were our orientation system. Remembering works very well in language.

You once said that *In C* is a kind of structured improvisation, that means it is performed differently depending on the situation, but there are also rules. What are the rules?

That's the next step. After we developed the figures, we started to test them in space. The layering of the figures creates a very complex structure for which you need a system of spatial organisation. In music, the score was adequate for the performing musicians. My choreographic score had to be complemented by spatial tasks and compositional tools, i.e., you can come together in all kinds of geometric figures – in a diagonal, a square, a triangle, a line. There is the idea of birds or of flocking, which means that groups come together and move in one direction like a swarm. There are 53 rules for spatial composition in total that can be applied during the performance, but they are not mandatory.

At the beginning of our rehearsals, this wasn't possible because we had to move at a distance. After the lockdown, the dancers could physically come in contact with each other again so I added that the figures can come into contact with each other and can thus also slightly be changed. In addition, there are chains, there is intensity, volume – making something very big or a little smaller – or making the movement run backwards, that is the figure retrograde. There is pause as a means of composition, which is very important because there is always condensation or congestion, traffic.

Do all the dancers rehearse all 53 choreographic figures or only some of them?

First of all, all the dancers have to learn all the figures and rules, and the basic rule in the performance is: it has to be chronological from 1 to 53, this is how Terry Riley already established it in his score. In doing so, all figures can be repeated as often as desired. The dancers and musicians decide individually how often they perform a figure. This is how these interwoven structures are created, as several figures always overlap. The only restriction is that one may not stand more than 4 to 5 figures apart. And one can't jump forwards or backwards. And the dancers can use the 53 rules of composition within this structure, depending on how it is necessary in the situation.

The dancers decide that individually or through dialogue?

It is a very complex structure which happens in *In C*, a kind of morphic field is created here. The dancers feel what their neighbour is supposed to do and either decide to go along or suggest something else. This also happens in larger groups. I would say, that there is a collective intelligence at work. The figures are units

Fig. 2 — In C, *Sasha Waltz & Guests, Terry Riley, Ensemble © Jo Glinka 2021*

that are precisely defined, each of them has its own time measure. Each figure is different, what connects them all is the basic beat in C major, which underlies the piece like a heartbeat. The figures must therefore be danced very precisely, but can then be varied again, repeated, or fragmented within the time structure.

For guest performances, the dancers are always recast, it is not only dancers of your company who dance. How does this passing on by other dancers happen?

We developed tutorials right at the beginning, so we filmed the individual figures in detail and explained them in the video. These videos also came about because during the pandemic, many of the dancers working with me lived elsewhere and could not travel, and so they were able to learn the piece through the video tutorials.

There are various phases for dancers to learn the material. In the first phase, the dancers receive the tutorials, so they can learn the figures very precisely. Then there is a workshop of at least two weeks to study the rules of composition, and of course, there are a lot of run-throughs with music, because the relation to music has to be established as well. It takes a lot of practice to dance *In C* as well as collective understanding, which is greater when dancers have danced together more often. But I also try to get the dancers to find new impulses, to make unusual decisions; this also keeps the group permanently awake. I don't want *In C* to become routine at some point, that it seems choreographed. I want to maintain this absolutely free, open moment of the decision, that is right for the space and for the group at this time.

Your website states: "How can we rethink artistic production?" Would you say that with *In C* you have rethought how you work yourself and with dancers? How you see stage art through the experience of digitality due to Covid 19?

Definitely! I have done large choreographies and also choreographic operas with elaborate stage design and costume. In the last few years – also regardless of Covid 19 – we have been thinking a lot about the climate change and started rethinking. How do we deal with our resources? This was important for me during Covid 19 and for *In C,* because the question arose: Will we still travel at all? And how will we be able to travel? Maybe only a few people? For *In C,* we created very simple costumes that everyone can pack in their suitcase. For the stage, we need only a dance floor and, if possible, a foil; both of them are usually available at the venue, we don't take it with us at all. So, we travel as lightly as possible.

In C is therefore also an answer to how we can save resources and how we can travel more sustainably. In addition, *In C* has another dimension. As a company, we still perform it in Berlin and on tour, but we also teach the material. And that is a new dimension because we don't necessarily have to travel everywhere and can reduce the amount of travelling. The transmission of material also has an educational effect. My thoughts on composition and space, which I have developed for many years, how I approach choreography, how I imagine a space, and how I work with the dancers are written in all 53 rules of *In C*. It is a system, an instruction manual – reduced and broken down in such a way that it can be conveyed relatively easily. And I didn't think of knowledge transfer like this before. Previously, I did choreographies that were very clearly written on and with individual dancer personalities, handovers weren't thus as important or didn't feel right. Meanwhile, I have handed over the pieces *Roméo et Juliette* but also *Körper* and *noBody* to other companies. With *In C,* it's completely different and I rather feel – this was from the beginning – that I had this desire for movement, for the body and for the energy, and I wanted to convey this experience of what dance can do. During the pandemic, we had such a negative relationship with our bodies, with other people, with closeness, I wanted to counteract that with something positive.

Fig. 3 (previous page) — In C, *Sasha Waltz & Guests,*
Terry Riley, Bang on a Can All Stars, Ensemble © *Sebastian Bolesch*

In 2023, you celebrated the thirtieth anniversary of your company. That is an unbelievably long time for an independent dance company and in itself a work of art to keep it going for so long – also financially. How do you imagine the future of an independent dance company in a digital world?

You can see it with *In C:* You can learn a choreography through tutorials, also digitally. But nevertheless, there is always a lack of information that can only be passed on in a purely somatic way. And the collective design of the space cannot be conveyed digitally. Complex spatial design is still difficult to establish, mistakes always happen. The space and the spatial design are the real problems with the digitisation of dance, not the exact movement. Notes and videos are indeed essential tools for sharing pieces, but I still think it is important that the human being and the physical contact are at the centre and that the body knowledge is passed on directly. I want to continue working on the body!

But there are great projects that move into the digital. Or hybrid forms, I find all that very exciting. However, I think that live performances with dance will continue to exist. This collective experience, which occurs through performers and the audience, remains special and unique for all participants, and it will continue to exist.

You hired someone for the position of an archivist about three years ago. Why did you start working with an archivist?

The first time I looked through my archive was in 2013, when I did an exhibition at the ZKM.[2] I started sorting through my material to get an overview. Because only I knew where everything was at that time, no one else. When I open a notebook, I know: On such and such a page, there's probably this and that. But you can imagine how much it has become over the years! I have simply realised that I need a different system of organisation, which is also accessible from the outside.

Fig. 4 (next page) – Sasha Waltz,
sketchbook for Sacre, *2013*
© *ZKM | Karlsruhe, photo Martin Wagenhahn*

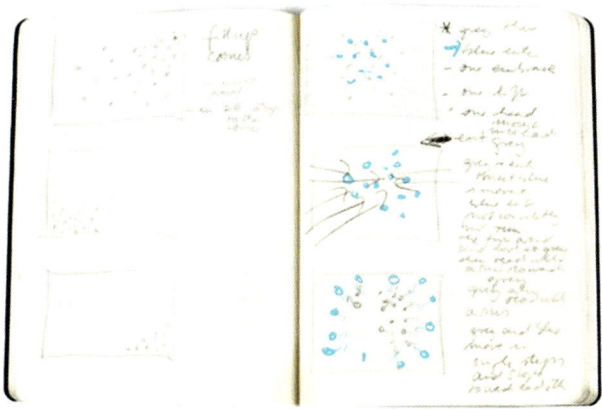

Have you also thought about putting your material into a publicly accessible archive?

No, it wasn't the idea to give my archive away somewhere, but to sort it; not only for me, but also for my collaborators, for repetiteurs who prepare the revivals of my pieces. Of course, the question arises: what happens to my archive in the end? Where does it go? I have also had the idea that parts of it are actually made accessible to the public. That there is a room where you can sit and look at videos or photos where the archive becomes alive. But we are not there yet. It has to grow slowly.

Peter Weibel[3] had asked me what I intended to do with my archive. But unfortunately, I couldn't give him an answer back then. I still don't know today. I haven't decided yet. At the moment, it's in good hands and we can access it digitally relatively quickly. I think that the archive also serves as a source of association for myself. It should be something that is still alive, that I am still in contact with. Not something that I file away and then that's it.

Do you draw on your archive when you make new pieces? Or do you always generate new material?

Usually, it's something new. But I have also looked into my old notebooks for some questions and looked through certain pages. And it can be also interesting to dive into a time past in the creation process. What did I work on there and how did I write it down and what drawings are still there? The past as inspiration, it is still in you!

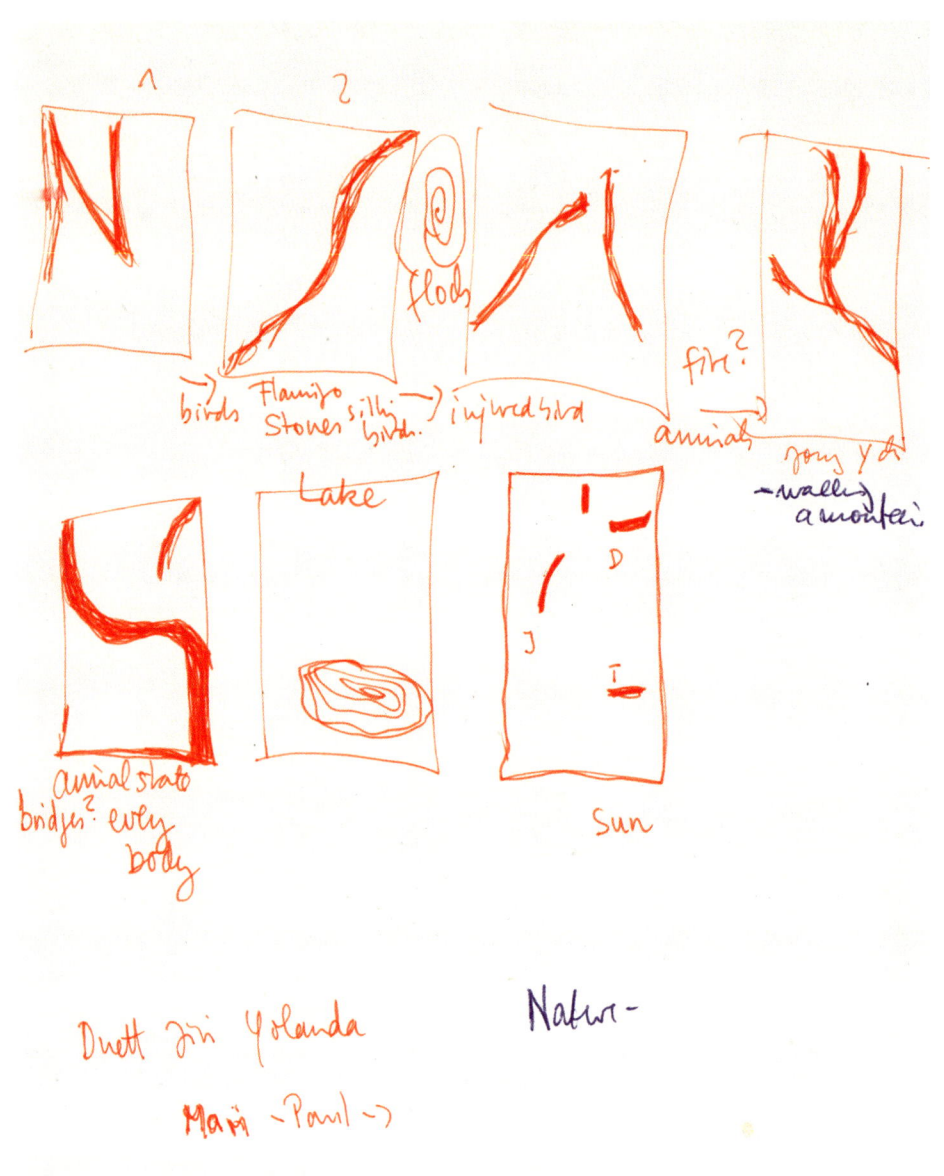

Fig. 5 — Sasha Waltz, sketch NATUR for SYM-PHONIE MMXX, 2019–2021

Besides photos, performance recordings or critiques – do you also want to make rehearsal material, your own or perhaps those of dancers or musicians you have worked with, available to the public?

I've had the idea of trying to break up a piece in this way: How is my working process? Where do you start? What kind of drawings are there? I draw an incredible amount, so I always first note movement in a drawing and then the word comes. Thus, there are a lot of notebooks. Some are beautiful, some are just a collection of sketches. So, the question is: what is interesting and what is uninteresting?

I always imagine my archive as something lively, in movement, quite openly accessible, with a sensual component, so that it also does justice to dance. It should be an archive that is about physicality and about space. How can we also bring this to life in the archive? An archive as a scenographic project. But as I said, I'm not there yet.

Dance archives of individual choreographers, whether Merce Cunningham, Pina Bausch, John Neumeier, or Hans van Manen, have one goal above all: the archive serves the reconstruction and passing on of the artistic work. You mentioned the need for physical passing on from dancer to dancer. How can I imagine such a transfer in 50 years? If this communicative memory no longer exists or if dancers of the first generation can no longer show and pass it on? Will the digital help? Will it help to have material that documents the rehearsal process? These are not only questions relevant to dance studies or dance historiography. They are also questions that address a culture of memory for dance. How can a culture of memory be created for a situational, contemporary art like dance?

Of course, we also thought about that. In the Pina Bausch exhibition[4], for example, I found it very interesting and revealing that there were her workbooks to see. This gives access to the thoughts, to a world behind the pieces. It is not always what we see that gives us new information. That's why I'm becoming more interested in language in dance. In very complex movements, when we move very far away from classical ballet, language is the only medium for me to describe the very specific qualities that we then look for in a scene or a particular movement, to fill in the gaps.

Maybe fifteen years ago, when we first thought about archives, our wish was actually – and we haven't done that until now! – that I speak about individual pieces in detail and we record that. Because sometimes drawings and sketches in workbooks are cryptic and the creation of choreographies is not very linear so that it's difficult to trace the process through these materials alone. But if you look back and summarise it again in your own words, it can give a lot of additional information. Especially when no one is alive who danced the performance. Text, language, narratives and records are important.

You once said: "The repertoire is the archive."
Would you still say that?

From the beginning of my career, I said that the pieces live when they are performed, so I wanted to develop a repertoire. I still think that. After so many years it just becomes difficult to maintain a large repertoire and keep it alive all the time. We had and still have a lot of different pieces in our repertoire, and I don't have a large ensemble. I always worked with freelancers. There was continuity, but also fluctuation, so you have to deal with that and it doesn't get easier the more pieces you want to keep alive. Nevertheless, repertoire is absolutely important for me. If you perform pieces again every two years or so, then the memory is still there in the body, and the dancers who have danced it can pass it on.

Do your pieces necessarily have to be passed on by dancers who have danced them? In ballet, this is done by the ballet masters.

I always have one or two repetiteurs, who usually danced the piece themselves and then became repetiteurs. In 2012, I transferred the piece *Körper*[5] to the Stockholm Ballet, and there was also a workshop of the original cast for the dancers of the Stockholm Ballet and the material was literally passed from body to body. That was very elaborate, but it is unnecessary if the pieces are well-documented.

There are many dancers and also dance scholars
who describe dancing as writing with the body.
Would you also see dancing as writing?

We don't describe, we dance. You always try to find an approach somehow. There are pieces where I have worked more visually.

You could also say drawing, which is perhaps even clearer than writing. In the end, for me it is an attempt to capture this transience. We can only transcribe with words and the word holds fast. But dance is too fleeting!

Some people say "writing" because they want to make it clear that dancing leaves traces.

But that's an illusion! There are no more traces when the dance is over. The traces are only in our memory and in our perception and in what the dancers have experienced. Ok, there may still be a video recording – but that doesn't really count. For me, dance is like a fragrance.

So, there can't really be an archive of dance? Dance can only be archived if it is transmitted medially, in writing or images?

I envy music for its notation. Of course, you can watch a video and if an interesting filmmaker records it, then maybe it's visually appealing and you think you've seen the piece. But I never feel like I've really experienced the piece when I have only seen a recording of it. I'll also tell you honestly, with video transmissions of concerts, too much is lost for me. But what we cannot record makes art for me: the collective experience in a performance. For me, that is the real thing. That's the reason why we continue to cultivate our art and don't just go digital. It's something non-material, it's vibrations; and it's something that we as spectators also feel with our bodies.

---

1   The interview was conducted on 2 May 2023 via *Zoom*.
2   Sasha Waltz. *Installations, Objects, Performances.* A special exhibition at the ZKM (Center for Art and Media Karlsruhe), 28 September, 2013 – 2 February, 2014.
3   Peter Weibel (1944—2023) directed the Center for Art and Media Karlsruhe from 1999 to 2023.
4   *Pina Bausch and the Dance Theatre.* 4 March to 4 July 2016 at the Bundeskunsthalle, Bonn, and from 16 September 2016 to 9 January 2017 at the Martin-Gropius-Bau, Berlin.
5   The choreography *Körper,* a co-production with the Théâtre de la Ville, Paris, premiered at the Schaubühne am Lehniner Platz in Berlin on 22 January 2000.

From Documenta to Performative Documentation
Annet Dekker

Documentation practices

The word "document" derives from the Latin verb *docere,* to learn, show and inform, as well as *documentum,* which signifies instruction and/or teaching. The root of the word shows that in the original Latin a document is not just an object, but rather a testimony, an example, an instructive demonstration of some principle or idea. Hence, "documentation" has been used to signify material that provides official information or evidence or that serves as a record, as well as the process of classifying and annotating texts, photographs, etc., and more recently as the written specification and instructions accompanying a product, especially a computer programme or hardware (Dekker 2018). While the first two meanings date to the seventeenth century it wasn't until the twentieth century that the profession of the documentalist was born. The first ideas about the relationship between a document and documentation surfaced in the writings of Belgian bibliographer and entrepreneur, Paul Otlet, and French librarian Suzanne Briet (among others) and developed into documentalist, library studies and later information studies (Day 2001). It was Briet who came up with the term *Homo Documentator* in the early 1950s, to distinguish between a librarian and a documentalist: *"It is not too much to speak of a new humanism in this regard. A different breed of researchers 'is in the making'. It springs from the reconciliation of the machine and the mind."* (Briet 2006[1951]: 17)

According to Briet, a librarian cared for the collection and developed a bibliographic apparatus, whereas a documentalist was paired with the researcher: under the influence of technology, they had become "a new breed of humans" (Briet 2006[1951]: 17). In her time, Briet was pioneering the profession of bibliographers, and perhaps even now her ideas are progressive. Not only did she see the relevance of the collaboration between the documentalist and the researcher, but she also expanded the notion of what constituted a document, and by breaking the trope of the written text she argued that a document could be *"any concrete or symbolic indexical sign [indice], preserved or recorded toward the ends of representing, of reconstituting, or of proving a physical and intellectual phenomenon"* (Briet 2006[1951]: 10). Using the word "indexical/indice" she placed the document in an organised and meaningful relationship with other material, and by emphasising documents as essential 'facts' or 'proof', she stressed their referential value. In other words, she saw documents as examples of things, or groupings of things, that would unfold in social and cultural spaces and hence derive meaning from the context of their creation and use. Briet was interested in the importance and influence of social networks and cultural forms that give value to documents.

In most museums, documentation is created by professionals; however, social networks are rarely taken into account when documenting the art that is collected. In addition to textual descriptions, photography has become the main method to document art. As José Ramón López pointed out, such photography captures a specific moment in time and freezes a particular perspective, point of view or experience: *"Photography, like museums, freezes things in time, stores them. Objects, like people, can reach eternity through it. Somehow, it reinforces, as it expands it, the idea of conservation, of the museum. Little by little, photography has become the modern temple of memory."*[2]

Since its inception, photography has been regarded as a tool for exploration and science (Wilder 2009). It is used to document landscapes, historical buildings, important events, societies and objects, either to illustrate scientific research, books and magazines, as evidence on which to base experiments or paintings, or to effect preservation efforts. Indeed, particularly concerning the latter, photographic images and textual descriptions have had a privileged place in the preservation and dissemination of art projects and have become the dominant way to reproduce art. Yet, even though documentation is at the core of museum practices, over the years methods to create it have evolved relatively little.

However, at the same time, artists' attitudes to documenting their work have evolved significantly: from elaborate notebooks to various video forms, and to seeing documentation itself as (part of) an art practice. Conceptual artist Sol LeWitt's detailed instructions on how to reproduce his large wall drawings are exemplary: in the art magazine *Artforum* he discussed in the 1960s how his diligent way of working was inherently conceptual, a process he described as: *"When an artist uses a conceptual form of art, it means that all of the planning and decisions are made beforehand and the execution is a perfunctory affair. The idea becomes a machine that makes the art."* (LeWitt 1967)

What would happen when taking the notion of machine documentation more literally? What if a machine makes art based on its documentation? What kind of data would a machine need? And would the result be closer to the dynamics of the art it tries to document? In other words, what happens in the interplay between human and machine? Or, as formulated by digital curator and researcher Katrina Sluis: *"What is captured in the act of photographic documentation? This has always been something of a troubling question, particularly when documenting art. Two forms of mediation – the artwork on the one hand, the photograph on the other – collide and produce a visual record in the form of a negative or digital image file. In this meeting between artwork and camera, the artwork's iconicity is emphasised whilst the photograph is rendered transparent, delegated the role of invisible carrier or container of visual information."* (Sluis 2022: 27)

In this article I will expand on how documentation practices have diversified to become what the Maltesian director of digital media Toni Sant has described as "the processes of documenting as a practice" (Sant 2017: xxi). As a consequence, documentation may affect the role of *Homo Documentator* as well as the art they document. For the purpose of this article, I'm particularly interested in the doing of documentation as a performative act and in how it becomes a network or assemblage that can be seen as forward-looking instead of a remnant of the past.[3] Hence, my focus will be on the *how:* how the documentation of digital art takes place and how it shifts from being documentation of, to being part of the art it tries to represent, or how in other cases it may turn into a new art project and thus becomes performative.

I describe digital art as a process of creation that is heterogeneous and involves incompatibilities, constraints, rules and a certain amount of improvisation in which its own structures can be continuously renegotiated (Dekker 2018: 20). Hence, digital art moves from art as a discrete, stabilised, original and authorial object, to art projects that can be characterised as:

– performative 'objects' that need to be executed to function properly and due to their changing context or the obsolescence of their hardware or software, have to be migrated or emulated to continue to work;
– distributed, in which (parts of) the project is scattered across different spatial, temporal and property regimes: elements can be part of multiple collections;

– proliferative and circulatory – such projects are replicated or reproduced in various contexts and don't necessarily exist as a final product or object, as the process (or network of other projects and people) constitutes the value of the project;
– processual, without a final state – here the art project may be (re)generated, and fragments or details of one project may lead to new projects;
– multi-authored, in which authorship is shared or becomes obfuscated.

What does it mean if these characteristics are translated to documentation practices?

Documentary documentation

Many performative, time-based and digital artworks are conceived of and developed in relation to societal factors which both shape and, on occasion, respond to the artwork. This means that, over time, the specific relational qualities of an artwork – the 'original' context for its production, exhibition and conservation – are neglected. Documentation can unify the different contextual elements of an artwork, for example, in a documentary in which text, images or videos explore the aesthetics and functioning of the artwork. While such documentary methods are highly diverse, a few years ago the Dullaart-

Fig. 1 — Constant Dullaart, Robert Sakrowski, netartdatabase, *https://net.artdatabase.org (screenshot).*

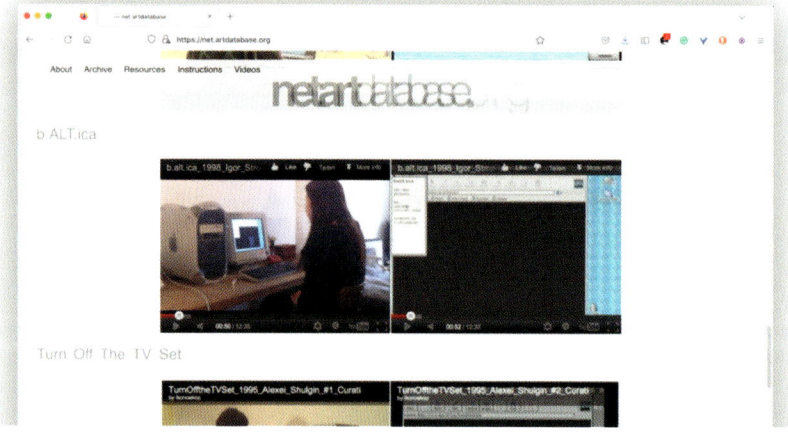

Sakrowski method tried to set a standard on how to best document net art (Spreeuwenberg et al. 2012). They proposed using a split-screen that showed both a screen recording and an over-shoulder perspective of someone browsing a website *(fig. 1),* thereby emphasising the work and the context in which it was viewed. The approach resembles the style of a conventional documentary in which the art project is shown in a factual and informative manner.

Publishing (online) is another form of documentation, as happened with *Naked on Pluto* by David Griffiths, Aymeric Mansoux and Marloes de Valk, a Facebook game created in 2010 that ceased to exist five years later due to changes in Facebook's regulations. Mansoux, together with artists/researchers Sophie Boschat Thorez and Dušan Barok, tried to gather all the loosely connected documentation scattered across the web, including texts, videos, photos and technical details of the project, in one space.[4] They approached *Naked on Pluto* as a discursive artwork that was documented in four ways:

– a dispersed archival repository that included the digital and physical material related to the artwork, i.e., articles, files, data;
– a series of public manifestations that ranged from public lectures to workshops and exhibitions;
– a narrative that favoured the presentation and experience of the game over its preservation;
– a description of the context in which the artwork was created and presented to situate it in its time and space, to provide a possible key to its comprehension in the future.

These four ways of documentation offer information about the process, how people interacted with the work, and the work's relationality.

For their documentation approach, the team used the notion of "preservation by publication" to emphasise that their preservation efforts were not based on the medium but rather on the conceptual impetus of the initial project, in this case, a problem-driven artwork, which they also referred to as artistic research.[5] This documentary practice shifts from showing only images or video, which would emphasise the technical or functional elements of an artwork, to creating a contextual overview that can include comments from the artists. By discontinuing the artwork, or even showing how it worked in a video, they hoped that emphasising the context in which the game was developed and functioned would provide future users with a better understanding of the context in which the artwork once thrived. An added advantage of the wiki was that they could compile an inventory to provide an extensive overview of all the technical details that could be used in the future as a basis from which new artworks or narratives could be developed.

Using video to document an artwork shifts the emphasis from merely a technical or functional overview to also include comments from others involved in the artwork, such as those who experienced it. Hence it is a strategy to better understand the context in which the artwork thrived. Such a form follows the conventions in documentaries to document primarily for the purposes of instruction, education, or to maintain a historical record. *Naked on Pluto* also followed this approach, but the team expanded it by bringing together the dispersed archive that was left after the artwork ended. The intention was not to embed or copy the actual material that was hosted on numerous websites. Instead, they followed a post-custodial practice, thereby shifting the balance of power in preservation. Linking to and contextualising the 'original' sources, rather than archiving them on a new server has the benefit that the material remains in its 'original' environment, at least for as long as those websites and links are operational. Publishing as preservation is therefore closely connected to the documentary format, albeit in the form of a wiki.

Documentation (as part) of the artwork

Documentary documentation can be seen as an interpretation of the art project, which may also replace the art project. However, documentation can also become an integral part of the artwork, as is the case with *Agent Ruby* (1999) by Lynn Hershman Leeson. *Agent Ruby* is described as an "artificial intelligent web agent" that responds to the input of users and data she[6] finds on the web. Eventually, Ruby is able to recognise the user's voice and respond to the perceived emotions, and likewise, her animated facial expression may be triggered by real-time web traffic.

Many digital artworks are experienced subjectively, and documenting how people react, especially to interactive art, is important to gain a better understanding of these artworks. Moreover, due to these interactions, the artwork can grow beyond its initial data set and potential function, and hence the documentation of the performances, including the changing engagement with the artwork, becomes relevant. SFMOMA exhibited *Agent Ruby* in 2013. However, because the project no longer functioned in the newer browser settings, Ruby could only respond based on the documented data in the database. Rather than updating the code to fit the settings, the historic interactions with *Agent Ruby* were shown. The exhibited version consisted of a custom-made code that visitors could interact with on a computer screen, and of binders and wall prints where they could explore dialogues from the twelve-year archive of audience interactions, referred to as *The Agent Ruby Files (fig. 2)*. This documentation made it possible to search for recurrent themes, technologies, and patterns in previous audience engagements.

Over time, due to users' questions and the data on the web *Ruby* changed her identity. When it no longer worked with the browsers, the museum turned to the documentation in its database. While *Agent Ruby* still exists online, its database doesn't grow anymore. To understand the initial development and change in *Ruby,* users can consult the documentation of its past interactions with the public. This shifts the status of documentation, which not only bears witness, or represents the work, but also becomes part of the artwork. *Agent Ruby* and *The Agent Ruby Files* are therefore both the same work and different iterations of it simultaneously, illustrating how documentation can define and become part of the artwork.

Fig. 2 — Lynn Hershman Leeson, The Agent Ruby Files, *SFMOMA, 2013.*

Generative documentation

Development and change in digital artworks are not unusual. Often these artworks evolve over prolonged periods of time and include user interactions but also generate numerous formats and manifestations, such as performances, talks and even research papers that circulate in different places. In these cases, the whole is more than the sum of the individual elements, as its – intentionally – sheer diversity and dispersion obscure the totality. While the documentation of such projects could add another level to this confusion, the term "generative documentation" can be applied to the convergence of these dispersed artworks.

mouchette.org (1996–present) by Martine Neddam is an example of such an approach.[7] The project started as an interactive website mimicking the diary of an age-proof 13-year-old girl, *Mouchette,* who expresses her thoughts on death, desire and suicide. The website can be accessed through an intricate navigation system, consisting of several image, audio and text compositions and various paths of interaction, including web questionnaires, games and fora. Yet, the artwork expanded to include live performances, installations, a variety of other websites and objects. As mentioned by Neddam: "It's hard to say what constitutes *mouchette.org.* Over the years I have lost track of all the performances, projects and objects that I made. But for sure, *mouchette.org* is more than just a website." (Neddam 2011)

Capturing the convergence of these components over time requires a proactive type of preservation, which Neddam herself refers to as "generative preservation" (Neddam 2016). The term "generative" addresses the ambiguity of the artwork, asking what it consists of, and how it evolves. It also emphasises the inaccuracy of notions that are commonly used in reference to an artwork, such as 'original' and 'unique'. In generative preservation, the distinction between the 'original' and its subsequent iterations is hard to make because earlier parts of the artwork and its documentation are reused or become part of a new iteration. Following this, generative documentation emphasises the evolving interactions as well as how documentation reproduces the artwork or transforms it into new artworks. Seeing *mouchette.org* as an expansive and pervasive project, including its documentation that is based on people's interactions, and the multiple other documentations of the project, it is both a performative site and its own archive, from which it keeps generating new projects. As such it is similar to how the artists of *Naked on Pluto* regarded their inventory on the wiki as a way to continue forking the project in new and potentially unexpected ways. However, rather than trying to create a standard index, *Mouchette* is more dispersed: in addition to the *mouchette* network and a separate website created by Neddam where members can become *Mouchette* (Dekker 2018), users also create their own projects. One such example is the Twitter account *botchette* – *@mouchettebot* by @larvapie (since October 2017[8]) in which an automated bot sent out several short messages every day that derive from *mouchette.org's* database – and hence, now a machine makes the documentation.[9] Although Neddam didn't set this up, she does regard it as part of the wider *Mouchette* network. Similarly, these creators usually make direct links to the website, forming a tightly knit network.

The documentation strategies of these artworks emphasise the "notions of growth and expansion instead of repetition or replication" (Dekker 2018: 93), where documentation becomes a propagating, generative mechanism that is aimed towards the future. As described by Gabriella Giannachi: *"This could be interpreted as a sort of cellular and potentially regenerative understanding of the relationship between digital art and documentation. Hence documentation could be visualised as a rhizomatic model [...] Documentation then is what is done to keep the artwork alive and to propagate the artwork via its documentation in space and time."* (Giannachi 2022: 135)

The notion of generative documentation challenges the conventional object oriented approach of art. However, whereas digital art evolves over time, its documentation remains static. While documentation can influence the experience and functioning of the artwork or play a role in its continuation and development, what does it mean for documentation to be performative?

Performative documentation

In 2016 I received an e-mail from Igor Štromajer, a well-known Slovenian artist who has worked as a performance and net artist since the 1990s *(fig. 3)*.

When opening the files, I saw two abstract cropped images, two gifs – one of someone sitting on a toilet and one of a roll of toilet paper – and a sound file of less than a second.

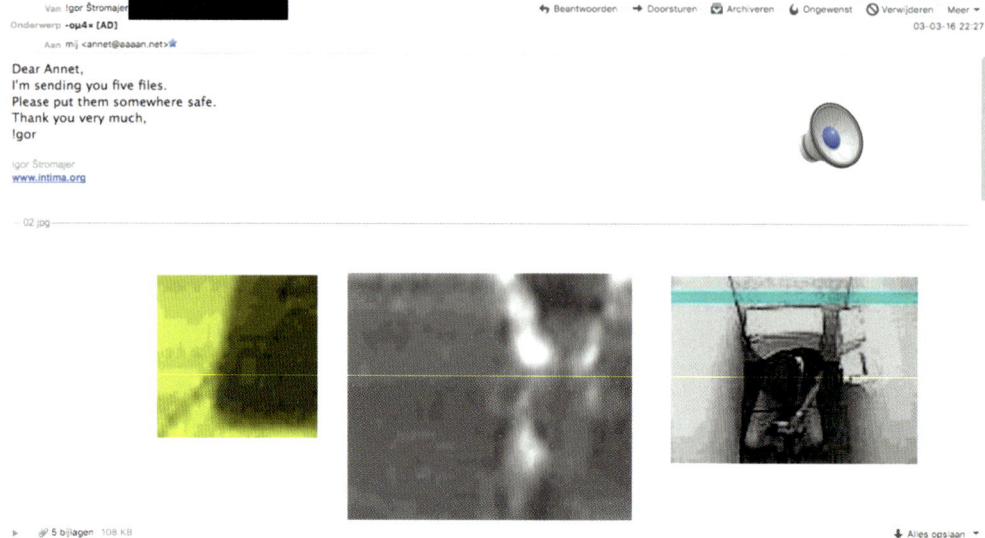

Fig. 3 — E-mail from Igor Štromajer, to the author, -oμ4×, 3 March 2016.

Two years later I received a similar e-mail asking me to keep the attached files, now encrypted, in a safe place. And again in 2020, I received an e-mail with yet more encrypted files. After the second e-mail I asked him about his practice, and Igor explained that *-oμ4x* (minus mu four times) was a "performative action" in which over several years, from 2016 to 2022, he would ask a decreasing group of people to keep several files safe. The files were a random selection from his earlier project *Expunction* (2011). *Expunction* was a performative project in which Štromajer ritually deleted a number of his classic net artworks that were produced between 1996 and 2007. To him, they did not look the same anymore because the context and settings of the web had changed. Štromajer preferred deletion to aesthetic loss, yet he did find several fragments and documentations of his artworks and he also documented his performance on a website.[10]

Expunction addresses questions of duration, accessibility and archiving of net art, which due to its inherent hardware and software challenges as well as those in its environment (such as browsers, players, apps, etc.), change or break down, resulting in it losing its functionality and hence its content. Yet, with the project *-oμ4x,* fragments and documentation become relevant in a new context. Although the autonomous images and files I received have little meaning, not in the least because they are encrypted, together with the e-mails they form a network that symbolises a promise, a proximity, that may be fulfilled one day.

As such, -oμ4x reflects the temporality of many digital artworks: a network is instigated by the first e-mail, but its development is ambiguous, prone to rupture or loss, and the result is open to speculation, depending on the actions of the recipients who don't know each other. The extended period of waiting for something to happen affirms the reality of the events that unfold, even if the outcome is open: it can disappoint but this is also the beauty of the work, because, as tromajer mentions, the project is: *"[…] a kind of a cycle, a durational, perhaps never-ending online performance with its natural rhythm: being constructed, deconstructed, then reconstructed anew, but this time differently. Who knows exactly what comes afterwards, but there is certainly no end to this cycle, because every trace, every move you make has its consequences."* (Štromajer in Sakrowski 2017)

Next to the technical files and encryption, which harbour their own technical specificity and agency, the social aspect of the act is important and answers the question of how documentation can become performative. The term "network of care" refers to the presentation or distribution of the project as public gifts, and hence choosing the circulation of close friends over commercial or established artworlds (Dekker 2018; 2022a). A network of care can emerge in response to an urgent issue, or form around an emotional connection, and it can be loosely described as:
– consisting of human and non-human actors that relate to each other (for potentially different reasons);
– based on a transdisciplinary attitude, an informal and open structure that is served by a combination of professionals and non-experts;
– using a common mode of sharing that is accessible to and can be (re)purposed by all; operating without the infrastructures of centralised archives and authorised custodians.

Although the notion of *networks of care* was initially used to better understand the preservation challenge of digital art, seeing documentation through the lens of this concept also facilitates the mapping of the different relations between documents, fragments, people and non-human actors. While -oμ4x demonstrates an engaged way of dealing with circulation and relations, in which the distributive effects are intentional even if what finally happens is unpredictable, the documentation proposes new modes of active engagement and creative use. The potentiality of the project is triggered by the e-mails and the fragmentary and encrypted files, i.e., the documentation (in which the e-mails also become documentation). The suspense or suggestion of infinity, or of being part of an adventure, may only become clear through engaging with it. Indeed, the documentation is hardly interesting in itself, but together and as part of a larger whole it is compelling because it conveys a suggestion of potentiality. Finally, the social aspect of the act is important here. The documentation (both the e-mails and the files) forms a network that may include points of convergence, yet these likely occur at an undecided moment when different actors find a point of connection, or shared interests, in which the roles of artist, audience, curator and conservator are allowed and sometimes encouraged to merge, which may lead in multiple other directions. The documentation is an invitation, a performative gesture to the future to continue the project.

In conclusion   Artists' documentation practices have diversified extensively, not only in their form but also in their function: with documentary documentation a video or other translation is made of a work, even though the work may still exist, either fully functioning or as fragments scattered around the web. This documentation functions as a memory or a historical document of what once was. With documentation as part of the artwork, documentation that is either generated in the artwork or as additional to the artwork (for instance floorplans or code) can at a certain point replace certain aspects of the work that malfunction, and hence also become (part of) it. With generative documentation, parts of the (potentially still functioning) artwork and its documentation are re-used. These fragments can lead to the ongoing development of the work or become part of a new iteration, and hence the work keeps evolving in unexpected directions. Finally, by considering documents/documentation as part of a network of care, documentation becomes performative and even an apparently meaningless fragment can become effective as a tool for transformation.

Clearly, there may be overlaps in the different categories, but the distinctions set up a proposition, foremostly as a way to open up and expand the concept and practice, and to emphasise the significance of shifting the notion of documentation from a past-facing documentary as a testament of an 'original' artwork, to understand documentation as future-facing while functioning through multiplicity. This means looking at and mimicking how digital art functions. Such documentation may become part of an existing art project, a new art project or suggest as yet undefined art projects. Moreover, doing documentation is about new socially organised networks in which different structures and systems, actors human and non-human coalesce around a shared interest. Such an approach also reinforces the characteristics of the artwork: embracing the openness, the unexpected and unstable relations that lead to a future-oriented practice in which custodial responsibilities and privileges are shared in ways that involve those who are affected by these artworks.

1. This article is an extended version of earlier articles, notably "Networks of Care" in *The Networked Image in Post Digital Culture,* edited by Andrew Dewdney and Katrina Sluis. London: Routledge, 2022, 189–207, and "The Qualities and Significance of Documentation" (co-authored with Gabriella Giannachi), MAP, Media Archive Performance #12, July 2022 (in particular the sections on 'Documentary documentation', 'Documentation as (part of) the artwork' and 'Generative documentation'). I want to thank my co-author Gabriella Giannachi, and the editors Andrew Dewdney and Katrina Sluis, as well as the publishers of MAP, and Routledge for the reproduction of the content.

2. Quote by José Ramón López on the exhibition website *Camera Obscured,* The Photographers' Gallery, London, 30 April to 20 June 1997, see *thephotographersgallery.org.uk/whats-on/camera-obscured-photographic-documentation-and-public-museum* (29/08/2023). The original reads: *"La fotografía, como el museo, fija en el tiempo, conserva, almacena. Los objetos, como las personas, pueden alcanzar la eternidad a través de ella. En cierto modo refuerza a la vez que amplia la idea de conservación, la idea de museo. La fotografía, poco a poco, se ha ido convirtiendo en el moderno templo de la memoria."* (López 1994: 13)

3. For more information about how digital art, or net art, functions and can be regarded as a network and assemblage, see Dekker 2018.

4. This project was part of the AHRC-funded research project Documenting Digital Art (2019–2023), a collaboration between University of Exeter, London South Bank University, LIMA, The Photographers' Gallery and The Australian National University.

5. All the information about the project can be read on a dedicated *Wiki* page: *monoskop.org/Naked_on_Pluto* (30/06/2023).

6. *Agent Ruby* is gendered as "she".

7. Martine Neddam coined the term "generative preservation" (Neddam 2016), from which Gabriella Giannachi and I derived the term "generative documentation" (Dekker and Giannachi 2022).

8. The Twitter bot closed down on 6 April 2023 due to new Twitter regulations by ending all large-scale API usage, which means that the bot can no longer function.

9. For more examples of how bots are used for documentation purposes, see Dekker 2022b. In recent years, examples of AI-generated artworks have become more common. Most of these systems use existing databases (including users' images and documentations) to create new artworks, write texts or curate exhibitions (Dekker 2023), which continues to upend notions of authorship, creativity and originality.

10. *intima.org/expunction/* (30/06/2023).

REFERENCES

Briet, Suzanne (2006[1951]): What Is Documentation? (Qu'est-ce que la documentation?), translated and edited by Ronald E. Day and Laurent Martinet with Hermina G.B. Anghelescu. Lanham, MC: Scarecrow Press.

Day, Ronald E. (2001): The Modern Invention of Information: Discourse, History, and Power. Carbondale, IL: Southern Illinois University Press.

Dekker, Annet (2023): Non-Institutional Contexts & Museum Challenges. In: Vince Dzieken and Anna Munster (eds.), The Encyclopedia of New Media Art, Vol. 3. London/New York: Bloomsbury, forthcoming.

Dekker, Annet (2022a): Networks of Care. In: Andrew Dewdney and Katrina Sluis (eds.), The Networked Image in Post Digital Culture. London: Routledge, pp. 189–207.

Dekker, Annet (2022b): The Tension Between Static Documentation and Dynamic Digital Art. In: Annet Dekker and Gabriella Giannachi (eds.), Documentation as Art: Expanded Digital Practices. London: Routledge, pp. 16–26.

Dekker, Annet (2018): Collecting and Conserving Net Art. Moving Beyond Conventional Methods. London: Routledge.

Dekker, Annet and Gabriella **Giannachi** (2022): The Qualities and Significance of Documentation. In: MAP, Media Archive Performance. Vol. 12, perfomap.de/map12/digital-archive-environments/the-qualities-and-significance-of-documentation (12/05/2023).

Giannachi, Gabriella (2022): The use of documentation for preservation and exhibition: The cases of SFMOMA, Tate, Guggenheim, MOMA, and LIMA. In: Annet Dekker and Gabriella Giannachi (eds.), Documentation as Art: Expanded Digital Practices. London: Routledge, pp. 133–144.

LeWitt, Sol (1967): Paragraphs on Conceptual Art. In: Artforum (online) artforum.com/print/196706/paragraphs-on-conceptual-art-36719 (12/05/2023).

López, José Ramón (1994): Procedimiento de archivo. In: PhotoVision 1994, pp. 6–14.

Neddam, Martine (2016): La préservation générative. In: Journée d'étude sur la préservation des arts et littératures numériques, Beaux-Arts, Paris (27 October). about.mouchette.org/preservation-generative/ (12/05/2023).

Neddam, Martine (2011): How to Be Pink and Conceptual at the Same Time. Amsterdam: SKOR.

Sakrowski, Robert (2017): EXPUNCTION. Deleting www.intima.org Net Art Works. A Conversation. In: Annet Dekker (ed.), Lost and Living (in) Archives. Collectively Shaping New Memories. Amsterdam: Valiz, pp. 159–172.

Sant, Toni (ed.) (2017): Documenting Performance. The Context and Processes of Digital Curation and Archiving. London/New York: Bloomsbury Academic.

Sluis, Katrina (2022): Documentation in an Age of Photographic Hypercirculation. In: Documentation as Art: Expanded Digital Practices. London/New York: Routledge, pp. 27–37.

Spreeuwenberg, Kimberley (ed.) (2012): Documenting Internet-based Art. The Dullaart-Sakrowski Method. Culture Vortex. Public Participation in Online Collections. Amsterdam: Institute of Network Cultures, aaaan.net/wp-content/uploads/2015/09/Documenting-Internet-Based-Art_FINAL.pdf (12/05/2023).

Wilder, Kelly E. (2009): Photography and Science. London: Reaktion Books Ltd.

The Scriptal Method and Choreography
Axel Malik

"Choreography is a curious and deceptive concept. The word itself, like the process it describes, is elusive, agile, and maddeningly unmanageable. To reduce choreography to a single denotation is to not understand the most crucial of its mechanism: to resist and reform previous definitions."[1] WILLIAM FORSYTHE

In and by my project, which I call *The Scriptal Method,* I attempt to release and completely disengage the manual motions of handwriting from the conditioned and standardised rules regulating the production of discrete, decipherable sets of typographic characters. What is aimed at is an untamed form of writing, disengaged from all its conventional functional contexts and thus liberated from its state of subservience: a form of writing that allows us to grasp script in its peculiar irregular identity, in its unpredictably sprawling potentiality and its autonomous self-centredness. Does script – of and by itself – possess a form of power to act, or even have its own programmatic agenda?

My characters, each written in a quick single stroke, constitute complex and clearly distinct enactments separately executed and existing separately from each other. Although they resemble each other and share a kind of commonality that establishes a connection between them, no genuine repetitions ever occur. In each case, their respective individual form as a coherent, logical figuration remains a singular occurrence, never to be repeated. And they can differ from each other substantially. The fact that they do so of their own accord, as it were, that the hurried, brief and rushed motions of my writing hand continuously result in such a degree of variety, is a phenomenon which I find difficult to comprehend. If I think about it, it seems unlikely enough to be virtually impossible. Yet is it not actually the case – against all odds?

In spite of their completeness – their implicit coherence as characters – and although many observers initially feel tempted to associate their form with instances of iconic representation, these characters are not drawn but written. As signs, they have no external point of reference, no semantic content – they refer to nothing beyond themselves. The characters I write neither make up the letters of an unknown alphabet, nor are they symbols. They neither amount to elements of pictographic script, nor do I bring to bear any kind of code in their writing.

And yet they are script; their having been written is obvious to any observer. But what is obvious, too, is that they cannot be read. Is this a fundamental feature, part and parcel of their essence, something that holds (and always will hold) true, whatever the circumstances? Does a script that cannot be read constitute a form of regress, a falling back to an earlier stage in the development of writing? Does my writing truly 'lack' decipherability? Is there something my characters actually lack, or is it rather the case that they, conversely, possess the additional potential to point towards something else that is made manifest exclusively by and through their form and their relationship to form?

Is this about rudimentary, vague forms that hark back to obsolete and long-forgotten states in the evolutionary history of writing? Or does my work also contain other progressive moments and new potentials that become apparent just now that handwriting as a practice is more and more on the vane? The aspect that lies at the core of my own motivation, the idea that preoccupies me and drives me to work, can be expressed by a seeming paradox – or at least by a most significant differentiation: By the observation that the characters I write and the sequences – the written 'texts' – which they form are unreadable, in that they cannot be read, though they are never illegible after the fashion of slapdash handwriting.

Unreadable vs. illegible – this contrast, and the tension that it implies, stakes out the field within which I move. I experience a pull, an urge, an attraction and a lack of footing. This elusive state of reeling instability is something I have been chasing after – something I have been trying to stalk up on and get into my grasp – ever since April 1989, when I commenced my work by putting on paper my very first characters. Since then, I have been writing daily; a core element of my project consists in the creation of consecutively paginated books, comprising by now more than 140 volumes with a total of over 30,000 pages – all of them unreadable though never illegible.

There was an initial key moment that I often describe as a positive shock because my understanding of writing and reading was turned completely upside down from one moment

Fig. 1 — Axel Malik,
The Scriptal Method, 2023.

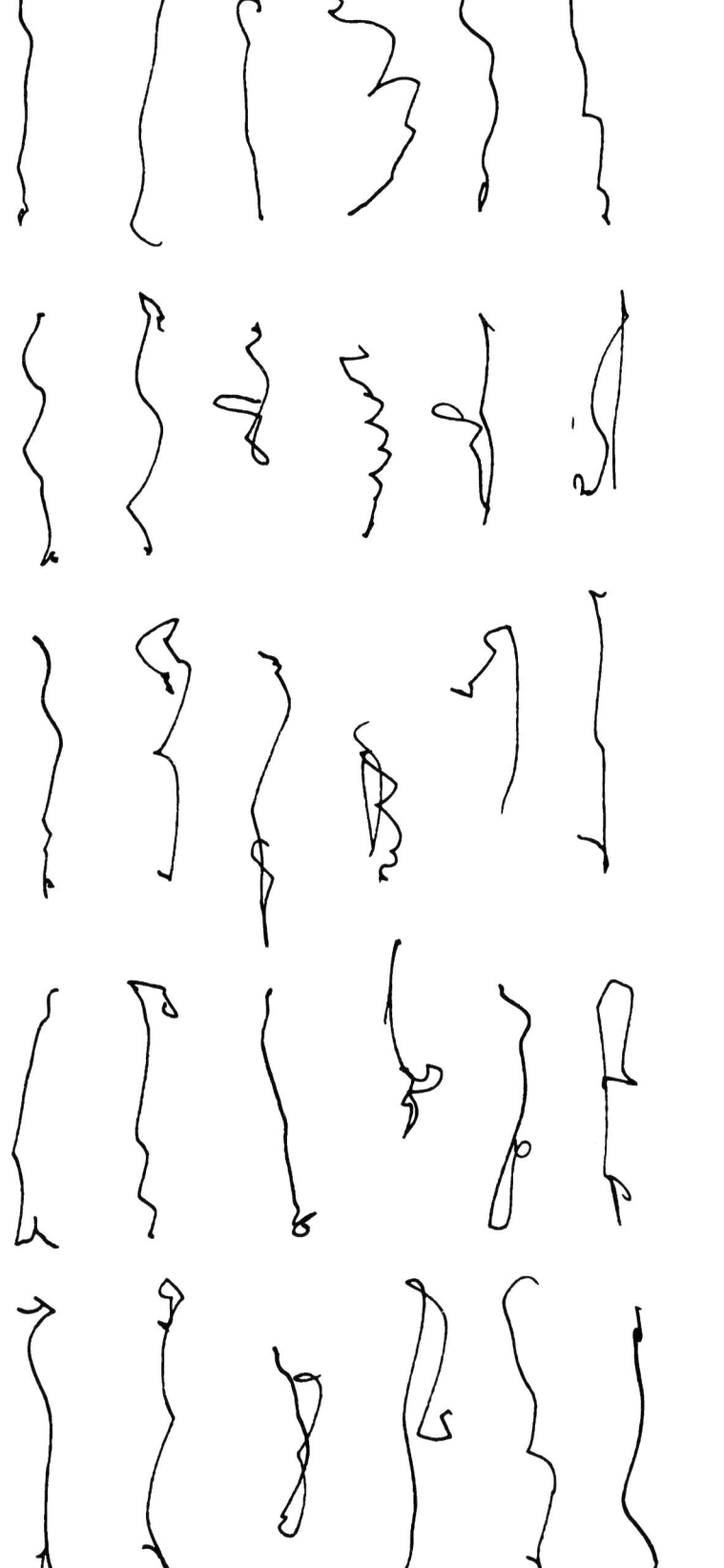

to the next. It seemed to me as if, once the leash was let off, so to speak, the particular motorics and flow of writing assumed control over the figures which my hand described, and they did so with such raw determination and resolve that I had no choice but to perceive their combination as an autonomous force, as something objectively given and independent of myself for all intends and purposes. Can this be an accurate description; can this be true?

As soon as they are no longer operating under the dictates of semantic content, the manual motions governing the writing process appear to strive for a kind of performative freedom of movement; they seem to crave variation and to avidly avoid repetition. I was shocked to note how these characters never repeat themselves, projecting instead an incessant rush of dynamic sequences – a vast panoply of complex modes of motion – while their uncontrollable, self-willed generative activity nevertheless results in creations of overwhelming density and clarity in terms of texture and line. Why this tendency towards an unlimited supply of characters, towards a potentially boundless reservoir of – for lack of any other term – textural structures or aisthetic texts resulting from their combination into sequences? What do they log, record or trace, these enactments whose perception alarms and attracts me so? That is: it attracts me magnetically to the deep rift spreading between similarity and dissimilarity that is to be witnessed in each and every character I write. And although it is me who write them, I do not conceive of myself as their author: I merely nudge their movement.

I ponder whether this undecipherable script could – or perhaps even should – be called a language. Could there be reasons – existential reasons – necessitating the development of a notation system in the form of a script, each of whose elements occurs only once? Could there be specific kinds of utterances, specific modes of expression whose articulation would require the use of exactly such a type of script? The utopian desire for such a script might stem from our living in a world that in its intensity and density lets us, moment by moment, experience both distinctness and indeterminacy. Each moment of our life is unique in its substance, mood and atmosphere – unrepeatable and without

Fig. 2 — Axel Malik,
The Scriptal Method, *2018.*

equal. Its distinctness, clarity and density, however, go hand in glove with a sense of openness that leaves us without something definite to cling to. There is no real foothold, only a reeling expanse of potentiality.

Over the first years, I considered my work as the keeping of a diary in the form of seismograms that trace the minutiae of these consecutive instances of stirred fluidity, recording them in writing. The way my characters spring up all in a flash, straight out of the moment's experienced immediacy, has motivated my work day by day, year by year, and still fascinates me to this very day.

A diary kept in this form is subject to a particular restriction: The sequences of induced motion[2] that it records, day by day, by means of the traces occasioned by consecutive scriptal events on the medium of paper, carry no date. Hence, the record consists of a durable tracing, or continuous material log, of certain sequential movements, none of which can retrospectively be attributed to an identifiable moment in time. It documents notable changes in the characters' structure as they have occurred over the years and indicates the specific momentum behind these modifications as that which governs the significant differences in their dynamics displayed by characters written at different points in time.

Unlike a traditional journal, however, it does not allow its user to establish what exactly has occurred on a specific day in the past. Nevertheless, when contemplating pages written in the past, I always can gather from them rather accurately the specific motion-related affective disposition I would have to put myself in if I meant to write characters that would continue the sequence I have before me without any blatant inconsistencies. The highly idiosyncratic manner in which an individual is attuned to and responds – as the specific motions of elements involved in resonance phenomena respond to each other – to the conditions of a unique moment as experienced by nobody else, exactly like it cannot be expressed in words. A form of writing, however, that focuses on its performance character and on the way its performance functions as a seismograph of the particular con-

Fig. 3 — Axel Malik,
  The Scriptal Method, *2023.*

ditions where it in itself (i.e. the corresponding performance in all its minutest aspects) is due, might furnish a structural language designed to fill this particular gap.

In contrast to instances of abstract doodling – a generally unintentional occupation that results in the tracing of diffuse and labyrinthine sets of visually underdetermined, ramifying lines, whose course and direction is virtually arbitrary – even those of my works into which I introduce extremely uncontrollable modes of writing and/or chaotic procedures (by trying to write as fast as humanly possible, for instance) owe their character to my striving for consistent processes and maximum compression. As manuscripts in and by which something specific is 'taken down', as it were, they are meant to be characterised by appositeness in the sense that their shape is supposed to fit, clearly and exactly, the precise conditions to which the movements of my writing hand respond. The moment of execution, the enactment, functions as a bottleneck that channels the 'now moment' of the state of induced motion then (and exactly then) current into the movements of the writing hand, which renders the former's suchness in a charged, condensed manner.

The fact that these writing movements, while referring to themselves, never peter out into unspecific, monotonous, stereotyped haziness, but – throughout the multi-layered subdivisions into which their trajectory can be analysed – maintain their precise, clearly defined and expressive character, suggests the rather mind-boggling idea that their apparently practically limitless capacity for lucid differentiation is due to a specific quality inherent to (at least a particular sub-set of) physiological motion spaces. Vertical acceleration may seamlessly transition into centripetal gyration, only to turn – within milliseconds and by means of a lateral swerve – into gliding, gather new momentum, fall into a downward spin and eventually nearly bury itself into whichever surface the writing materials that are used in that instance may provide. Yet these atoms of motion do not appear isolated, they do not meet the eye as separate fragments, but amalgamate into the form, the character that is brought about by their succession – while despite their amalgamation they none-

Fig. 4 — Axel Malik,
   Super-Signs, *2020.*

theless never stand to lose their respective individual identity. They mutually expose and emphasise each other, while they – in stark contrast to what is observable in instances of inattentive our automatic writing – never lose their poise, never lose track of their surroundings, as it were.

Comparing several individual characters with each other, a look at the line that delineates them not only reveals the variety of vastly different characters and structures which the latter generates. It also lets us perceive to which extent the way they differ from each other does indeed make a difference. In my view, their astounding variety is indicative of an underlying principle predicated upon the quality of excessive abundance.

Some very specific individual characters – which I call super-signs *(fig. 4)* – turn out to display in their design such an amount of complexity, combined with definiteness, such a degree of aesthetic persuasiveness and self-evidence that whoever has seen them will, even after years, as soon as they see them again, immediately realise that they have come across exactly this particular sign once before. At the same time, it is completely impossible to visualise such a character's exact shape by means of recollection and imagination, even if those who attempt to do so close their eyes after having scrutinised the phenomenon for a significant while.

The characters' inherent restlessness and independence, to which their inaccessibility and intangibility are due, lie at the bottom of their inability to be read. Yet this inability does not constitute any kind of deficiency, but, quite conversely, is inextricably linked with the special potential they possess – just as the latter is linked with both the reasons for and the effects of their being unreadable. The unreadable characters do not lack the ability to be read; instead, they are overabundant in features to relate to and matters to be dipped into. Owing to their overdetermination – in the sense that they confront us with an unlimited number of distinctions – which is part and parcel of their always individual and unfailingly unique shape, they are capable

Fig. 5 — Axel Malik's work on the screen during the conference Material Goods *at Kampnagel, Hamburg, 2023.*
Fig. 6 — Axel Malik and Harald Kimmig, Tectonics, Concert, *installation and writing performance, 2008/2012.*

of lending material form to infinite variety itself, to boundlessness and interminability – and, what is even more, to do so with succinctness and exactitude.

The source code which organises the consecutive movements involved in the characters' execution remains hidden, invisible; it defies sense perception. Sometimes the characters hover on the edge of an inscrutable void, in whose abysmal turbulence I recognise something of my own innermost Self. To put it in slightly more prosy terms: Not only does script belong to us, but we, in turn, also belong to its realm and to a certain extent partake in its nature. The question I address to the written character, the latter also addresses to me.

In my view, everything I have just mentioned in relation to my artistic project also pertains to the sphere of dance – as illustrated, for example, by the question whether x (for x read "unreadable script" or "dance", respectively) can be a language. The concepts of "body", "movement" and "(potential absence of) rigid codification" – with all the tensions, frictions and all the explosive force their discussion implies – definitely serve as connecting factors. Despite the multitude of conceivable correlations and overlaps arising from the fact that both – my scriptal method and dance – are concerned with motion processes, with their sequence, their expression, their intensity and quality, as well as with the question of who or what exactly induces, directs and controls their execution, I would, however, like to emphasise the filigree, minute and subtle character of the gestures performed in writing. By medium of a usually point-shaped writing tip, minimal gestures deliver their impact on a two-dimensional surface. In each instance, the particulars of the specific way in which the hand moves – and as whose trace there is left a very specific line on the respective writing medium – defy observation, since the movement is too short, too fast and too minute for the eye to follow. All writing hands look more or less alike; they do not strike as being imbued with – or being able to impart – any particular aura of their own. Exaggerating a little, one might say: in writing, the immediate impulse responsible for the *gestalt* of that which is written cannot be traced back to the writing hand.

Fig. 7 — Axel Malik, Choreographies in the Unreadable, *200 × 300 cm, 2017.*

Saying that somebody writing (fast) is letting their "hand dance" – or even that their "hand dances" (as if of and by itself) in the act of writing – seems to employ a feasible metaphor. Exactly which analogies or commonalities between the two phenomena could be quoted in order to motivate this figure of speech – or which differences could be pointed out in order to stress its inherent fallacies – amounts, at least in my opinion, to a question that brooks no comprehensive and satisfactory answer. Nevertheless, the fact that the metaphor immediately suggests itself points towards promising opportunities in an approach that aims to elucidate either activity by comparing it with – and distinguishing it from – the other.

Bodies moving through space leave an impression, but they leave no lasting trace; their movement does not result in a written text or any other form of manifestation post festum. Bodies speak to other bodies, continuously, not least in dancing. Writing, in contrast, is marked by withdrawal; it is a retreat.

Due to the extreme complexity of their body articulation, human beings move (simultaneously!) on several levels, their limbs, joints and muscles push out, are retracted, bend and rotate in different directions, while the different layers, as it were, in which their motion occurs, always permeate and affect each other. Writing, even if continued over time, results in a stable, two-dimensional writing-image or mise-en-page.

Script documents something, arranging itself in lines and strictly linear architectures. Bodies on stage – even if we occasionally call them figures or characters – are not written onto a carrier medium; their action – and also their presence – leaves an impression, but neither does the former provide us with, nor does the latter amount to an instance of mise-en-page.

Yet although it is thus impossible to neglect the differences in spatial, temporal and physical structure that exist between the provinces of writing and dance, it is precisely this observation of existing differences that makes the concomitant observation of manifold intriguing correspondences between them, and the perception that intriguingly similar questions can and ought to be addressed to them, appear so exciting.

Fig. 8 — Axel Malik,
    Shoe rail, *2023.*

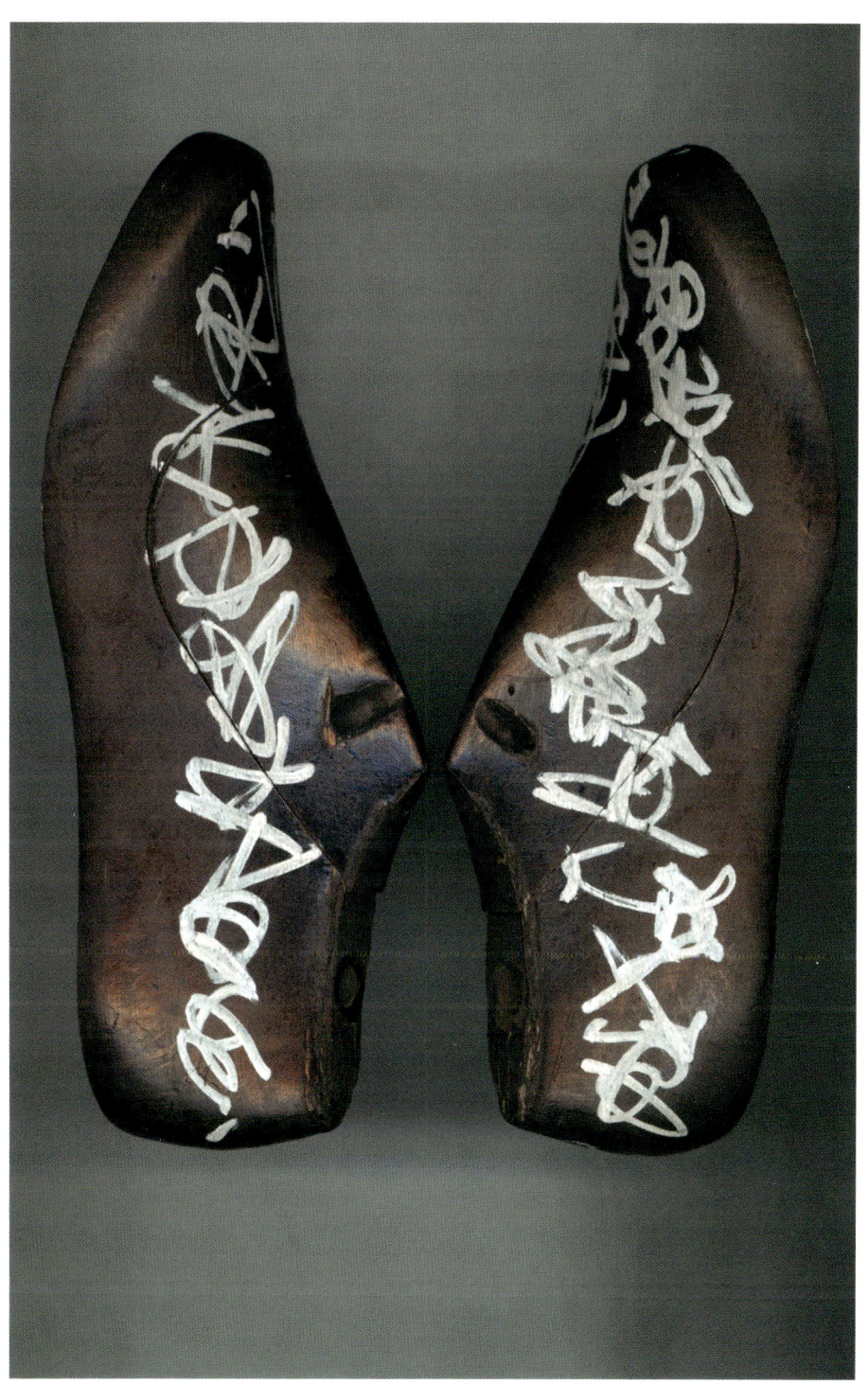

Between 2008 and 2012, I collaborated with the composer and violinist Harald Kimmig – who integrates body movements into the performance of his playing that are strongly reminiscent of dancing moves – on a sequence of performances meant to synchronise and align musical, dance-related and scriptal-performative elements. And it was during this our dialogical project that I began to introduce the idea of choreography into my own artistic considerations. Up to then, the concept had possessed rather little appeal for me.

Understanding choreography as an open perspective in the quest for convincing logic and increased expressiveness can result in fundamental changes in one's work processes, which, in turn, then may result in a fundamentally different outcome – no matter whether the latter consists in a strikingly different piece of writing or in a completely different kind of performance. Choreography does not by force of necessity have to follow and establish ordering principles, but it can also bring to bear destabilising ones. In doing so, it exposes itself to a certain risk, in that it tests the limits of what can ultimately be achieved by testing the limits of what can be controlled. Exactly with moments of utter unreservedness, when all bounds are shed and any firm foothold is dispensed with, there rests a potential to touch upon freer and more potent structures of relation. And as abstract as this may sound at first – since what is in question here involves, at least at first glance, neither more nor less than certain (sequences of) rhythms, characters, gestures, signs and signals – on closer consideration it becomes clear that it falls to exactly those said relations to further our sense of presence and to initiate change.

Our idea of meaning owes much too much to our concept of semantics – an insufficiency which the ongoing digitalisation of our world only serves to aggravate. My work, in contrast, is dedicated to the exploration of architectures within the sphere of the unfamiliar. Movements reflecting this dedication are like vectors that bend accurate trajectories, forcing them into directions that are wild and free, but consciously embraced and tenderly pursued. The aspects of easy lightness and condensation that are inherent to them preclude all unshakeable certainties and do not brook any prefabricated recipes, whereas every loss of control is immediately acted out.

TRANSLATED *from German by Ekbert Birr*

---

1 William Forsythe, Choreographic Objects. In: Steven Spier (ed.) (2011): William Forsythe and the Practice of Choreography. London, New York: Routledge, pp. 90–93, here p. 90.

2 "Induced" in the sense that each motion is attuned to and responding to the individual moment much in the manner of resonance phenomena, where one item in its vibratory motion responds to the motion of another item to which it has a harmonic likeness.

Notational Iconici
Spatiality, Time: Th
Creativity of Artif
Flatness

Sybille Krämer

1 The "cultural technique of flattening" – a productive capacity?

The material turn is more than just a turn to the concrete embodiments and the empirical, thing-like character of cultural objects. To discover cultural materialism implies new attention to the processual nature and the performativity of producing, circulating and using cultural artefacts. Material and performative turn are mutually connected; they work towards each other. In this context, the concept of "cultural technique" acquires a new epistemic dignity.

In the German discussion, with the founding of the Helmholtz Center for Cultural Technology[1] in Berlin in 1999, the concept of cultural technology acquired a new theoretical signature. In contrast to a discourse in the humanities that all too readily identified culture with immaterial goods and values, the aim was to focus humanities research more strongly toward the materiality, mediality and technicity of its objects. Cultural techniques are considered to be routinised procedures in dealing with symbolic and technical artefacts that sediment themselves in everyday practices. Mastering cultural techniques provides a basis for social participation as well as for social differentiation and exclusion. Cultural techniques are crucial resources of scientific and artistic practices and underlie and enable higher-level cognitions. The following considerations reflect on a widespread dimension of cultural techniques that largely, albeit not exclusively characterises the epoch of modernity. I refer to it as the "cultural technique of flattening". The term flattening is not intended in a pejorative and derogatory sense: rather, artificial flatness implies a great and creative potential for scientific and artistic work.

All forms of presenting and displaying alphanumeric literacy, which usually are connected with writing, reading and calculating, have an attribute that – strangely enough – has hardly attracted attention in the humanities. It is the ubiquity of two-dimensional projections, representations and displays indicating the indispensability of illustrated, inscribed surfaces or animated screens. Perhaps this artificial flatness is of almost anthropo-technical ubiquity, if not universality: That which the invention of the wheel opens up for physical mobility, the invention of the inscribed surface is for mobility in the intellectual realm. At this point, we have to avoid a misunderstanding. There is no empirical two-dimensionality. All corporeal things in our lifeworld – no matter how flat they may be – are three-dimensional; yet we practically treat inscribed and illustrated surfaces as if they were flat. From skin tattooing, cave paintings and ornaments, to the invention of pictures, writings and maps, to scoreboards and television screens, and finally culminating in the computer screen, tablet and smartphone: artificial flatness runs like Ariadne's thread through our cultural practices past and present.

We are familiar with the rhetoric of depth: thinking that is inspiring and fertile has to be deep; being oriented to surfaces, by contrast, is discriminated as superficial, if not intellectually taboo. But in contrast to what the narrative of depth recommends all sciences, many arts, complex technology and architecture, and last but not least administration of big organizations are simply inconceivable without the use of surfaces as organising displays and informational representations. What are the reasons for this significant productivity of artificial flatness? What is the artifice of its creativity? The following considerations try to offer an answer. But first, we have to relativise our picture of forgetting surfaces in the Humanities as an unquestioned tendency. In some humanistic research areas, we can find already hints about how methodologically to rehabilitate surface orientation.

2 Methodological privileging of surfaces – a new "turn" in parts of the Humanities?

In the shadows of the material and performative turn – but closely connected to both – an interest in surface orientation is becoming apparent. It can be identified as a research trend in quite different academic fields. The following still incomplete list can provide some references:

FLAT ONTOLOGY: In social theory, Theodore Schatzki (2003, 2016) develops a flat ontology of society, whose practices do not diversify into a multitude of levels, but rather take place on only one level.

SURFACE SIGNIFICANCE OF LANGUAGE: In parts of linguistics, the construct of a "language behind speech" is dispensed and the prioritisation of competence and deep structure is discarded in favour of linguistic performance and surface significance (Linke and Feilke 2009).

SURFACE READING: In text theory, the model of symptomatic reading, orienting the meaning of a text to the interpretation of what is unsaid and hidden behind the visible iconicity of the text is mitigated and criticised in favour of a manner of reading that is orientated to the sensuously visible signature of the text (Best and Marcus 2009).

NOTATIONAL ICONICITY: In the theory of writing, scripts are not considered solely in terms of their potential for representation; rather, the phenomenon of notational iconicity is elaborated as the epitome of the materiality, perceptibility and operativity of writing (Krämer 2003).

DIAGRAMMATOLOGY: The role of diagrams and graphs is explored in science, art, engineering, architecture and administration. Diagrams show mostly invisible concepts and relations by perceptible relations drawn on paper (Krämer 2016b; Stjernfelt 2008).

STUDIES IN THEATRE, DANCE AND MUSIC underline the role of choreography, script and musical scores. The relationship between the medium of writing and artistic potential is explored. (Klein, Barthel and Wagner 2011; Celestini, Nanni, Obert and Urbanek 2020)

SCREENOLOGY: Film studies examine the development and potential of screens in terms of media archaeology; interface studies analyse and construct the intersections of human-machine interactions. (Hutamo and Erkki 2004)

MEDIA PHILOSOPHY: Vilém Flusser elaborates a phenomenological approach to media theory under the title *In Praise of Superficiality* (1995).

DESIGN THEORY reflects on design as a surface-oriented form of controlling the world of everydayness. (Hellmann 2014)

INTERFACE STUDIES analyse and construct the intersections of human-machine interactions.

3 Artificial flatness: the transfiguration of time into space and vice versa

How can we explain that the reduction of three-dimensionality to two-dimensionality is not simply a loss, but also a great advantage?
I want to offer two answers.

BODY REFERENCE: Our embedding in the world is oriented along three perpendicular axes connected to our corporeality: the difference between right/left, above/below and front/behind. What lies behind us usually remains – without a rear-view mirror – a domain that is beyond our visibility and control. The invention of inscribed mobile surfaces – especially when connected to the medium of paper – creates a format that is in front of the eyes, can be grasped and manipulated with the hands and easily be distributed and shared with others. An artificial space has emerged that is completely visible, manipulable, controllable and, moreover, mobile. Bruno Latour has drawn attention to this in his essay on "immutable mobiles" (Latour 1990). But we want to go one step further – and thus also beyond Latour – in understanding this immutability and moreover mobility in terms of the potential of flattening out.

MEDIA PERSPECTIVE: Media – as we want to put it on the horizon of our messenger model (Krämer 2015) – are in the position of a third party, situated in between heterogeneous poles, fields or systems and creating a nexus without thereby eliminating the structural difference between the mediated instances. We describe this position of connecting and transmission between the heterogenous by the model of the messenger, without wanting to anthropomorphise and personify the institution of the mediator. If we insert the cultural technique of flattening into this media perspective, something is striking: time is usually considered one-dimensional; you cannot be in different places simultaneously. And space is – with reference to our lifeworld – considered to be three-dimensional. Having this in mind we see: artificial flatnesses two-dimensionality is a medium that is in between the one-dimensionality of time and the three-dimensionality of space and is thus able to bridge the gap. What follows is that it is possible to translate time sequences into spatial configurations and vice versa. Our epistemic, artistic and everyday practices generate innumerable examples for this time-space-metamorphosis. For example, the timeline and timetables of historians translate events into definite points, the phonographic writing transforms oral speech into the spatial constellation of letters, choreography, music notations or computer programming offer instructions for performances of humans or machines.

It is important to emphasise that the mutual translation of time sequences into spatial constellations and vice versa has not to be interpreted as a mapping or even mimesis of a previously already given state. Rather, it is a matter of transfiguration; what is transfigured undergoes an instant transformation and brings about new ways of being and acting and new potentials and risks. Transfiguration originally is a religious term; it refers to the metamorphosis of the corporeal Jesus of Nazareth into the transfigured, heavenly figure of Christ as God's son, experienced by the apostles on a mountain. Here we use the word transfiguration in a secular sense, underscoring that transfiguration is always more than a mere transmission and translation. It embodies a kind of ontological shift, a change in the mode of being.

4 Phenomena and concept of operational iconicity

I would like to introduce the phenomenon of transfiguration with three examples: the artificial use of shadows; the logic of geographical maps; the perspective of notational iconicity.

4.1 Artificially used shadows

The shadow is the natural form of two-dimensional projection, but also a prominent origin of the cultural technique of flattening. Gaius Plinius Secundus (1st century CE) in *Naturalis Historia* describes a legend: The daughter of the potter Butades produces an image of her departing lover by drawing his silhouette on a wall. She uses the flattening potential of shadows. By accentuating the outlines of shapes, things are deprived of their corporeal volume. Through the use of the graphic line, the silhouette becomes the record of shadowy disembodiment. At the same time, however, it also creates a new modality of physicality and materiality: graphism. Drawn graphism is a corporeality sui generis and is not subject to the temporal disappearance of the shadow. The potter Butades later produces a three-dimensional sculpture following his daughter's shadow drawing. Pliny's legend of the origin of pictorial art shows how the irrevocable passage of time is potentially averted through spatialisation. For us, it is relevant that transfiguring the shadow into an image creates the existence of a new kind of object: art and artefacts.

The spatialisation of time also plays a role in ancient sundials: the epistemic use of silhouettes. As we all know, the hours of the day are readable through the lengths of the shadows cast by illuminated things: the shorter the shadow, the higher the position of the sun. Vitruvius (1st century BCE), a Roman architect and theoretician, describes the functioning of an ancient sundial in his *Ten Books on Architecture*. A GNOMON or pointer is placed in a hole within a network of lines that is subtly constructed as a diagram based on astronomical observations and mathematical calculations. The shadow cast by the GNOMON onto this network of lines, the

ANALEMMA, allows the hours of the day and the months of the year to be ascertained. What matters most is not the recording of the shadow – as in the legend of Butades's daughter – but rather the shadow's successive mobility and changes as it moves across the diagrammatic field. The cultural use of the silhouette indicates the importance attached to the act of spatialising temporality.

4.2 Is Gerhard Mercator's world map a Eurocentric project?

The second example refers to different modes of representing the world with "realistic" geographic maps. In 1569, Gerhard Mercator designed a map of the world that is a familiar sight to us all today. From the equator to the poles, the areas represented on the map increase in relation to their factual size, so that northern regions appear disproportionately large compared to equatorial regions. *(Fig. 1)*

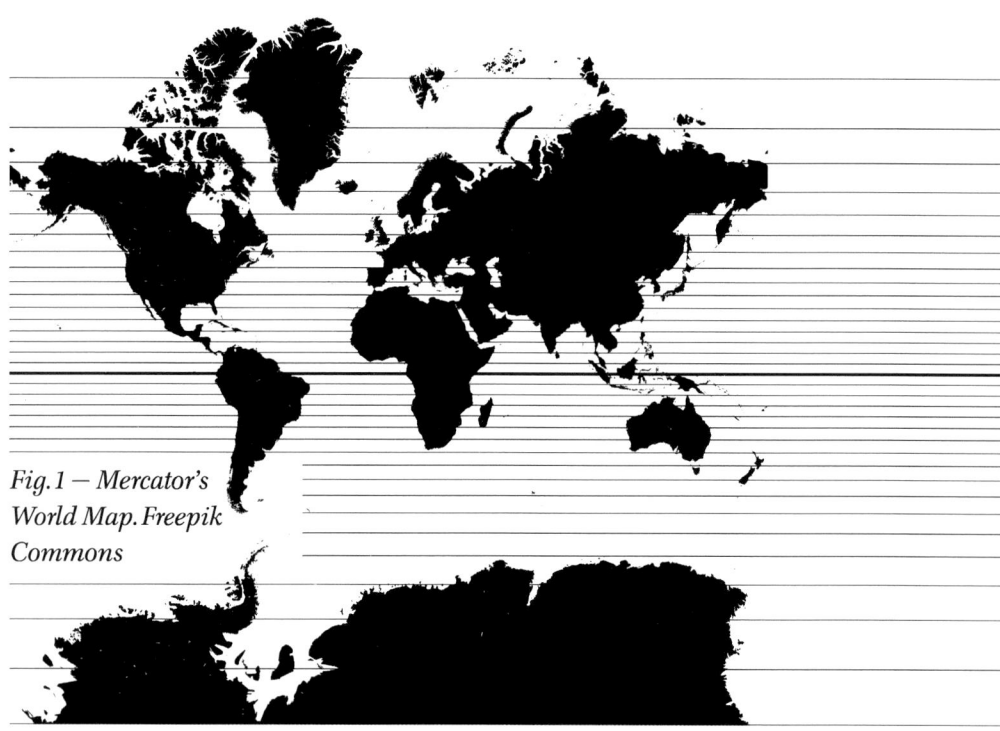

Fig. 1 – Mercator's World Map. Freepik Commons

The modern accusation that this map reflects a Eurocentric view of the globe was not long in coming. And in 1974, Arno Peters developed a map projection that claimed to represent real geographical conditions. *(Fig. 2)*

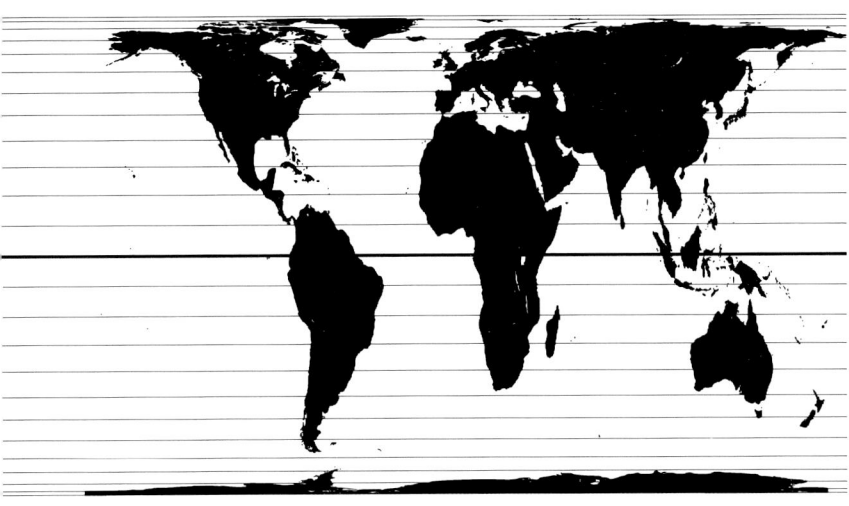

Fig. 2 — Arno Peter's World Map.
Wikimedia commons

What is important here is that the distortion on Mercator's map was not the result of a political programme but rather a necessary logical-mathematical side effect. Mercator's map was not simply a "world picture"; rather, it served as a praxeological instrument of navigation. We can explain Mercator's method of projection using an image. Imagine a globe. A paper cylinder is wrapped around it like a coat and the paper only touches the globe at the equator. A light emanating from within the globe casts shadows of the continents on the paper. If the cylinder is cut open at a certain point, then the result is Mercator's map. The angles in the array of longitudinal and latitudinal lines are thus equal, but the areas are not, as it is impossible for a map to visualise correct angles and correct areas at the same time. A practically useful projection of the earth's surface on a plane is only possible as a distorted illustration, and it is the practical purpose of the map that determines the kind of distortion preferred. Mercator's map makes it possible for the loxodrome or rhumb lines – virtual lines that spiral around the globe – to appear as straight lines. Once a navigational course has been determined by means of this map, ships can then be steered on a constant bearing over a non-marked ocean with nothing but a compass. The Mercator projection is still the basis of nearly all nautical and aeronautical charts today.

4·3 Notational iconicity

For all too long, writing was considered to be oral language written down and thereby fixed. This phonetically oriented concept, the idea that writing is registered oral discourse is problematic; we call this view the phonographic dogma. Its problem is the alphabet-centred and thus Eurocentric interpretation of how to conceptualise writing. Within the framework of the phonographic dogma, writing is definitely interpreted as a language and not as a picture. It's a kind of secondary language, referring to speech as the first language.

Writing, however, is a hybrid, composed of dimensions partly rooted in language-like and partly in image-like attributes. Moreover, the iconic dimension is not just its visuality, but its spatiality rooted in a two-dimensional configuration. The creative potential of writing is based on the two-dimensional visual arrangements of graphic signs on surfaces: not only linear following the left/right (or vice versa) direction, but also using the second dimension of top/down directionality.

Emerging from the graphic interplay of point, line and surface, scripts are sui generis symbolic systems that can, but do not have to, be used to represent language. Musical notations and dance notations, chemical formulas, logical, and numerical notations, and last but not least the binary alphabet of 0 and 1, as well as programming languages being not languages but scripts: in all of these forms, the writing fulfils artistic and epistemic tasks without directly referring to oral languages. Spatially operating on surfaces is essential for understanding writing's creative potential.

Let's look at an example, handed down as a narrative, of how the mathematician Carl Friedrich Gauß (1777–1855) as a nine-year-old schoolboy solved an arithmetic problem. How would you add up the first 100 numbers? The young Carl Friedrich Gauß did it like this:

i $1+2+3+4+5+ \ldots +97+98+99+100$

This can now be rearranged by permuting the places and combining summands into:

ii $(1+100) + (2+99) + (3+98) + \ldots + (49+52) + (50+51).$

A visual situation has arisen showing the same sum in every bracket:

iii   (101) + (101) + ... + (101) + (101)

Since there are 50 brackets the solution is:

iv   101 x 50 = 5050

Numbers are theoretical entities; they have no spatial position. Nobody has ever "seen" a number. However, by operating not with numbers but with spatially localised graphic signs on paper, their spatial positioning and permuting can in turn be transformed into a tool of arithmetic work. The medium for depicting numbers is transfigured into an instrument for performing calculations. A complex mental activity is not done inside the head but executed externally through a regular manipulation of signs, which consists of moving and regrouping their spatial positions. The paper with its spatial directionality participates in the solution.

5 Digitality

The example of cartographic navigation in particular suggests the question of what happens when inscribed and illustrated surfaces are transformed into electronically networked interfaces. No doubt: digitisation draws on the cultural technique of flattening and radicalises this technique.

5.1 Computer-independent digitisation

What do "digital" and "digitisation" mean? Basically, digitisation is a process in which a continuum is discretised into individual elements in such a way that these components can be encoded independently of one another and combined more or less arbitrarily. In this generalised perspective, the alphabet already constitutes a modality of digitising: the fluxus of oral speech is broken down into discrete letters.

It is no coincidence that the alphabet was not only used to transcribe spoken language but also served as a mathematical sign language. The invention of letter algebra by François Viète[2] (1540–1603), for example, made it possible for algebraic rules to be written down in a universally valid way for the first time and thus to be taught and learned. It is no coincidence that the dual numbers, invented by philosopher Gottfried Wilhelm Leibniz (Leibniz 1966), were also called the binary alphabet. Leibniz's dual numbers of 0 and 1 not only reduced the decimal number system to just two characters but later became the prototype of digital coding in general. *(Fig. 3)*

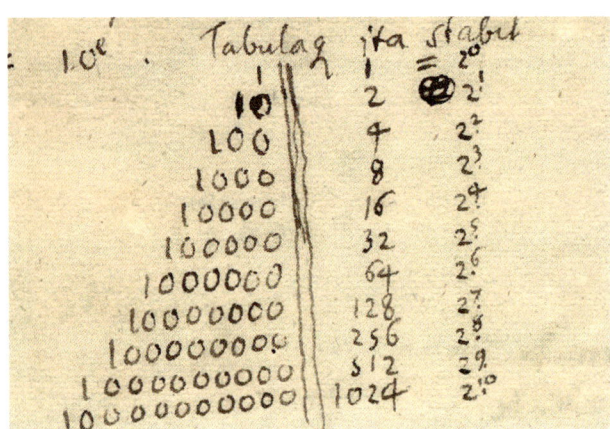

Fig. 3 — Gottfried Wilhelm Leibniz, Binary numeral system De Dyadicis, *ca. 1703. Gottfried Wilhelm Leibniz Bibliothek, Hannover, call number* LH XXXV, III B1, Bl. 1–4.

5·2 Programming computers

In 1843, about ten years before Carl Friedrich Gauß died, the mathematician Ada Lovelace (1815–1852), the daughter of Lord Byron and Anne Noel-Byron, wrote the first running computer programme in table form. In collaboration with Charles Babbage, who invented and designed his "Analytical Engine" as a pure paper design, Lovelace realises that a universal machine is sketched and described by Babbage, which is to be turned into a special – for example, arithmetic – machine by feeding it with written signs and instructions. Lovelace designed the first – in principle fully functional – computer programme in the form of a table. *(Fig. 4)*

Each horizontal row corresponds to the overall state of all machine parts; the vertical columns separate the machine parts from each other and instruct how each part is changing if a new operation is performed. Lovelace recognises that the transfiguration into an arithmetic machine is only one of many options. She emphasises that just as algebraic patterns are created by her arithmetic programme, a programme for generating musical patterns, i.e. a machine for composing music, would also be possible.

5.3 Contemporary digitality

What happens if the inscribed surface turns into an electronic interface? Contemporary digitisation can be characterized by at least four conditions:

> ALGORITHMICISING
> DATIFICATION
> NETWORKING
> VISUALISATION

Our present society is situated in a field characterised by this framework. Completely new potentials but also risks emerge for which there is no forerunner and model to be found in the embryonic digitality of alphanumeric literacy. I would like to explain this very briefly using one of the four factors as an example: changes in the nature of the algorithmic.

Al Khwarizmi (ca. 780–850), a Persian Islamic scholar, brought the Hindu-Arabic numerical script to Europe, thereby introducing the possibility of calculating by manipulating written signs without any further physical tool like an abacus or a reckoning board. Al Khwarizmi's proper name in its Latin version condensed – in the following centuries – to the term "algorithm". Algorithms are computational rules for schematically processing a problem, which can be written down as a sequence of characters and can then also be solved by mechanically transforming these characters – whether realised by humans or machines.

But with the current development of Big Data and Deep Learning, what was originally just a rule for solving problems is now transforming into a method of prediction, with which past data can be used to infer future possibilities: problem-solving algorithms have become predictive algorithms (Finlay 2014). And they are used to forecast trends in almost all fields of society and to provide decisions in medicine, insurance, "curated shopping", companies, and so on. However, the internal models developed during the training and testing stages of the learning algorithms can no longer be extracted or deduced from their output: the problem of Black Boxing arises. Bruno Latour's statement is well known: Black Boxing is *"[…] the way scientific and technical work is made invisible by its own success. When a machine runs efficiently, when a matter of fact is settled, one needs to focus only on its inputs and outputs and not on its internal complexity. Thus, paradoxically,*

Diagram for the computation by the Engine of

Number of Operation	Nature of Operation	Variables acted upon.	Variables receiving results.	Indication of change in the value on any Variable.	Statement of Results.	Data				
						$^1V_1$ ○ 0 0 1 ▢	$^1V_2$ ○ 0 0 2 ▢	$^1V_3$ ○ 0 0 4 ▢	$^0V_4$ ○ 0 0 0 ▢	$^0V_5$ ○ 0 0 0 ▢
1	×	$^1V_2 \times ^1V_3$	$^2V_4, ^2V_5, ^2V_6$	$\{^1V_2 = ^1V_2, ^1V_3 = ^1V_3\}$	$= 2n$	...	2	n	$2n$	$2n$
2	−	$^1V_4 - ^1V_1$	$^2V_4$	$\{^1V_4 = ^2V_4, ^1V_1 = ^1V_1\}$	$= 2n - 1$	1	...	...	$2n-1$	
3	+	$^1V_5 + ^1V_1$	$^2V_5$	$\{^1V_5 = ^2V_5, ^1V_1 = ^1V_1\}$	$= 2n + 1$	1	...	...	...	$2n+1$
4	÷	$^2V_5 \div ^2V_4$	$^1V_{11}$	$\{^2V_5 = ^0V_5, ^2V_4 = ^0V_4\}$	$= \dfrac{2n-1}{2n+1}$	...	...	...	0	0
5	÷	$^1V_{11} \div ^1V_2$	$^2V_{11}$	$\{^1V_{11} = ^2V_{11}, ^1V_2 = ^1V_2\}$	$= \dfrac{1}{2} \cdot \dfrac{2n-1}{2n+1}$	...	2	...	...	
6	−	$^0V_{13} - ^2V_{11}$	$^1V_{13}$	$\{^2V_{11} = ^0V_{11}, ^0V_{13} = ^1V_{13}\}$	$= -\dfrac{1}{2} \cdot \dfrac{2n-1}{2n+1} = A_0$	...	...	...	...	
7	−	$^1V_3 - ^1V_1$	$^1V_{10}$	$\{^1V_3 = ^1V_3, ^1V_1 = ^1V_1\}$	$= n - 1 \ (= 3)$	1	...	n	...	
8	+	$^1V_2 + ^0V_7$	$^1V_7$	$\{^1V_2 = ^1V_2, ^0V_7 = ^1V_7\}$	$= 2 + 0 = 2$	...	2	...	...	
9	÷	$^1V_6 \div ^1V_7$	$^3V_{11}$	$\{^1V_6 = ^1V_6, ^0V_{11} = ^3V_{11}\}$	$= \dfrac{2n}{2} = A_1$	...	...	...	...	
10	×	$^1V_{21} \times ^3V_{11}$	$^1V_{12}$	$\{^1V_{21} = ^1V_{21}, ^3V_{11} = ^3V_{11}\}$	$= B_1 \cdot \dfrac{2n}{2} = B_1 A_1$	...	...	...	...	
11	+	$^1V_{12} + ^1V_{13}$	$^2V_{13}$	$\{^1V_{12} = ^0V_{12}, ^1V_{13} = ^2V_{13}\}$	$= -\dfrac{1}{2} \cdot \dfrac{2n-1}{2n+1} + B_1 \cdot \dfrac{2n}{2}$	...	...	...	...	
12	−	$^1V_{10} - ^1V_1$	$^2V_{10}$	$\{^1V_{10} = ^2V_{10}, ^1V_1 = ^1V_1\}$	$= n - 2 \ (= 2)$	1	...	...	...	
13	−	$^1V_6 - ^1V_1$	$^2V_6$	$\{^1V_6 = ^2V_6, ^1V_1 = ^1V_1\}$	$= 2n - 1$	1	...	...	...	$2n$
14	+	$^1V_1 + ^1V_7$	$^2V_7$	$\{^1V_1 = ^1V_1, ^1V_7 = ^2V_7\}$	$= 2 + 1 = 3$					
15	÷	$^2V_6 \div ^2V_7$	$^1V_8$	$\{^2V_6 = ^2V_6, ^2V_7 = ^2V_7\}$	$= \dfrac{2n-1}{3}$	...	...	...	...	$2n$
16	×	$^1V_8 \times ^3V_{11}$	$^4V_{11}$	$\{^1V_8 = ^0V_8, ^3V_{11} = ^4V_{11}\}$	$= \dfrac{2n}{2} \cdot \dfrac{2n-1}{3}$					
17	−	$^2V_6 - ^1V_1$	$^3V_6$	$\{^2V_6 = ^3V_6, ^1V_1 = ^1V_1\}$	$= 2n - 2$	1	...	...	...	$2n$
18	+	$^1V_1 + ^2V_7$	$^3V_7$	$\{^2V_7 = ^3V_7, ^1V_1 = ^1V_1\}$	$= 3 + 1 = 4$	1	...	...	...	
19	÷	$^3V_6 \div ^3V_7$	$^1V_9$	$\{^3V_6 = ^3V_6, ^3V_7 = ^3V_7\}$	$= \dfrac{2n-2}{4}$	...	...	...	...	$2n$
20	×	$^1V_9 \times ^4V_{11}$	$^5V_{11}$	$\{^1V_9 = ^0V_9, ^4V_{11} = ^5V_{11}\}$	$= \dfrac{2n}{2} \cdot \dfrac{2n-1}{3} \cdot \dfrac{2n-2}{4} = A_3$					
21	×	$^1V_{22} \times ^5V_{11}$	$^0V_{12}$	$\{^1V_{22} = ^1V_{22}, ^0V_{12} = ^2V_{12}\}$	$= B_3 \cdot \dfrac{2n}{2} \cdot \dfrac{2n-1}{3} \cdot \dfrac{2n-2}{4} = B_3 A_3$					
22	+	$^2V_{12} + ^2V_{13}$	$^3V_{13}$	$\{^2V_{12} = ^0V_{12}, ^2V_{13} = ^3V_{13}\}$	$= A_0 + B_1 A_1 + B_3 A_3$	...	...	...	...	
23	−	$^2V_{10} - ^1V_1$	$^3V_{10}$	$\{^2V_{10} = ^3V_{10}, ^1V_1 = ^1V_1\}$	$= n - 3 \ (= 1)$	1	...	...	...	

Here follows a repet

| 24 | + | $^4V_{13} + ^0V_{24}$ | $^1V_{24}$ | $\{^4V_{13} = ^0V_{13}, ^0V_{24} = ^1V_{24}\}$ | $= B_7$ | ... | ... | ... | ... | |
| 25 | + | $^1V_1 + ^1V_3$ | $^1V_3$ | $\{^1V_1 = ^1V_1, ^1V_3 = ^1V_3, ^5V_6 = ^0V_6, ^4V_7 = ^0V_7\}$ by a Variable-card. by a Variable card. | $= n + 1 = 4 + 1 = 5$ | 1 | ... | $n+1$ | ... | |

Fig. 4 − Ada Lovelace's Programme for Charles Babbage's
Analytical Engine for calculating the Bernoulli numbers *(1843).*
© *Magdalen College Libraries and Archives, Daubeny 90.A.11*

bers of Bernoulli. See Note G. (page 722 et seq.)

		Working Variables.					Result Variables.		
$^0V_8$ 0 0 0 0 ▢	$^0V_9$ 0 0 0 0 ▢	$^0V_{10}$ 0 0 0 0 ▢	$^0V_{11}$ 0 0 0 0 ▭	$^1V_{12}$ 0 0 0 0 ▭	$^{11}V_{13}$ 0 0 0 0 ▭	$^1V_{21}$ B_1 in a decimal fraction. ▢ B_1	$^1V_{22}$ B_3 in a decimal fraction. ▢ B_3	$^1V_{23}$ B_5 in a decimal fraction. ▢ B_5	$^0V_{24}$ 0 0 0 0 ▢ B_7
...	...	...	$\frac{2n-1}{2n+1}$						
...	...	...	$\frac{1}{2}\cdot\frac{2n-1}{2n+1}$						
...	...	...	0	....	$-\frac{1}{2}\cdot\frac{2n-1}{2n+1}\ A_0$				
...	...	$n-1$							
...	...	...	$\frac{2n}{2}=A_1$						
...	...	...	$\frac{2n}{2}=A_1$	$B_1\cdot\frac{2n}{2}=B_1A_1$	....	B_1			
...	...	...	....	0	$\left\{-\frac{1}{2}\cdot\frac{2n-1}{2n+1}+B_1\cdot\frac{2n}{2}\right\}$				
...	...	$n-2$							
$\frac{2n-1}{3}$ 0			$\frac{2n}{2}\cdot\frac{2n-1}{3}$						
...	$\frac{2n-2}{4}$ 0	...	$\left\{\frac{2n}{2}\cdot\frac{2n-1}{3}\cdot\frac{2n-2}{3}\right.$ $\left.-A_3\right\}$						
...	...	...	0	$B_3 A_3$	....	......	B_3		
...	...	...	....	0	$\left\{A_3 + B_1 A_1 + B_3 A_3\right\}$				
...	...	$n-3$							

rations thirteen to twenty-three.

| ... | ... | ... | .... | .... | .... | ...... | ...... | ...... | B_7 |

the more science and technology succeed, the more opaque and obscure they become." (Latour 1999: 304)

With the progress of so-called Deep Learning technologies, which underly almost all sophisticated data technologies from spam filtering to speech and face recognition, the realm of non-knowing is increasing. A lot of the machine's internal processing – so to say: it's "knowing how" – can no longer be transformed into human-recognisable "knowing that".

The new profile in the use of algorithms is only one example of significant changes in the transition from alphanumeric to digital literacy. How does the role of writing change as artificial flatness evolves into an electronic interface? While there is an embryonic digitality already to the alphanumeric, the ongoing networking and datafication transfigure the modality of artificial flatness. New forms of writing emerge like activatable links, the QR code or Radio Frequency Technologies (RFT), all of which are indispensable for the Internet of Things. Time and movement are implemented into the stable structure of notational iconicity. The character of writing changes by adopting self-movement and operational processuality implemented in the interface. We have to concede that the phenomenon of two-dimensional spatialisation undergoes a radical change based on the implementation of time into artificial flatness. Our assumption at this point is that a dimension of depth, a third dimension, returns on whose amputation and annulment the cultural technique of flattening once was built.

6 Transfiguring the idea of flatness by implementing time

By digitally implementing time into the inscribed surface, we have to modify our idea about spatial flatness. Here we want to offer just one example going beyond the invention of new forms of writing. The topic is the advanced form of digital storage technology, the so-called "Bigtable" (Chang et al. 2008). The problem that Bigtable has to solve is that webpages are constantly changing, while others remain unchanged. If search algorithms could limit their search to the modified files only, this would significantly reduce search time. The Bigtable database, developed in 2004 and used in Google Maps, Google Earth, YouTube and others, is based on exactly this principle. *(Fig. 5)*

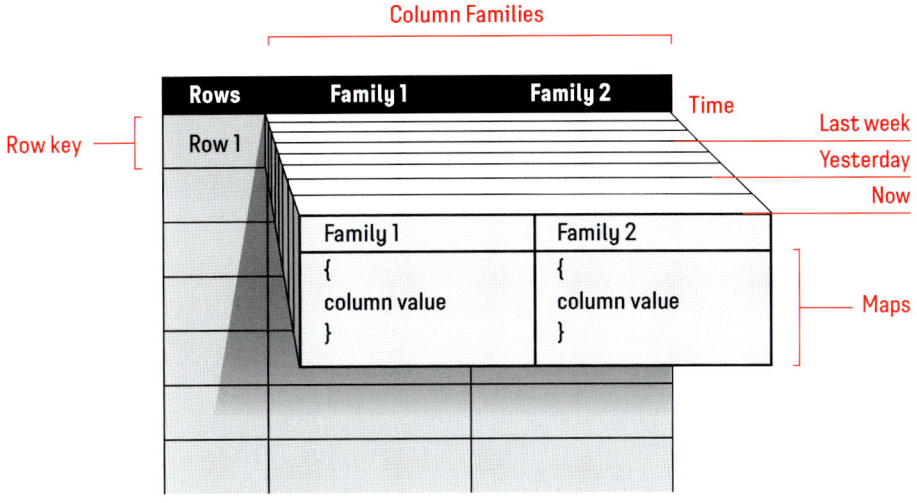

Fig. 5 — Bigtable Data Base: Time as a third dimension, besides the spatial registers "column" and "row". livebook.manning.com/book/google-cloud-platform-in-action/chapter-7/40

It is informative to look at the diagrams offered to demonstrate Bigtable's principles: As usual, the two-dimensional mapping of the database contains horizontal rows and vertical columns; but in addition – and that's the point – a timestamp for temporal indexicalisation is inserted as the matrix's third dimension. Search algorithms are thus enabled to consider only the most recent versions of the data. A digital search query can now deliver real-time results even for the largest data corpora. The phenomenon of real-time is precisely what we want to emphasise because it offers a new form of experiencing time.

Since the theory of relativity, we speak of "space-time" and use this term to emphasise that the three dimensions of space and the one dimension of time form a continuum together. In classical physics, space and time were independent of each other. Metaphorically expressed: classical 'space' was conceived like a container, which can be filled or emptied over the course of time. But the four-dimensional continuum of space-time indicates that space and time are interconnected and no longer absolute and independent quantities. Yet when time is implemented in the electronic interface, then the physical reality of four-dimensional space-time is transformed into a human-created digitised three-dimensional space-time, in which two spatial dimensions and one temporal dimension form a three-dimensional ontological modality. This idea of transfiguring and simultaneously reducing four-dimensional space-time to a three-dimensional modality of flat space intertwined with temporality is still speculative in character, it is a hypothesis at best. Further research on that speculative issue is necessary.

The idea of implementing time in inscribed surfaces seems purely conceptual and abstract, but it has immediate consequences for the human perception of time. With three-dimensional space-time, a novel modality of time emerges: computer-generated real-time or micro-temporality (Miyazaki 2012). There are many studies on computer-generated micro-temporality. Here, only its phenomenal impact is of interest. The time of a computer operation can no longer be perceived by humans as a temporal interval, as a time-consuming event. It appears instantaneous while for the computer, it still constitutes a time gap. The philosopher Henri Bergson distinguished two forms of time: the objectively measurable, spatialised time and the subjectively experienced continuous duration of time (Bergson 2001). But a third form of time is emerging: computer-generated micro-temporality. We can only articulate and express, but not debate this idea here. We want to make a last step in returning to our concept of notational iconicity, to the flatness of images and non-electronic writing by introducing Axel Maliks "written pictures".

7 Axel Malik: displaying notational iconicity

Axel Malik, who accompanies the Hamburg Cluster of Excellence "Understanding Written Artefacts" as a visual artist, says about himself in a lot of conversations: "I write."[3] *(Fig. 6)*

Fig. 6 (previous page) — Axel Malik's
Schreibflächen © *Axel Malik*

He works with surfaces, some as high as floor levels, others so small they can be bound into books. In obsessive labour, he populates light backgrounds with individual characters resembling writing. Often – though not always – Malik follows the strict arrangement of two-dimensional textuality. There are lines separated by white spaces, often columns. There are blank spaces between characters as well as white margins that limit and circumscribe the artistic text-like object. At a first, distant glance, what we see is similar to the textual form of writing – not too much different from how we experience ordinary notational iconicity. *(Fig. 7)*

Fig. 7 — Axel Malik's Diaries *volumes 1 to 9.*
In: Axel Malik 2003, n.p.

And yet something is radically different. Each of these written characters is individual, a singularity, and has, therefore, no lettering or type character. For writings, as Jacques Derrida (1988) insisted early on, consist of repeatable signs. Iterability is the defining feature of writing. The operational dispositif of doing written work consists of using a limited repertoire to open up an unlimited number of possible combinations. Moreover, writings have an external reference. But Malik's signatures are self-sufficient, referring to nothing but themselves. This creates an unsurveyable, extensive universe of miniature signatures that can be looked at, but not read. Here, nonwriting is represented in the mode of notational iconicity. Writing is not camouflaged but unmasked in its notational iconicity. What is aesthetically gained with these graphic objects?

From a philosophical perspective, Malik exposes the mostly hidden and suppressed aspects of the script's materiality, sensuality, and tactility. Usually, reading and interpreting are regarded as the supreme ways of dealing with text. Within this hermeneutic paradigm, including its orientation towards deep rhetoric, the perceptibility, materiality and operativity of the notational iconicity are mostly disregarded and ignored. Malik gives aesthetic expression to these repressed dimensions of notational iconicity, which are mostly forgotten in academic discourse.

8 Conclusion

In the wake of the material and performative turns, approaches of methodologically acknowledging the relevance of surface dimensions of cultural artefacts are emerging. The "cultural technique of flattening" participates in this tendency. The use of artificial flatness is perhaps an anthropotechnical universal. Modernity is based on the ubiquitous use of illustrated and inscribed surfaces. Spatial two-dimensional relations are applied to represent mostly non-spatial issues to display, manipulate, control and share knowledge and artistic experience with others.

The concept of notational iconicity refers to the materiality, spatiality, perceptibility and operativity of writing. It is not only the visuality and iconicity but the spatiality that matters. The phonetic dogma that writing transcribes colloquial speech, as well as the absolutising of the hermeneutic attitude to interpretative depth behind a text's appearance, disregards and marginalises the significance of notational iconicity.

The creative functions of language-independent graphic signs in the sciences (logic, formula, number writing) as well as in the arts (choreography, musical notation) and technology (blueprints, programming) are to be acknowledged as achievements of writing, especially constituting modernity. The concept of writing must be stripped of the phonetic dogma according to which writing is only what oral communication records. Thus, Eurocentric alphabetcentrism can be overcome, as well as the degradation of iconic dimensions, which are inherent to all – even alphabetic – writings.

Digitalisation and datafication radically change artificial flatness because time and movement are introduced into the fixed structure of written signs on a screen. A third form of time is emerging: computer-generated micro-temporality.

---

1 The Hermann von Helmholtz Zentrum für Kulturtechnik was founded by eight Berlin scientists working in very different disciplines: Horst Bredekamp, Art History; Jochen Brüning, Mathematics; Wolfgang Coy, Computer Science; Friedrich Kittler, Cultural Studies; Sybille Krämer, Philosophy; Thomas Macho, Cultural Studies; Bernd Mahr, Computer Science; Horst Wenzel, Medieval Studies.
2 See Vietae 1646/1970.
3 See above Axel Malik's contribution to this chapter. (Note by the editors)

REFERENCES

Austin, John Langshaw (1962): How To Do Things With Words. Oxford: Clarendon Press.

Bergson, Henri (2001): Time and Free Will: An Essay on the Immediate Data of Consciousness (1889). Mineola: Dover Publications.

Best, Stephen and Sharon **Marcus** (2009): Surface Reading: An Introduction. In: Representations, vol. 108, No. 1, pp. 1–21.

Blumenberg, Hans (1986): Die Lesbarkeit der Welt. Frankfurt am Main: Suhrkamp.

Bogen, Steffen (2005): „Schattenriss und Sonnenuhr. Überlegungen zu einer kunsthistorischen. Diagrammatik". Zeitschrift für Kunstgeschichte, 68, 2, pp. 153–176.

Chang, Fay et al.: Bigtable: A Distributed Storage System for Structured Data. In: ACM Transactions on Computer Systems, Vol 26, Issue 2, 2008, pp. 1–14.

Chia, Xinji and Martin **Pumera** (2018): Characteristics and performance of two-dimensional materials for electrocatalysis. In: Nature Catalysis 1, pp. 909–921. doi.org/10.1038/s41929-018-0181-7

Derrida, Jacques (1988): Signature Event Context. In: Limited Inc, tr. Samuel Weber, Evanston: Northwestern University Press, pp. 1–23.

Finlay, Steven (2014): Predictive Analytics, Data Mining and Big Data. Myths, Misconceptions and Methods. Basingstoke: Palgrave Macmillan.

Flusser, Vilém (1995): Lob der Oberflächlichkeit. Für eine Phänomenologie der Medien. Mannheim: Bollmann.

Gombrich, Ernst H. (1995): Shadows: The Depiction of Cast Shadows in Western Art. London: National Gallery.

Gumbrecht, Hans Ulrich and Ludwig **Pfeiffer** (eds.) (1994): Materialities of Communication. Stanford: Stanford University Press.

Huhtamo, Erkki (2004): Elements of Screenology: Toward an Archaeology of the Screen. In: Iconics, Vol 7, pp. 31–82.

Krämer, Sybille (2003): Writing, notational iconicity, calculus: On writing as a cultural technique. Modern Language Notes – German Issue 118 (3). Johns Hopkins University Press, pp. 518–537.

Krämer, Sybille (2015): Media, Messenger, Transmission. An Approach to Media Philosophy. Amsterdam: Amsterdam University Press 2015.

Krämer, Sybille (2016a): Is there a diagrammatic impulse with Plato? 'Quasi-diagrammatic-scenes' in Plato's philosophy. In: Sybille Krämer and Christina Ljungberg (eds.), Thinking with diagrams. Boston, Berlin: de Gruyter, pp. 161–178.

Krämer, Sybille (2016b): Figuration, Anschauung, Erkenntnis. Grundlinien einer Diagrammatologie. Berlin: Suhrkamp.

Krämer, Sybille (2021): Media as cultural techniques: From inscribed surfaces to digital interfaces. In: Jeremy Swartz and Janet Wasko (eds.): Media. A Transdisciplinary Inquiry. Bristol, UK and Chicago, USA: intellect 2021, pp. 77–86.

Krämer, Sybille (2022): Reflections on 'operative iconicity' and 'artificial flatness'. In: David Wengrow (ed.): Image, Thought, and the Making of Social Worlds. Freiburger Studien zur Archäologie & Visuellen Kultur Bd. 3. Heidelberg: Propylaeum, pp. 251–273.

Krämer, Sybille (forthcoming): Should we really 'hermeneutise' the Digital Humanities? A plea for the epistemic productivity of a 'cultural technique of flattening' in the Humanities. In: Theorytellings: Epistemic Narratives in the Digital Humanities. Journal Cultural Analytics.

Latour, Bruno (1986): Visualisation and Cognition: Drawing Things Together. In Henrika Kuklick (ed.): Knowledge and Society Studies in the Sociology of Culture Past and Present. Jai Press, vol. 6, pp. 1–40.

Latour, Bruno (1990): Drawing Things together. In: Representation in Scientific Practice, ed. M. Lynch and S. Woolgar. Cambridge MA: MIT Press.

Latour, Bruno (1999): Pandora's hope: essays on the reality of science studies. Cambridge, Massachusetts: Harvard University Press.

Leibniz, Gottfried Wilhelm (1966): Herrn von Leibniz' Rechnung mit Null und Eins. Siemens Aktiengesellschaft (ed.). Berlin, München.

Linke, Angelika and Helmuth **Feilke** (eds.) (2009): Oberfläche und Performanz. Untersuchungen zur Sprache als dynamische Gestalt. Tübingen: Niemeyer.

Lovelace, Ada Augusta (1843 [1961]): Notes by A.A.L. (Augusta Ada Lovelace). In: Taylor's Scientific Memoirs, Vol. III, pp. 666–731; reprint: P. Morrison and E. Morrison (eds.), Charles Babbage and His Calculating Engines: Selected Writings by Charles Babbage and Others. New York: Dover Publications 1961.

Malik, Axel (2003): Axel Malik. Katalog zur Ausstellung in der Dombibliothek Hildesheim. Freiburg: schwarz auf weiss.

Miyazaki, Shintaro (2012): Algorhythmics: Understanding Micro-Temporality in Computational Cultures. Computational Culture 2, 2012. *computationalculture.net/algorhythmics-understanding-micro-temporality-in-computational-cultures/* (23/10/2023).

Nake, Frieder (2008): Surface, Interface, Subface. Three Cases of Interaction and One Concept. In: Uwe Seifert, Jin Hyun Kim and Anthony Moore (eds.): Paradoxes of Interactivity. Perspectives for Media Theory, Human-Computer Interaction, and Artistic Investigations. Bielefeld: transcript, pp. 92–109.

Plinius Secundus the Elder, Gaius (1997): Naturkunde / Historia Naturalis vol 1–37: Vol 35: Farben, Malerei, Plastik, ed. and transl. Roderich König with Gerhard Winkler. Düsseldorf and Zürich: Artemis & Winkler.

Saussure, Ferdinand de (1967): Grundfragen der allgemeinen Sprachwissenschaft. 2nd ed., Berlin: De Gruyter.

Schatzki, Theodore R. (2003): A new societist social ontology. In: Philosophy of the Social Sciences 33 (2), pp. 174–202.

Schatzki, Theodore R. (2016): Praxistheorie als flache Ontologie. In: Hilmar Schäfer (ed.), Praxistheorie: Ein soziologisches Forschungsprogramm. Bielefeld: transcript, pp. 29–44.

Schechner, Richard (2002): Foreword: Fundamentals of Performance Studies. In: Nathan Stucky and Cynthia Wimmer (eds.), Teaching Performance Studies. Carbondale: Southern Illinois University Press, pp. I-X

Stjernfelt, Frederik (2008): Diagrammatology: An Investigation on the Borderlines of Phenomenology, Ontology and Semiotics. Dordrecht: Springer.

Vietae, Francisci (1646/1970): Vietae Opera Mathematica, collected by F. Van Schooten. Leyden: Elzévir 1646. Reprint Hildesheim and New York: Georg Olms Verlag 1970.

Vitruvius (1964): Vitruvii de architectura libri decem (Zehn Bücher über die Architektur), trans. and ed. Curt Fensterbusch. Darmstadt: Primus.

Archivi
Perfor
Act

ng as
mative

anarchivTANZ
deufert+plisc

anarchivTANZ started 2016 and since then it continues to happen in Berlin, Bonn, Brussels, Cologne, Curitiba, Dubai, Düsseldorf, Dresden, Essen, Istanbul, Krefeld, Los Angeles, Mülheim, Munich, New York, Potsdam, Reykjavik, Schwelm, Singapore, Tel Aviv and Viersen. It is not a performance, but emerges out of a combination of Workshops, Ballroom and Community Work. It is more of a situation with people where deufert&plischke work with communities to collect, write, read and dance all those personal relations, memories and experiences people have with dance. They work in dance studios, retirement homes, ballrooms, book clubs, schools, theaters, on the street ... people dance, draw and distribute favorite movements and write personal letters to dance. With the favorite movements of a city a local ballroom is organised to celebrate dance! Over the years the project became very complex, with some thousands of letters and favorite movements, with many artists contributing ... the project grew as an archive and in the same time the material resisted to be stored – there is a sense of anarchy within the material.

August 20, 2018

Dear Dance,

I love to dance as it allows me to forget everything else and enjoy movement. To quote another:

- Let's Face the Music and Dance!

Darrol Stanley
73
Los Angeles, CA

dear dance,

you are the gateway to my most liberating
experiences — spiritually, emotionally + socially.
as a kid, I could not talk to people, but
I could dance! you often make me feel primal,
sometimes, orgasmic. you are so sensual, provocative
+ infinite! i'm sorry if i don't spend
enough time with you. thank you for never
needing to understand, analyze. or judge me.
i love you beyond reason.
xxxxxxxx chloe

6.10.19
dance nucleus
singapore

11.4.16

Lieber Tanz

Ich mag dich, du bist sehr nett und sehr
frech. Ich mag nur paar Sachen von dir
und das ist Hiphop und in Hochzeiten
tanzen wie zum beispiel Haley.

Sonst Mag Ich Dich Nicht TanzEN
Es Tut MIR LEID BRUDA.

Du Bist schon 100 Jahre
Alt RESPEKT.

mit freundliche Grüße
dein Görkem

Lieber Tanz,
ich bin dir so dankbar. Du hast
mich ins Leben, in die Lebendigkeit
gebracht. Du hast mir eine Stimme
gegeben und die Möglichkeit mit mir, der
Welt und anderen in Kontakt zu kommen.
Durch dich erzähle ich meine Geschichte.
Mit dir spüre ich den Wind, die
Erde unter meinen Füßen, ich fliege.
Ich spreche mit den Sternen und du
bist meine Sprache.
Wieso bin ich nun so sprachlos geworden?
Wieso bin ich verstummt? Sprechen werden
macht verletzlich, dem wertenden Blick
der anderen ausgesetzt, das schert dich
aber nicht, oder? Ich weiß schon, was du
mir sagen wirst – Mädchen tanz!
Tanz deinen Tanz – okay, okay.
Thank you

Shushan, März 2022

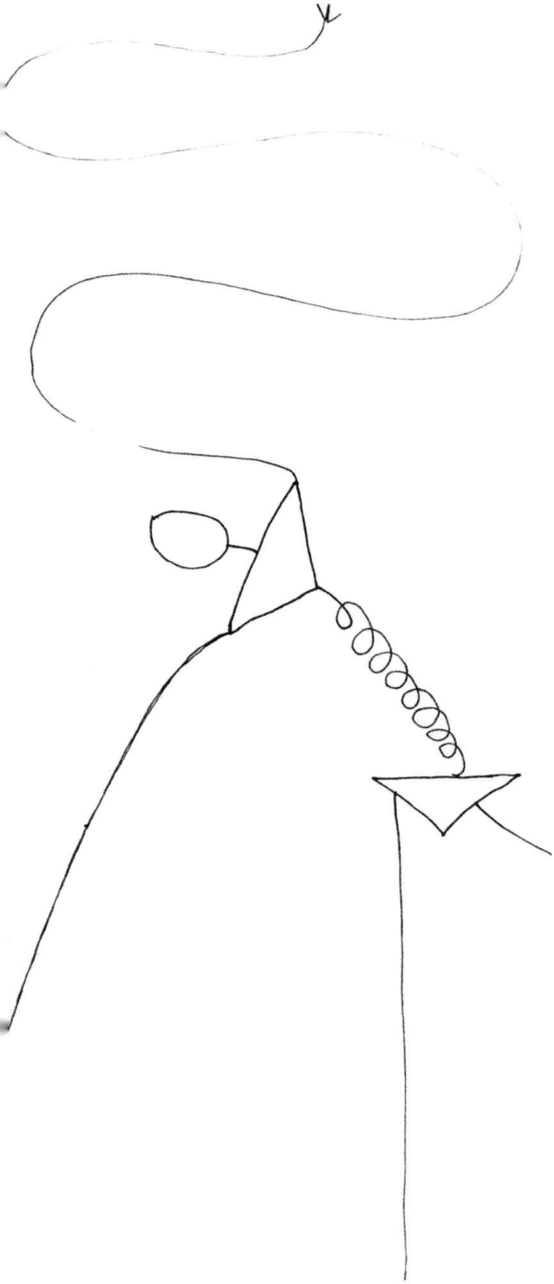

Dear Dance,

I do. I do. I... do... I really do.
I mean... I ~~should~~ could. I could do.
Because I did.
So I should. I could and I should.
~~So I might~~. I mean... I might.
Yeah. I think I might.
That might do.
Don't you think?
Oh. You do not...
But you did! You did say 'I do'!
When you said 'I do' to me and not
do anything, what are you doing?
In ~~#~~ doing the do, what is being done?
I do and ~~#~~ do and do.
But I do not know what I have done.
Maybe I ~~haven't~~ have done too much.
Maybe I haven't done enough
But I will.
I will do it. I will keep doing it.
I will to do it.
I promise
                                    ˣ Daniel Kok

Reykjavik, 2019
17.11.19

~~Dr.~~ Dear Dance

I just wanted to say thank you.
I should have done it earlier I know.
You should know that you've fundamentally
changed me, or more correctly
shaped me. Both physically and mentally
I will try to be better about communicating
that to you.

There is no place I feel more powerful
confident capable and sexy as I
do when I'm with you

Best á dansgólfi

പ്രിയ നൃത്തമേ,

നീ എന്നും മനോഹരമാണ്! നിന്നെ ഈ ലോകത്തെ അത്ഭുതമെന്നെ സന്തോഷത്തിന്റെ പകിട്ടാർന്ന ഓരോട്ടങ്ങ ങ്ങളാണ്. നീ എന്നും നിറഞ്ഞ് നിൽക്കട്ടെ ദുഃഖവും ദുരിതവും നിറഞ്ഞ മനുഷ്യന്റെ ഹൃദയത്തിൽ സന്തോഷ കുളിർമഴ പെയ്യിക്കാൻ. നീ ഉള്ളിടം ഉത്സവമാണ് നിന്റെ താളങ്ങൾ ഈ ഭൂമിയിൽ ചിരി ഉണർത്തും നീ ഒരിക്കലും മരിക്കാതിരിക്കട്ടെ. കോവിഡ് എന്ന ദുരന്തം നൃത്തങ്ങളെ ഇല്ലാതാക്കിയെങ്കിലും നിന്നെ പൂർണമായി തകർക്കാനൊന്നും എന്ന് തന്നെ എന്റെ ഹൃദയത്തിന്റെ സ്പന്ദനങ്ങളും വിചാരിക്കുന്നു. നീ എന്നും എന്റെ അടഞ്ഞ മനസ്സിനെ ഉണർത്തി ഉത്സാഹമുള്ളതാക്കുന്നു. നിന്റെ ചുവടും പരക്കുന്ന ശോക മനസ്സുകളെ ശാന്തമാക്കുന്നു. നീ എന്നും എല്ലാ പ്രായക്കാരുടെ മനുഷ്യന്റെ സന്തോഷത്തിന്റെ ഭാഷയായിരിക്കട്ടെ! നീ എന്റെ മനസ്സിന്റെ രഹസ്യഅറയിൽ ഒതുങ്ങി നിൽക്കാതെ അങ്ങു! ആരും അറിയാത്ത ഒറയിൽ ഇരുന്നും കാക്കും. ഒതുങ്ങി നിൽക്കാതെ പുറത്തേക്ക് വരിക. ഞാൻ അതിനുവേണ്ടി ഓരോരോ അവസരങ്ങൾ കണ്ടുപിടിക്കും. എന്ന് നിന്റെ ഏറ്റവും നാണമുള്ള കൂട്ടുകാരി, വിദ്യാലക്ഷ്മി.

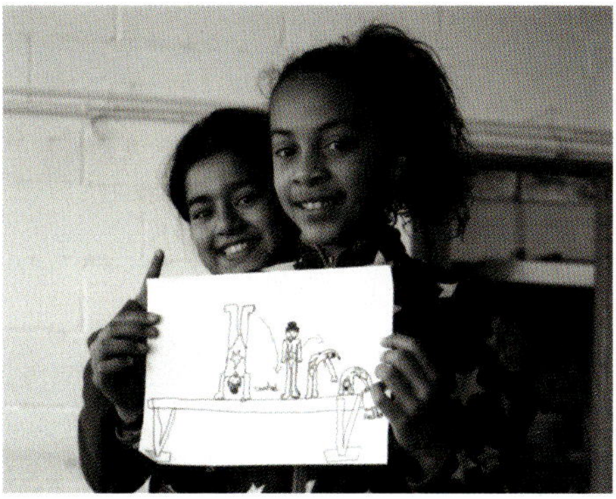

12.07.2019
ISTANBUL, BEŞİKTAŞ, BİMEKAS
17:30

DEAR DANCE,

I'M PAUSING. HESITATING. TO WRITE TO YOU. BECAUSE YOU WERE THERE FOR ME WHEN THERE WERE NO WORDS, TO DESCRIBE, WHAT I WENT THROUGH. SLIDING THE ROUNDABOUT OF LOVE, LIFE, AND MAYBE WATERMELONS.

I CANNOT THANK YOU ENOUGH BUT I DON'T WANT TO THANK YOU IN WORDS.

NOT THAT I CAN. THEY FAIL ME ANYWAYS.

YOU MADE ME WHO I AM.

TRULY YOURS,

G.E.

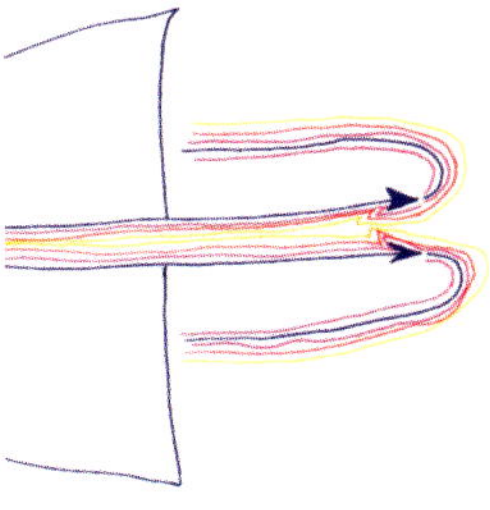

Liebe Tanz

Können Sie bitte auf dem Wasser und auf der Treppe Tanzen?

Schöne Grüße
Reza

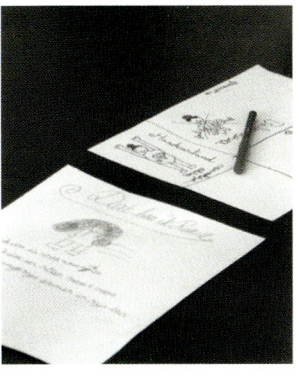

12. nóv 2019

Elsku dans,

Ég er í skólanum og við vorum að tala um þig, vinna með þig og mig langaði til að láta þig vita. Það var svo gaman að sjá þig í gær, það var svo óvænt og skemmtilegt. Það væri gaman ef þú kíktir oftar á mig ég finn hvað þú gerir mér gott. Mér finnst stundum eins og ég geti ekki ða- megi ekki hringja í þig, eins og þú hljótir að vera upptekin einhvers staðar annars staðar með einhverjum öðrum. Við erum náttúrulega meira svona kunningjar en þess vegna vildi ég skrifa þér og spyrja-: Viltu vera vinkona mín? Ég vil hafa þig í lífi mínu, ég þarf á þér að halda. Ég vona að þér finnist þetta ekki of dramatískt ða intens. Takk fyrir spjallið í gær, hittumst hjótt aftur. Þín Sigga

DEAR DANCE.

Singapore
9th Oct 2019

Thank you for ~~bringing out~~ bringing so much joy to my children. It brings me back to forgotten freedom and sense of expression. You remind me that sometimes there are no words ~~moments~~ for expression and your body just feels it. I hope to see you soon again.

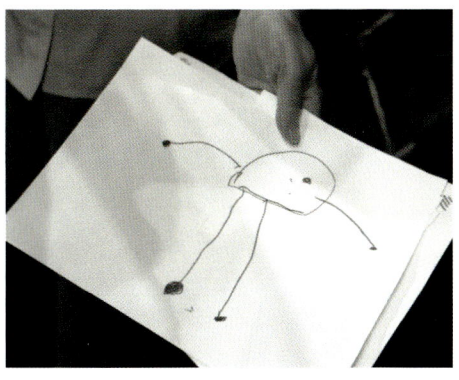

Dear Dance ♡ AZMI

It was a pleasure to ~~have~~ meet you today. I got to meet with some beautiful souls. They taught me, reminded me, played with me, moved me to places I had not met yet. I loved the beats (drum beats) reminded me of heart spaces. It was lovely to engage openly, feeling absolute freedom or what one perceives as freedom in mind. There were lot of teachers and the fun part of having learned how to STEAL OR IMITATE was also something that you brought out to FOCUS or probe into. Moments of movement is what I would take away TODAY. For that I have deep GRATITUDE to DANCE.

Dear Dance,

I don't know who you are
but thank you for
letting me think about
being a stick, a truth
or the wind.

        Love,
            Miki

Querida Dança,

Eu gosto muito de dançar, posso fazer isso por horas. Sem parar. É o que me faz bem.

Dançar é o que faz a alma se conectar ao corpo e ligar entre a mente.

Dance com tudo, especialmente com o coração.

Dance do seu jeito sem se avaliar, sem pensar e sem julgar.

Ache o seu espaço e o seu lar de dança.

Alimente a sua Alma.

E não pare de tentar.

Quando você dança a vida dança de volta.

E se precisar de ajuda olhe o espelho.

E o mais importante é amar. E aprender amar a dança.

        Gabriela 🍍

Dear Dance,

It has always been a mystery to me... watching them express all their feelings through you... and showing their real self through you. I used to envy that.

Can you help me become that, too?
Become myself, the fun cool boy while dancing.
I am working on that, and hopefully will get their soon.

BTW, thanks for contributing to my happiness every time, while I am in front of my bedroom mirror, after a smile from her, an achievement at work, or a small win. Really thanks for that, you do a good job making me feel better... and I do a good job making you

Best regards,
Abdo
10/12/2021

Lieber Tanz,

hier spricht ein Leidenschaftlicher Anhänger deines Geistes. Mehr muss ich nicht sagen. Lass uns Taten sprechen.

Lieber Tanz,

nun treffen wir uns wieder. Es gab Jahre, in denen wir zusammen waren, und es gab Jahre, in denen wir getrennte Wege gegangen sind. Aber ich habe immer an Dich gedacht. Du bist schön, du enthüllst meine Seele, die normalerweise von anderen Menschen gefesselt ist. Aber mit dir kann ich ehrlich sein.

Jetzt, wo wir uns wieder getroffen haben, weiß ich, dass ich Dich nicht mehr verlieren möchte, denn du gibst mir so viel Kraft. Du lässt mich ich selbst sein. Danke, dass es Dich in meinem Leben gibt. Ich werde versuchen, Dich nicht gehen zu lassen.

28.04.2022
Irina Shutova

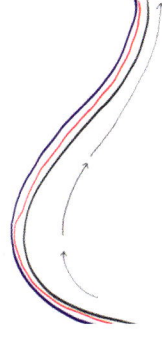

Dear Dance,

We have a strange relationship, and I apologize that sometimes when people ask me if I like to dance that I say "Sometimes, but not really." I have awful memories associated with you (talent show mishap, middle school socials gone wrong) but I am frequently reminded of the joy that you can inspire. Also, thanks for giving my cousin a career. That was kind of you.

See you later port-ups,

Keith

Dear Dancer

We Buddhists believe the first act was sound but the first response was dance --- bodhisattvas emerged from the earth dancing to the beat of the human heart

Gavin Glynn
National Square Dance Champion 1984

Archiving the Body, Cultural Memory and the Practice of Intangible Cultural Heritage
Aleida Assmann

The general topic of the essays in this volume is the performing arts, in particular their processes of production, documentation, mediation and archiving. It is a firmly established consensus that the central medium of these ephemeral performing arts is the human body itself. In the light of a material turn, however, more dimensions of this embodied cultural art form and its history are discovered. In performances, Gabriele Klein writes, *"not only human actors come into view, but also different materialities and forms of embodiment: In addition to physical gestures, movements and figurations, artefacts (such as costumes), things and objects (props), spatial arrangements (stage sets) and acoustic-visual media (sound, video clips played on stage) are also significantly involved in the performative acts."* (Klein 2023: 294)¹

In my contribution, I want to open up a wider historical and theoretical context for these questions by linking them to the emergence of the concept of cultural memory and the category of intangible cultural heritage. At the same time, I focus on the performing arts as an important stimulus to rethink the dynamics of material and immaterial heritage in Western consciousness and to decolonise the idea of cultural memory.

What is meant by the material turn?

The material turn is offered by the editors of this volume as a beacon for our joint intellectual endeavour. In order to learn more about this turn, I turn to Doris Bachmann-Medick's influential publications on academic 'turns' (Bachmann-Medick 2016, 2006). In her books, she discusses the interpretative turn, the performative turn, the iconic turn, the postcolonial turn, the spatial turn and the translational turn, but a material turn is not part of her collection.² There is excellent information available on the internet, however, which explains the material turn's object, origin and aims. Its main object is to *"write nature, bodies, and things into the humanities"* and thus to create a wider and connected framework for the research of arts and cultures.

*"The performative turn focuses on doing art instead of reflecting upon artistic end products; the affective turn focuses on the bodily aspects of artists and viewers; the material turn focuses on the agency of artistic material itself. The material turn has been called a paradigm shift in the humanities as it encompasses the former two, and focuses on what has been made most passive: matter."*³

Matter is therefore what matters most. The project of redefining matter is part of a programmatic strategy: to transcend foundational binaries of Western thinking such as culture versus nature, spirit versus matter, or human versus environment. When looked at in this way, the material turn becomes part of a post-anthropocene worldview that includes the human rather than placing it outside or at the centre of our focus. By avoiding exclusionary dichotomies, the material turn emphasises a monistic worldview that takes great care to be inclusive and comprehensive. Its transdisciplinary perspective is relational; it combines methodologies and connects the humanities, the natural sciences and the evolution of technologies. The Wikipedia article on the *Materiality Turn* offers this concise answer to my question:

"In short, the material turn is a theoretical stream covering what is expected to endure across time and space, or what is temporally and spatially constituted through everyday activities, i.e. tools, objects, artefacts, technologies, built spaces, bodies and embodiment and their relationships with organizations and organizing."[4]

This definition encourages me to relate the question about the performing arts and the material turn to the concept of "cultural memory" as it was developed by Jan Assmann and myself in the 1980s. Under this term, we started to look for a language and methodology to describe cultures as human investments in objects and practices in order to endure across time and space. In 1979, we began to research and discuss these questions systematically in a comparative perspective within a group of experts from different disciplines, representing different historical periods and cultures. Our special focus was the medial and material conditions of cultural transmission and the dynamics of remembering and forgetting within societies, nations and religions.

The rise of media studies, semiotics and the concept of cultural memory

In the 1960s and 1970s, a new type of media studies emerged at universities, which had a considerable impact on the project of "cultural memory". Important impulses at that time came from England and Canada. The authors were cultural anthropologists and classicists who often engaged in their comparative studies beyond the European perspective. One of them was Jack Goody. His anthology on *Literacy in Traditional Societies* from 1968 entered our library in 1986 in the new series, translated by Friedhelm Herborth under the title *Entstehung und Folgen der Schriftkultur.* Other relevant texts came from the Toronto School, such as Eric Havelocks' *Preface to Plato* (1963) and *The Muse Learns to Write* (1986), which dealt with the beginnings of the alphabet in Greek culture. And we must not forget the pioneers of the recovery of oral traditions of South Slavic Epics on the Balkan, starting with Milman Parry and his student Albert Lord who carried on the ethnographic study (Lord 1960), and the Jesuit priest Walter Ong with his influential *Orality and Literacy: The Technologizing of the Word* first published in 1982.

These books were landmarks on our way towards "cultural memory". In all of them, the fundamental question of the mediality of culture and tradition was at stake. A genuine interest in both written and visual art forms such as film, theatre or dance, considered media with different technological, social and cultural infrastructures, was deepening. All this happened at a time of technical transformation when huge computing centres were turned into neat and handy PCs in private homes. It was surely no coincidence that this new digital media awareness arose between the 1960s and 1980s when the digital technological rupture was beginning to undermine compact concepts of tradition, and, at the same time in different African countries, new decolonised states were re-inventing themselves and reconstructing their heritage.

In creating our concept of "cultural memory", we profited also from another inspiration of the 1970s that came from semiotics, at the time the most influential and inclusive approach to languages, media and communication in terms of sign systems. Our heroes were two semioticians at Tartu, Jurij Lotman and Boris Uspenskij who defined culture as *"the non-hereditary memory of the community, a memory that is relying not on genes but expresses itself in a system of constraints and prescriptions."* (Lotman 1971: 6) Lacking the support of genetic transmission, cultural systems need a specific economy of external symbols and cultural frames to pass on the relevant heritage. With such acts and symbols, humans create symbolic frameworks that support the social cohesion of smaller or larger groups and communities. These symbolic frameworks transcend the individual life span by creating an ongoing communication between the living, the dead and future generations of the group. Within the extended temporal horizon of meaning production that we call "cultural memory", participants of groups have access to the past in the present and can hope to reach the yet unborn in the future. Thanks to these frameworks or infrastructures, cultures don't have to start from scratch in every generation. They are standing on the shoulders of giants whose knowledge they can use and reinterpret. Culture, in this sense, is a temporal framework for the communication of a group across the abyss of time. The new concept and vocabulary, we hoped, would help us to forge a new form of cultural studies, based on comparing cultures by studying the infrastructures of their memory-systems in a non-Eurocentric perspective. We were interested in a historical view that was not enmeshed in a modernist ideology of evolution, progress and development as derived from the works of Hegel.

Jan Assmann's and my first premise was: there is no culture without memory. Every culture depends on preserving and passing on knowledge of key events, values and practices. Another premise was: individual memory is embedded in social memory. And a third: no human being lives only in the present. In more or less conscious ways, human life is shaped by the past, constituting a resource that is reshaped in the present to provide orientation for the future. The impact of the past can either be positive or negative; in the latter case, the key to a better future is through a reassessment of the past.

Orality and literacy – different types of cultural memory

When we started our research to further explore these questions within a circle of friends and colleagues, we invented a new topic and our own forms of collaboration strictly outside the structure and premises of the universities. Picking up the thread of recent publications, we chose *Schrift und Gedächtnis* (Writing and Memory), thus creating for our analysis a typological distinction between cultures that use writing and those that use extended forms of mnemotechnics (Assmann and Hardmeier 1983).[5] An intellectual hype had been created by post-modern theorists such as Jacques Lacan, Jacques Derrida and Hans-Ulrich Gumbrecht in the 1980s around the term "écriture", which lent itself to extensive philosophical and psychoanalytical elaborations. Our pairing of writing with orality went in a different direction. Our focus was on the absence or presence of the body. Writing allowed a form of communication that was premised on the absence of the body, while orality represented the other end of the emphatic presence of the body as its central medium of presentation and communication. Together with the presence or absence of the body, we focused in this constellation on different temporal dimensions and their respective media: preservation via material signs and symbols in space *(Sicherungsformen der Dauer)* and preservation via repetition of acts and practices across time *(Sicherungsformen der Wiederholung)*.

With these premises, further research questions were on the agenda: how do oral and written cultures secure the knowledge that is essential for their survival? How do oral cultures differ from cultures that use writing? How do oral cultures change when writing is introduced as a new pillar of transmission? Does one form of cultural literacy displace the other or do they overlap and coexist? And what strategies of power and counter-memory are possible under these circumstances?

Outsourced or embodied? The precarious state of embodied memory

Indigenous and Western cultures differ in the way that they build up long-term temporal structures. Western societies outsource their memory in grand institutions: they are based on a history that is preserved and exhibited in texts, libraries, museums and archives. Indigenous memory cultures hand down their cultural heritage in a completely different way. They make the body the medium of memory. The body itself is the archive; in the body and through the body the tradition that is important for the group is inscribed, performed, preserved and passed on. In these cultures, human memories have to bear the burden and responsibility. Techniques of memory and rhythms of regular repetition support the memory in creating continuity and carrying the life of the community into the future.

In 1960, the Malian writer and ethnologist Amadou Hampâté Bâ gave a speech before the UNESCO. He addressed a global audience when he said: *"In Africa, when an old man dies, it is a library burning."* (Hampâté Bâ 1972, no page). At the time, the pace of modernisation and globalisation accelerated considerably in Africa, which led not only to the extraction of resources and the extinction of natural species but also to the loss of cultures, languages and traditions.

In this historical context, Hampâté Bâ alerted the world to the precarious status of memory cultures, which are not backed up by strong and permanent institutions such as monuments, museums and archives, but exist solely in the embodied performance and in the elaborate practice of passing them on from generation to generation, requiring constant repetition and the specialised skills of mediators. In societies that are thrown off their traditional track by external circumstances or internal upheavals, the vital knowledge of tradition within the group is no longer secure. What is interrupted can break off and be lost forever, which disrupts the vital contact with the ancestors.

It took almost half a century since Hampâté Bâ's speech until UNESCO developed criteria to valorise this embodied form of tradition and to protect it with a new legal term as *"intangible cultural heritage"*. It was this new term that finally in 2003 helped to put the embodied variant of cultural heritage on an equal footing with Western cultural memory and its material infrastructure. Until then, the quality of cultures had been measured exclusively by the yardstick of material legacies of Western cultures. In a lecture on Africa, Hegel denounced its inhabitants as *"void of history and unenlightened beings"* (Hegel 1961: 163, translation Aleida Assmann). For him as for many after him, Africans, equipped with griots, bards and folklore, had no equivalent for museums, archives or libraries. They had no cultural heritage, no historical consciousness and thus no place in world history.

With the concept of intangible cultural heritage, UNESCO initiated an important process of decolonisation of the West and emancipation of memory cultures. It was finally acknowledged that there are not only material but also immaterial media of cultural memory, and that cultures are also sustained across generations and centuries through performances and practices, through singing and dancing, music-making and storytelling, cooking and pottery, rites and festivals. There is a book behind this shift toward intangible cultural heritage. It was published in 2003 by Diana Taylor and titled, *The Archive and the Repertoire. Performing Cultural Memory in the Americas.* I had the opportunity to have a conversation with Diana Taylor at the University of Zurich in June 2018.[6] A student of mine, the Junior

Professor Ana Sobral, had organised the event. For me, it was a welcome opportunity to revisit an abandoned path of our research after almost 40 years.

Diana Taylor grew up in Northern Mexico and taught performance studies at New York University's Tisch School of the Arts. She comes from a white family but has experienced the (im)material cultural border and political power imbalance between the northern and southern hemispheres of the Americas since her childhood. Therefore, her research is part of a wider movement that works toward decolonising Central and South America and to building a socio-political counter-memory.

"He who writes will stay", was a slogan of the German post office when it still existed and advertised itself *(Wer schreibt, der bleibt!).* The same is true for archives: those who create and use archives have political power; archives are powerful weapons of colonialism. Writing supports the status of elites and defines national identity; those who have no access to archives remain invisible and silenced in the history of the victors.

While Jan Assmann and I explored the media of cultural memory at the beginning of the digital revolution and delved into the study of cultures based on writing, Diana Taylor explored the forms of embodied cultural memory. While we worked with terms like canon and censorship, her key concepts were performance and repertoire. She asked: *"How does expressive behavior (performance) transmit cultural memory and identity?"* (Taylor 2003: xvi) The term performance encompasses concrete acts of performance and stands more generally for a form of culture that takes place and renews itself in performing communal action. The term thus marks not only a particular form of tradition and transmission, but also stands for a specific episteme: a genuine form of knowing, of world-experiencing and world-making. Hampâté Bâ himself referred to this particular episteme connected to embodied performances. He found clear words for it that are reminiscent of Socrates's words in Plato's Phaidros dialogue:

"Writing is one thing and knowledge is another. Writing is the photography of knowledge, but it is not knowledge itself. Knowledge is a light which is in man. It is the heritage of all the ancestors knew and have transmitted to us as seed, just as the mature baobab is contained in its seed."[7]

The concept of performance has opened up new perspectives in various disciplines and has fundamentally transformed our concept of culture. Its amazing productivity is clearly related to its broad spectrum of meanings ranging from the theatrical and spectacular as a salient performance for spectators to forms of general participation in social scripts and habitualised actions on the stage of everyday life. The performative turn has also upset our hierarchies. In the new digital media age, performance gained priority, shaping personal and collective life, while the cultural impact of the print age, which enabled individual expression and independent thinking waned.

The performative turn is important because it has opened up a new perspective on embodied practices of cultural translation and transmission. A key to the specific memory behind staged performance is the repertoire. Repertoire is the memory archive of the body. Performances work as powerful acts of transfer, conveying social knowledge, memory and a sense of shared identity through repeated, or *"twice-behaved behavior"* (Schechner 1985: 36). The repertoire is the personally embodied stock and collectively owned store of knowledge that individuals in a group can own and access. Participation in performance differs widely and offers varying degrees of interaction and intensity, such as joining the singing of a song either with all the verses or only the chorus, or only by humming along with the melody.

Mnemosyne and mnemonics: building up a repertoire

The word *remembering* is ambiguous. Neuroscientists distinguish the autobiographical or episodic memory from the declarative or semantic memory. The one is the place where we gather our subjective experiences and emotions through which we become individuals and distinguish ourselves from others, while the other is the place where we store what we learned and know. To better understand the quality of performance, we need a third form of memory besides episodic and declarative memory, namely mnemonics. Mnemonics are an integral part of intangible cultural heritage and a prerequisite for the celebration of traditions. The term stands for a specific art of remembering in the form of continuous practice or physical training. For bards, griots and other singers of tales, the performance of the collective epic is a life-time-job and responsibility. In many communities, when celebrating their feasts, the cultural memory is more equally distributed in the group. An example is the Jewish *Seder* Ritual in which all are connected in a shared cultural participation. Though booklets with the liturgy are available, everybody at the table is able to sing and follow the Biblical story as it is performed and sensuously experienced every year.

Mnemonics is also a vital part of artistic performances, which involves a specific training. It is a knowledge and a skill that is acquired and retained in order to be reproduced at will. There is no performance without rehearsal; any professional performer who enters a stage, be they musicians, actors or dancers, need to be physically and mentally equipped with roles, notations, choreography and other specific practices. Because it precedes performance and is removed from perception, it is the most intangible part of the intangible cultural heritage.

An interesting example of the art of creating and acquiring a body memory behind the stage is a text by choreographer Sasha Waltz (Waltz and Sandig forthcoming 2024), who, together with her team, develop their own immaterial scripts in order to make dance figures recognisable and durable for repeated performances. Gestures and movements are identified by the dancers as recognisable shapes and figures; they are given names to find their way into the archive of their bodies. Waltz draws attention to the fact that in Greek mythology Mnemosyne, the goddess of memory, is the mother of the nine muses. Each muse thus relies on a specific kind of memory. The muse of dance, Terpsichore, not only represents the dance but is also often depicted with a lyre and a plectrum, indicating the music that accompanies the dance. Here is Sasha Waltz's description of the role of mnemonics as a collaborative process of naming and remembering:

"In the rehearsal room, as a mystically demarcated district of a secular present to which the audience has no access, the birth as well as the giving of a name for a movement takes place as a clandestine act. The rules of this interplay are not set by any of the participants: the names fly to the movements, arise sometimes from the libretto of an opera, the architectural circumstances, then again from spontaneous association and imagination." (Waltz and Sandig forthcoming 2024)

The names for movements and gestures are created in the group and improvised, but as precise tokens, they function as mental images in the body memory, thus helping to coordinate and control the sequence of dance movements in the process of the performance as a joint activity.[8]

Memory of the World – recording and archiving the ephemeral

William Shakespeare's stagecraft is an outstanding and timely example of an intangible cultural heritage and its safeguarding. In his last play from 1611, *The Tempest,* he himself, in the role of Prospero, bids farewell to his art and stages the show as intangible cultural heritage. When the magic of the performance is over, nothing is left of the stage spectacle. It is like waking up from a dream, arriving in another world. Behind the wizard Prospero looms the even more powerful wizard Shakespeare, the creator of all the actors, pulling their strings and directing their destinies. In this role, the playwright bids farewell to the theatre and his audience. He refers to the play within the play in order to comment on his own farewell from the stage:

> *Our revels now are ended. These our actors,*
> *As I foretold you, were all spirits and*
> *Are melted into air, into thin air:*
> *And, like the baseless fabric of this vision,*
> *[…] the great globe itself*
> *[…] shall dissolve*
> *And, like this insubstantial pageant faded,*
> *Leave not a rack behind.*[9]

The concept of intangible cultural heritage cannot be expressed more clearly: when the show is over, everything is gone and no trace remains of what has been experienced. For Shakespeare, the ephemeral quality of the show is only a premonition of the non-durability of the whole theatre and the world as such. The Latin motto was inscribed on the front of his theatre: *"Totus Mundus agit histrionem"* (the whole world acts out a play).

We would in fact have no idea of Shakespeare and his stage work today, had not his acting company given him a posthumous gift, and that is the great folio complete edition of his plays, which appeared seven years after his death. The two editors, John Heminges and Henry Condell, laid the foundation for Shakespeare's afterlife by giving his works a durable and material form. This is the only reason why the Globe's tradition did not end and his plays are still performed and adapted in series all over the world. In 2023 we celebrate the 400-year anniversary of this first edition of his works as a unique Memory of the World. Shakespeare's afterlife therefore rests on two pillars that complement each other: the safeguarding of his plays in print as a durable form of material, externalised storage, and the continuous embodied repetitions in theatres; in other words: on page and stage.

Archiving of the body with the help of new technology

The performances of immaterial cultural heritage rely on an embodied mnemotechnic; they use the body itself as an archive. But this mnemotechnic stands and falls with the body; and when the body disappears, it must be replaced, otherwise the continuity of this cultural form breaks down and is lost forever. In a conversation, the German theatre director Andrea Breth brought home to me the inexorable temporal logic of intangible cultural heritage: *"Once you're gone"*, she said to me, *"there will be still your books on the shelf; once I'm gone, the shelf will be empty."* The stage may be an eternal space, but it immortalises no one. The performances are ephemeral; they automatically dissolve, leaving *"not a rack behind"*.

Before the technical possibility of recording music and moving images, no performances made it into Western cultural memory. The German composer Clara Schumann (1818–1896), for example, was a world-class pianist who travelled from performance to performance, impressing audiences on stage for 60 years of her life – yet nothing of her art has survived to reach us. As technologies were developed to record and preserve sounds and moving images, the gap between excarnate and incarnate culture has become surmountable. Digitisation, the chronologically last and now most current recording technology, creates an afterlife for performances to be heard and viewed in the private mode of print culture. A video is a recording and not a performance, but with the help of these documents a history of performances can be written, and even ephemeral arts like dance gain the dignity of a university subject. Cultural memory has been remarkably expanded through the new media. Now, more than a rack remains after the performance, namely a whole library of records and DVDs of the performative arts. Page and stage are on an almost equal footing, as both are now archivable as memory of the world.

Western cultures have relied on material duration in space for safeguarding their cultural heritage, while indigenous cultures have chosen another path: they ensured their cultural heritage through repeated performances in time. What has come to an end is dissolved and disappears. To secure it across time, it must be repeated, from performance to performance and from generation to generation.

Material and immaterial heritage

Throughout this essay, I have worked with binary oppositions to analyse different forms and dynamics of cultural memory. But on second thought, material and immaterial cultural heritage are not so easily divided. Indeed, what is written in granite promises long durability, and what one possesses in black and white can be carried home with confidence. But that is only one side of the coin, because repetition, rereading, updating and renewal – altogether actions in which the temporal dimension comes into play – are no less important for memory. Cultural memory, like individual memory, is therefore dependent on external impulses or triggers. What is permanently stored in museums, archives and libraries must be triggered on certain occasions, i.e., repeatedly read, exhibited, performed, staged, discussed, in short: reactivated. Just as there are monuments in space, there are monuments in time, which is just another name for feasts, memorial days and anniversaries. Such appointed dates serve several functions. They create occasions for a re-encounter with a historical or mythic event, which is renewed, reviewed and updated within the present. In historical anniversaries, a society assures itself of the central turning points and lasting impulses of its history; these dates form a framework for critically reviewing and negotiating the collective self-image, offering occasions for personal participation in events, debates and reflections that update and critically renew the historical consciousness of a society.

What is permanently fixed and stored, however, recedes into an ever greater temporal distance. If it is not re-presented and discussed in general public, it loses its relevance and becomes inert. It is therefore futile to play these two modes off against each other because they are complementary to and dependent on each other. Acts of repetition are important modes of refreshing and renewing what is remembered, both for the individual as well as for a society as a whole.

---

1 Translation Aleida Assmann.
2 See also a retrospective assessment of the various turns by Doris Bachmann-Medick (2017).
3 The Material Turn in the Humanities, *nwo.nl/en/projects/275-20-029*, issued by the Dutch Research Council (13/09/2023).
4 Materiality Turn, Wikipedia article: *en.wikipedia.org/wiki/Materiality_turn#:~:text=In%20short%2C%20the%20material%20turn,their%20relationships%20with%20organizations%20and* (13/09/2023).
5 The volume opened up a series of meanwhile twelve titles relating to general topics of culture in a comparative perspective.
6 Reenacting, Recoding, Reinscribing: The Body as Archive in Art and Performance. Round Table Discussion with Aleida Assmann, Rebecca Schneider and Diana Taylor, Cabaret Voltaire, Zurich, 4 June 2018, organised by Ana Sobral.
7 *quotefancy.com/amadou-hampate-ba-quotes* (13/09/2013).
8 See the interview with Sasha Waltz in this volume (note by the editors).
9 William Shakespeare, *The Tempest,* Act 4, Scene 1, 148–156. In: Shakespeare 2011.

REFERENCES

Assmann, Aleida and Jan Christof **Hardmeier** (eds.) (1983): Schrift und Gedächtnis. (Archäologie der literarischen Kommunikation I). Munich: Fink.

Bachmann-Medick, Doris (2017): Cultural Turns: A Matter of Management? In: Wendelin Küpers et al. (eds.), Rethinking Management. Management – Culture – Interpretation. Wiesbaden: Springer, pp. 31–55.

Bachmann-Medick, Doris (2016): Cultural Turns: New Orientations in the Study of Culture. Berlin, Boston: de Gruyter.

Bachmann-Medick, Doris (2006): Cultural Turns. Neuorientierungen in den Kulturwissenschaften. Reinbek bei Hamburg: Rowohlt.

Goody, Jack (ed.) (1968): Literacy in Traditional Societies. Cambridge: Cambridge University Press. German translation. (1986): Entstehung und Folgen der Schriftkultur. Transl. Friedhelm Herborth, Frankfurt am Main: Suhrkamp.

Hampâté Bâ, Amadou (1972): Aspects of African Civilization (Person, Culture, Religion), translated by Susan Hunt, 2; *academia.edu/49073084/Aspects_of_African_Civilization_Amadou_Hampate_Ba* (13/09/2023).

Havelock, Eric (1963): Preface to Plato. Cambridge: Harvard University Press.

Havelock, Eric (1986): The Muse Learns to Write. New Haven: Yale University Press.

Hegel, Georg Wilhelm Friedrich (1961): Vorlesungen über die Philosophie der Geschichte. Stuttgart: Reclam.

Klein, Gabriele (2023): Performanztheorien. In: Beate Hochholdinger-Reiterer, Christina Thurner and Julia Wehren (eds.), Theater und Tanz. Handbuch für Wissenschaft und Studium. Baden-Baden: Rombach, pp. 289–296.

Lord, Albert (1960): The Singer of Tales. Cambridge, MA: Harvard University Press.

Lotman, Jurij (2019): Culture, Memory and History. Essays in Cultural Semiotics. Edited by Marek Tamm. London: Palgrave Macmillan.

Ong, Walter Jackson (1982 [2002]): Orality and Literacy: The Technologizing of the Word. Reprint New York: Routledge.

Schechner, Richard (1985): Between Theater and Anthropology. Philadelphia: University of Philadelphia Press.

Shakespeare, William (2011): The Tempest. In: The Arden Edition, eds. Alden T. Vaughan, Virginia Mason Vaughan. London: Bloomsbury Academic.

Taylor, Diana (2003): The Archive and the Repertoire. Performing Cultural Memory in the Americas. Durham, N.C.: Duke University Press.

Waltz, Sasha and Jochen **Sandig** (eds.) (forthcoming 2024): Sasha Waltz & Guests. Berlin: Hatje Cantz Verlag.

Absent and Abund
Arte(povera)facts
Sasha Portyann

> "You know you are a foreigner
> when you talk about the socio-political role of the artist and your tutor tells you, you'd better decide if you want to be Florence Nightingale, Joseph Beuys or an artist."
> MARLENE DUMAS, *You know you are a Foreigner*

While working on this article, I received the following request from the Moscow Museum of Modern Art, where my colleagues and I were about to perform the archive-related performance Soviet Gesture[1]: *"[…] would it be possible to record the performance for the museum's media archive? If it is ok with you, we will specify in the contract that the footage will solely be used for archival purposes and will not be uploaded to our website or social media platforms. In addition, they* [archivists] *would like to bring in a photographer, however, only if you and the other participants are comfortable with it."* (translated from Russian by the author)

My first instinctive reaction misinterpreted their intentions, thinking that they would not allow us to use the recordings or photos for our purposes. Perhaps the misunderstanding was due to postmemory flashbacks, the implicit mistrust that many independent, not yet well-established artists often develop towards institutions (see Stiles 2021), or the experience of living in a repressive political regime where, by default, you are not allowed to do things without explicit permission.

Upon re-reading the message, I realised that this could be the moment: the first time in my artistic career that an institution unambiguously invited me to contribute work to their archive, thereby creating an artefact for future generations to reflect upon. Is it my moment to enter the "hall of fame", as Ada Mukhina (2020) puts it in her video essay *How to sell yourself to the West?*

My thoughts wandered further: What could be the reasons behind such a proposal? Could it be related to Russia's ongoing war of aggression against Ukraine? Since the onset of the full-scale invasion, cultural actors and institutions seem to be showing increased concern about the legacy they might leave behind, especially in the face of a potentially apocalyptic future. Or are my colleagues and I just old enough to be considered worthy to be archived? And above all, do our colleagues in Ukraine have an opportunity now to archive what is going on in their cultural landscape? Or are they simply satisfied with the occasional chance to present and see performances?

So, returning to the question of artefacts: What art archives from 2022/2023 will remain in Ukraine and Russia, respectively? In Palestine and Israel? In Afghanistan, Syria, Iran, the USA or Europe? Will we later draw conclusions about the presence or absence of the dance scene in a particular country based on the abundance or absence of artefacts? And what do we even mean when referring to a dance scene in such different cultural and political environments?

Dance archives or mere collections of artefacts?

When we discuss dance archives, we are often referring to carefully curated private collections, some of which later became state-supported archives. As Aleida Assmann distinguishes, cultural memory is formed by active and passive remembering practices. She states that active practices, related to the selection and collection of certain artefacts, can lead to the creation of the canon that eventually finds its way into museums and academic curricula. In contrast, passive practices consist of accumulation, the non-curated aggregation of artefacts, which often end up in archives – non-spectacular storehouses (Assmann 2008: 98–99). These archives lack entertaining components, which are crucial for museums, as they allow them to navigate their range of purposes, which can be education, commemoration, activism and bourgeois leisure routines (see Procter 2021).

In archival practices, the intention to narrate a particular story and prioritise one kind of artefact over others is considered a serious intervention and corrupts the objectivity of the archive in question. Usually, such cases take place during periods of authoritarian political regimes, when governments tend to manipulate history for their political benefits (see Assmann 2008; Spieker 2021; Taylor 2003). However, in case of the personal archives of established dance artists, similar practices of biased narratives and of engaging in self-mythologising seem not to be an object of criticism. According to anecdotal references, famous artists pass over their personal archives to public institutions along with inventory lists and detailed descriptions of what should be presented and how. Such an approach has more in common with an attempt to create a canon.

Moreover, a certain level of selection exists in every analogue archive and is even considered necessary: *"more or less regulated destruction of records is the prerequisite for the archive's ability to accept new accessions."* (Spieker 2021: 36) This process may be valid as long as it does not selectively target a specific group. Since this kind of targeting has become widely debated and investigated in recent times, the *"structural mechanisms of exclusion in terms of class, race, and gender"* (Assmann 2008: 106) cannot be disputed anymore.

Conceptual artists have addressed the issues of preservation practices as well as archival hierarchies through multiple acts of intentional destruction or transformation of the artefacts to the extent that they no longer retain their integrity. Describing the destruction or transformation of potential artefacts and real archival documents, Sven Spieker (2021: 35–36) refers to it as *"archivophobia"* – as opposed to *"archivophilia"*, which is manifested in the creation or adoption of the archives by artists with the intention to fill in the gaps and to reconstruct the *"histories that were repressed or expunged from the official record during the period of communism"*. Both *archivophilia* and *archivophobia* transform the concept and political mission of the archive from a *"static container of information"* to a *"dynamic process of knowledge formation"* (Spieker 2021: 35).

Most of the dance archives are situated in the West-European territories and contexts, which tend to have a rather traditional understanding of 'the archive' with very particular and often non-transparent procedures of adding new materials to collections. However, there are projects addressing this issue of gatekeeping that attempt to undo questionable traditions. For instance, first the *Mime Centrum Berlin*[2] and later the *Tanzforum Berlin*[3] have, since 2000 and 2014, respectively, been regularly documenting an extensive though not exhaustive number of *"current projects by renowned Berlin choreographers and young artists, as well as productions shown within the scope of established Berlin dance festivals"*.[4] The approach of showcasing the experiments of young artists together with full-scale funded productions by renowned choreographers serves to record a broad depiction of the range of activities that take place in Berlin. The website of *Tanzforum Berlin* presents an archive of video trailers, and full-length video documentation of the performances is handed over to three public institutions, though full access to the recordings is only possible in the *Media Library for Dance and Theatre* (the former *Mime Centrum Berlin*) for visitors not affiliated with a university.[5]

Of course, each approach and practice mentioned reflects the political realities and values of the respective actors. However, there is also a certain infrastructure that either allows or restricts the development of different kinds of projects.[6] While acknowledging the significance of the remarkable community and cultural efforts that have enabled participants to achieve recognition and develop more sustainable structures, it is crucial to remember that there can be also other contexts. For instance, coming from Russia, whose authorities prefer declaring democratic principles rather than implementing them (see Guriev and Treisman 2022), where acts of solidarity and any form of civil or political cooperation could potentially result in imprisonment, I consider even the opportunity to propose a grassroots cultural project to authorities a privilege (let alone the prospect of receiving funding for it). Similarly, I perceive the opportunity to establish a collection or an archive as a manifestation of another level of privilege.[7]

Having said that, it is worth noting that there is an implicit academic consensus regarding the understanding of a dance archive. The nature of bureaucratic formalities still accommodates a range of contexts. From the self-curated archives of well-established artists to archives of unfunded venues, self-organised platforms (SDVIG, PLAST), or the dispersed archives of dissolved institutions (GAKhN) – the matter of the artefacts matters due to their power of legitimisation.[8]

Dance (canon) studies

Most of the archives discussed in dance studies are collections – the outcome of active selection processes and aiming to establish a canon that constructs a hierarchy of heritage, culture and value. The goal of culture that contains hierarchy *"has always been to move downward from the height of power and privilege in order to diffuse, disseminate, and expand itself in the widest possible range"* (Said 1983: 9). It is not surprising, then, that the geography of the scenes, actors and stars in the dance canon strongly correlates with the infrastructure of active and relevant networks. This correlation is a stark reminder of the world map during the colonial era, emphasising that *"debates about the 'ephemerality' of performance are, of course, profoundly political"* (Taylor 2003: 17). Anonymous social media accounts express similar concerns in the internet memes shown on *fig. 1 & 2* below:

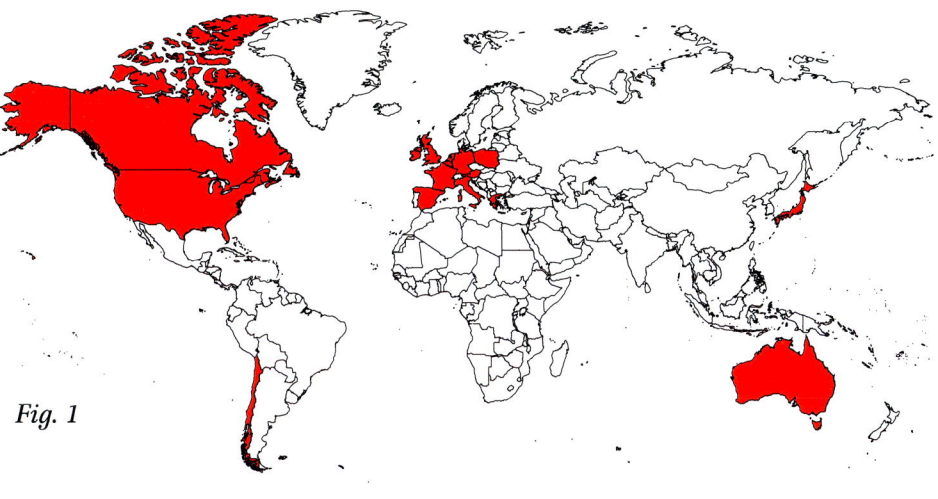

Fig. 1

Fig. 2

Fig. 1 (previous page) — Source: Twitter account @MemesCentraI
Fig. 2 (previous page) — Source: Instagram account @somatic_based_content_only

In addition to the unequal recognition and representation, existing dance (canon) archives contribute, in turn, to the creation of a canon of archives. They serve as a blueprint, illustrating what an archive should encompass: items such as recordings, posters, awards, articles, and reviews in media. Interestingly, a professional artistic cv is supposed to consist of similar parts, representing education, projects (including videos), awards (as a symbol of recognition by the professional community) and press coverage (recognition of a broader audience). It seems as if the idea of potentially archivable content is already integrated into undergraduate education, where young artists are taught what to include in their cv. The knowledge system that shapes this type of education is entirely indoctrinated with the paradigm of modernity. As a student in the dance department of *Vaganova Ballet Academy* (2011–2013), which had a focus on contemporary dance, I studied art and dance history of the twentieth century, both of which can be traced back to the beginning of the modern era. In our curriculum, the dark sides of modernity were not addressed, and all dances that did not fit into the paradigm of modernity were labelled ethnic, folk, etc., confirming the following observation by Madina Tlostanova: *"Once the idea of modernity was created, it legitimized the system of knowledge that created it. Both became instruments for disavowing other systems of knowledge and pushing other historical processes outside modernity"* (Tlostanova 2015: 40). One may argue that the topic I am addressing is too emotionally charged and / or region-specific; but indeed, as Tamara Hundorova puts it, *"a perspective like this, from the point of view of the periphery, is global"* (Hundorova 2022).

And yet the peripheries are not homogeneous. Particular canons of different regions reflect the hierarchies and inequalities within those regions. Art scenes operating in a realm of a shared political past and present have produced distinct canons and infrastructural advantages. For example, prior to the Russian invasion of Ukraine, there was a notable disparity in opportunities for artists holding Russian and Belarusian passports. This difference was so significant that many artists from

Belarus considered becoming citizens of Russia to gain access to the same resources, which is reminiscent of similar patterns exhibited in postcolonial regions (Mukhina 2020). The same refers to cultural products of post-Soviet countries: they became part of the local and often global canon if they were produced in the Russian language, or by artists based in Moscow and in Saint Petersburg. Otherwise, such regional cultural productions were presented as the folk art of national minorities, without the cultural and political weight required for the canon.

"Secondary empire Russia, balancing between semi-peripheral and peripheral status in the world system, follows the rule of regressive transformation of imperial difference into colonial difference. This two-faced empire in the view of its victorious rivals, seen in reality as a colony, soon becomes aware of this status and responds with aggression and denial both towards its stronger imperial rivals and toward its own colonial others." (Tlostanova 2020: 28, translated by the author).

Domestic and international cultural policies operate similarly to how canonical artworks are consumed: *"normative and formative texts, places, persons, artefacts, and myths [...] are meant to be actively circulated and communicated in ever-new presentations and performances"* (Assmann 2008: 100). Within the realm of dance, Russian ballet stands as a perfect example of the cultural canon, demonstrating that the performative aspects of dance pieces, even in case of ballet, fail to resist change (see Taylor 2003: 20). Due to the corporeality of dance, its preservation heavily relies on repetition. To maintain the canonical repertoire and techniques, ballet routines and choreographies must be taught, learnt and regularly practised in studios by dancers. These multiple repetitions of physical actions often lead to an amplification of certain features over time. These features are then perceived by interpreters as canonical aspects of that dance or technique. Over generations, this trend has resulted in canonical ballet pieces becoming rather a simulacrum: subsequent iterations are derived from copies of copies and the original is not only dissolved in the myriad of repetitions, but the concept of originality itself becomes irrelevant (see Baudrillard 1994). The evidence of this transformation can be easily seen in recordings of canonical ballet pieces like *The Dying Swan*[9] or *Little Swans*[10] from various years and locations throughout the twentieth century.

Wrong optics, biased methodology

Any depiction of a dance, whether it is a picture, sketch, photo or video recording, captures only a fraction of the actual movement. The quality of muscle tone can be perceived from a photo, but not the quality of movement. Moreover, each dancer possesses their own unique movement quality, which is heavily influenced by the physical capabilities of their joints and muscles, their dance training and, to a significant extent, the cultural environment where the dancer was raised (Kamanan 2021: 89). Dancers who transition from one technique to another, or even from one dance school to another (retaining the same technique) know that the inner map of the body and the way certain movements are articulated can differ tremendously. What may be reminiscent of a tendu movement in a picture can in fact be informed by completely different corporealities, having no correlation with one another.

In the post-Soviet context, the most famous example of such misinterpretation is the phenomenon of folkdance ensembles such as the Igor Moiseyev Ballet. Ironically, this internationally known brand name reflects the essence of Moiseyev's approach much more sincerely than its domestic Russian title, the *Igor Moiseyev State Academic Ensemble of Folk Dance* (author's translation). The depiction of folk dances in this ensemble's shows is not just transformed in a way that allows the performance of these acts as a stage dance; rather, the movements themselves have been altered to match the ballet movement training. By undergoing this kind of transformation, the movement loses its corporeality. The logic, the inner map of the body, the significance of the interaction in relation to space and others, the cosmology of traditional folklore and the topographical role of dancers as well as their body manifestations in the related mythologies – all of these aspects are lost in a folk dance performed as a ballet. Igor Narskij (2018) observes that when folklore is only used as a raw source material for the creation of new folk dances, the accumulation of repertoire goes hand in hand with an increase in standardisation. He also notices that *"folk dances in the USSR were invented in a similar fashion to how choreographers did in other countries during the twentieth century, and this was not limited to totalitarian regimes."*[11]

The inaccurate embodiment of a certain movement happens not only in folk dance but also in modernist techniques.

Such inaccuracies may easily go unnoticed by spectators, dance researchers or critics, but they are widely discussed among practitioners of dance and certainly addressed in further training. For instance, the new cast of the Trisha Brown Dance Company struggled to perform a particular part of the choreography, which they were learning from a video recording, until a member of the former cast came and explained the logic of the articulation of one particular movement.[12]

The unfolding of modernity not only changes the physicality of the movement but also extinguishes the climactic potential of dance. Bakhtin (1984) points out the transformative aspect of carnival and especially of laughter in the folk art of the European Middle Ages, particularly due to its ability to temporarily abolish existing hierarchies. Later, Enlightenment and Romanticism abandoned the carnival grotesque, leading to the idealisation of still images, and the transformative potential of art was lost. This trend can be traced to the present time, revealing aesthetic and social hierarchies.[13]

The approaches to researching dance vary depending on whether the focus is on academic knowledge production or physical movement exploration. Many corporeal aspects of dance tend to elude inclusion in academic discourse. Methodologies, rooted in the visual analysis as well as the value paradigm oriented on the material objects tended to be adapted to analysing dance rather than created out of its inherent logic. The assumption that we completely know something based only on its outward appearance has proven to be problematic from the postcolonial perspective (Procter 2021) as well as from the perspective of embodied knowledge. Artefacts and archives become ambiguous concepts when it comes to dance and performance, especially considering the power dynamics of the art field in its tendency to create canons.

As a dance practitioner, I find research aiming to articulate what dances convey on the meta-level to be inspiring and informative. For example, Kuryumova (2020) elaborated on the concept of physicality models that refer to the philosophical discourse of embodiment. Reid (2018) also continues to attempt to grasp the non-iconographical message of the image in dance, acknowledging that the current canon of the modern period considers only Western aristocratic and theatrical dance, without taking into account non-aristocratic and non-Western dance or popular dance. Dances lying beyond the Western canon often possess a complexity that defies existing scholarly language, the disparity in both the quantity and quality of academic scholarship devoted to dances within and beyond the Western canon is an issue that must be addressed (see Kealiinohomoku 1969). To access knowledge that surpasses the confines of modern epistemology, the presence and agency of researchers endowed with life experiences steeped in diverse paradigms, modes of knowledge production, worldviews and sense-making processes become not only valuable but indispensable.

What texts make us dance?

The most important question about dance archives from the practitioner's point of view remains the same: Is the knowledge an archive holds relevant to the current concept of movement and dance? What kind of artefact do dance practitioners consider informative for their work? Is this knowledge accessible and circulating?

Puzzled by these questions and trying to grasp an intangible identity left by a generation of dancers working in Moscow and Saint Petersburg, my colleague Dasha Plokhova and I conducted artistic research in the archive of the Choreological Laboratory of the State (Russian) Academy of Artistic Sciences (GAKhN).[14] Inspired by previous research on the same subject by Misler (2011) and Sirotkina (2011) we first explored the iconographical approach, supported by historical narratives, and eventually focused on textual sources. Our sources were the archived minutes of the laboratory meetings. These protocols were created by the members of the laboratory out of bureaucratic necessity: the "Choreological Laboratory" was a department of the GAKhN and it was supported by the state, which required reports and proofs of activities.

We found the textual sources particularly valuable and have intentionally focused exclusively on them due to the following reason: However impressive the collections of photographs and notations are, the precision of the depicted movement, coupled with a critical attitude towards the dramatic outcomes of the movement disciplines in question, leaves little room for dance experimentation that could inform contemporary dance practice. This is the reason for the lack of interest among dance artists in photo collections and notation systems, while most acknowledge the importance of video sources (Kamanan 2021, Wolińska 2021). From a practical point of view, there is a great difference in the amount of information that can be retrieved from a video compared to photos and notation.[15] There can be no illusions about the quality and quantity of kinetic information that can be extracted from static visual artefacts. Additionally, the reconstruction of a movement from a static image and dance notation is a very time-consuming task. At the same time, the explicit absence of any visual reference as well as the discursive nature of the minutes provoke creative speculation and invention of the dance scores. Pursuing our goal to undo the hierarchal potential of both text and the proposed methodology, we have created a card game that can be used to produce an immense amount of absurd scores. The mission of the project is to share the content of our research in a form that encourages dance practice as well as further artistic investigation.

From the publications curated and written by other dance artists, such as described below, one can conclude that practitioners are more interested in when, why and what for people dance, rather than how they do it. It seems that many artists who were educated in the episteme of modernity, who studied Western dance canon, feel the necessity of bringing back that aspect of dance *"that was developed to facilitate bonding with other humans outside of one's bloodline […] with cooperation being a key skill in those processes"* (Wolińska 2021). Several articles in different issues of *a Dance Mag* (for instance Dirik 2020; Aoun 2019) refer to the empowering function of dances and their ability to enhance the political agency of communities, while others discuss the phenomenological perception of the body in regional festivals and how it influences pain perception (Jirasakwittaya 2019), real experiences of recovering after stroke and returning to dance classes (Meskaoui 2019), or the ethics of the gaze in club culture (Corkish 2019).

I suggest that although these texts are not in line with the academic tradition of knowledge production, their attempt at *"de-linking from the rhetoric of modernity and the logic of coloniality"* (Mignolo 2007: 463) is very effective. The content and strategies of such publications communicate the possibility of *"placing theory and the lifeworld on the same axis as the practices of decolonisation in everyday writing, thinking and activism"* (Tlostanova 2020: 26, translated by the author). The following examples demonstrate how important this line of research may be.

The first example of how the dance practices and their epistemes work comes from my experience with dance and activism. As a practitioner, I contest the seemingly logical proposition that *"the joy of the rhythmic activity [...] helped overcome the fear of confronting predators and other threats, just as marching music has pumped up soldiers in historical times"* (Ehrenreich 2007: 26). Dancing with Sevi Bayraktar, who was teaching dances from Turkey's protest landscape, we have noticed that in grassroots dances (including folk tradition) the first step often starts with the weak beat (upbeat), as opposed to the strong beat (downbeat) that is emphasised in marches.[16] Therefore, from a practical perspective, folk dances and marches operate on opposite poles of the political aspect of embodiment: in order to follow the dance that starts ahead of a beat (upbeat), a dancer needs to be more attentive to the people around them. Marching music, in contrast, does not induce this complexity of relations: everyone makes a step on the strong, loud downbeat, altogether – no particular attention or embodied intelligence is required.

Another case of collective embodied intelligence rooted in folk dance tradition appeared during the protests against military mobilisation in 2022 in the Sakha Republic of the Russian Federation. The group of predominantly female protesters engaged in a traditional form of circle dance, and encircled the armed group of riot police, depriving them of their power.[17] Thus, the initial idea about the simplistic connection of dance, rhythm and protest is re-shaped as soon as one starts to get to know and participate in the multitude of real dance practices.

Conclusion. From absence to the void and vā

Considering the political geography of intangible and archivable cultural heritages and the history of their hierarchical relations, what conclusions can we draw from the respective absence and abundance of the artefacts? What type and amount of information can be extracted from artefacts? And who possesses an appropriate methodology that aligns with the knowledge system the artefacts embody? Do those who are informed in the related semiotics have access to the artefacts in question? Will the knowledge produced in other-than-Western epistemes find its way to academic publications? What emerges from the void these yet-to-be-addressed questions have shown exists?

In artistic practice, we frequently immerse ourselves in a plenitude of questions by choice. The abundance of input creates a state of constructive confusion that may allow us to perceive relations and connections which seem to be absent or simply do not make sense in the logic of the dominant knowledge system. There are concepts in other-than-Western epistemes which embrace those phenomena. The most recent one I have learned about is the *Sāmoan concept of vā* which is a *"space between, the between-ness, not empty space, not space that separates but space that relates, that holds separate entities and things together in the Unity-that-is-All, the space that is context, giving meaning to things"* (Van der Ryn 2017: 220).[18] This concept aligns with the strategies of creating more space in between, offering more room for creative speculation. Through this, dance artists can *delink* from the existing hierarchy of knowledge, encouraging creative corporeal research (see Mignolo 2007). This perspective also allows us to reconsider the archival space, transforming it from an empty container waiting to be filled, into an ever-evolving network of relations awaiting discovery. Moreover, it facilitates a re-evaluation of both the archivable materials and the inherent value of artefacts.

Whether surprising or not, writing this article helped me reflect upon my emotional confusion caused by the fact that the documentation of our performance mentioned in the beginning didn't happen – the museum was unable to organise either video or photo documentation. As a result, despite remaining institutionally unarchived, the abundance of audience responses and Instagram posts remain in the constantly evolving internet archive and in the void of people's memories.[19]

---

1   Soviet Gesture. Research-in-progress since 2015, *sashaportyannikova.com/soviet-gesture* (15/06/2023).
2   *mimecentrum.iti-germany.de/* (11/08/2023).
3   *tanzforumberlin.de/en/* (23/07/2023).
4   *tanzforumberlin.de/en/* (23/07/2023).

5   *archiv.mimecentrum.de/* (11/08/2023).

6   As an example, the above-described documentation activity in Berlin is supported by the administration of cultural affairs of the Berlin Senate, which correspondingly leads to the prioritisation of documenting Senate-funded projects ahead of any other *(tanzforumberlin.de/ueber-tanzforum-berlin)*.

7   This privilege may be connected to the prosperity of the country that provides resources for such activities, or to the personal wealth of private collectors (see Assmann 2008: 98). The cultural and historical value of such collections and archives is (in)disputable, especially in light of the revealed practices of their financing, which raises questions about possible art-washing/toxic philanthropy (see Bayer 2022).

8   SDVIG – Performing Arts Studio, *sdvig.space/contacts/* (15/06/2023); PLAST – The Platform for Contemporary Dance, *plast.dance/archiv-diel-podla-sezon.php* (15/06/2023); GAKhN – the State Academy of Artistic Sciences (1921–1930, Moscow, Russia). For further reference see e.g., the special research project website of the University of Bochum, in German: *gachn.de* (15/06/2023). More GAKhN documents are held in the Russian State Archive of Literature and Art (RGALI, Moscow), and in private collections.

9   *The Dying Swan:* Anna Pavlova (premiered in 1904), *youtu.be/tkFSBkl9mmo* (14/06/2023); Plisetskaya (1975), *youtu.be/Wpk7Kx4dt-U* (14/06/2023); Svetlana Zakharova (2010s), *youtu.be/PKwsG7gS2r0* (14/06/2023).

10 *Little Swans,* 8 performances for comparison (online) *youtu.be/uPwSndlRpg8* (14/06/2023).

11 Narskij 2018: chapter 2.2, paragraph 10; see also chapter 2.3, paragraph 12. Translated by the author.

12 Personal conversation with Elena Demyanenko, March 2018.

13 Traces of the grotesque tradition were still present in the folk culture in Soviet Russia after the Revolution of 1917. At that time, dance caricatures, "political grotesques", were very popular and appreciated by the public much more than any organised gymnastic practices. Usually, they were performed in the form of a "living newspaper" (Sokolskaya 2000: 370).

14 The outcome of this research was presented in the form of the book *Manual for the Practical Use of a Dance Archive: Experiments in Choreology, or Where the Soviet Gesture Has Led Us* (Plokhova and Portyannikova 2020).

15 The limitations of extracting embodied information from video recordings were discussed above, see section "Wrong optics, biased methodology"; see also Taylor 2003: 20.

16 Sevi Bayraktar: Diaspora temporalities – gathering through dispersing. Workshop at Tanzquartier Wien, 13–15 January 2023; *tqw.at/en/event/diaspora-temporalities-bayraktar/* (21/08/2023).

17 Varlamov News from 25 September 2022; *t.me/varlamov_news/34389* (14/06/2023).

18 For the concept of *vā*, see Pelenakeke Brown. In-Between Space, Movement, and Time. *kampnagel.de/produktionen/pelenakeke-brown-in-between-space-movement-and-time* (14/06/2023).

19 Collection of Instagram stories related to the Soviet Gesture project: *instagram.com/stories/highlights/17993251399947058/* (13/06/2023).

REFERENCES

Aoun, Anas Abou (2019): From Nakba to Dabka. In: a Dance Mag, Vol. 2, pp. 75–78.

Assmann, Aleida (2008): Canon and Archive. In: Astrid Erll, Ansgar Nünning (eds.) Cultural memory studies: an international and interdisciplinary handbook. Berlin, New York: Walter de Gruyter, pp. 97–107. *doi.org/10.1515/9783110207262.2.97*

Bakhtin, Mikhail (1984): Rabelais and His World. Bloomington: Indiana University Press.

Baudrillard, Jean (1994): Simulacres et simulation: Simulacra and simulation: the body in theory. Ann Arbor, MI: University of Michigan.

Bayer, Waltraud M. (2022): Filantropija.ru | Kunst- und Museumsstiftungen der Moskauer Wirtschaftselite. Zenodo. *doi.org/10.5281/zenodo.6631165* (13/08/2023).

Corkish, Lucy (2019): Skeptical Gaze. In: a Dance Mag, Vol. 2, pp. 24–27.

Dirik, Hêlîn (2020): Hand in Hand. In: a Dance Mag, Vol. 3, pp. 18–21.

Dumas, Marlene (2014): Sweet Nothings. London: Koenig Books.

Ehrenreich, Barbara (2007): Dancing In The Streets: A History of Collective Joy. New York: Metropolitan Books.

Guriev, Sergei and Daniel **Treisman** (2022): Spin Dictators: The Changing Face of Tyranny in the 21st Century. Princeton: Princeton University Press. *doi.org/10.1515/9780691224466.*

Jirasakwittaya, Pascha (2019): Purity Though Pain. In: a Dance Mag, Vol. 2, pp. 6–9.

Hundorova, Tamara (2022): How Peripheries Talk Amongst Themselves. In: SONIAKH digest. *soniakh.com/index.php/2022/12/23/hundorova-how-peripheries-talk-amongst-themselves/* (11/06/2023).

Kamanan, Christelle Ahia Marie-Laure (2021): Change from the bottoms. In: Kasia Wolińska (ed.), Danceolitics. Berlin: Uferstudios GmbH, pp. 87–100.

Kealiinohomoku J. W. (1969): An anthropologist looks at ballet as a form of ethnic dance. Impulse 1969/1970, pp. 24–32.

Kuryumova, Nataliya (2020): Contemporary dance in the culture of the XX century: a change in the models of physicality. St. Petersburg: Lan, The Planet of Music.

Meskaoui, Zéna M. (2019): Re-Pairing. In: a Dance Mag, Vol. 2, pp. 32–37.

Mignolo, Walter D. (2007): DELINKING: The rhetoric of modernity, the logic of coloniality and the grammar of de-coloniality. In: Cultural Studies, Vol. 21, No. 2–3. pp. 449–514. *doi.org/10.1080/09502380601162647.*

Misler, Nicoletta (2011): Vnachale bylo telo [In the beginning was the body]. Moskva: Iskusstvo--XXI vek.

Mukhina, Ada (2020): How to sell yourself to the West. *junge-akademie.adk.de/en/articles/ada-mukhina/* (13/06/2023).

Narskij, Igor (2018): Kak partija narod tantsevat uchila, kak baletmestery ej pomogali i chto iz etogo vyshlo: Kulturnaja istorija sovetskoj tantsevalnoj samodejatelnosti (How the party taught the people how to dance, how the choreographers helped them, and what came out of it). Moskva: Novoe literaturnoe obozrenie.

Plokhova, Daria and Alexandra **Portyannikova** (2020): Rukovodstvo po prakticheskomu primeneniyu tanceval'nogo arhiva "Opyty horeologii", ili Kuda nas zavel "Sovetskij zhest" (Manual for the Practical Use of a Dance Archive: Experiments in Choreology, or Where the Soviet Gesture Has Led Us). Moscow: Garage Museum of Contemporary Art.

Procter, Alice (2021): The Whole Picture: The Colonial Story of the Art in Our Museums & Why We Need to Talk about it. London: Cassell.

Said, Edward W. (1983): The World, the Text, and the Critic. Cambridge, Massachusetts: Harvard University Press.

Sirotkina, Irina (2011): Svobodnoe dvizhenie i plasticheskij tanec v Rossii (Free movement and plastic dance in Russia). Moscow: Novoe literaturnoe obozrenie.

Sokolskaya, Ariadna Leonidovna (2000): Plastika i tanec v samodejatel'nom tvorchestve (Plastic And Dance In Amateur Art). In: Ksenija Georgievna Bogemskaya et al. (eds.), Samodejatel'noe hudozhestvennoe tvorchestvo v SSSR (Amateur Art in the USSR). St. Petersburg: DB, pp. 356–399.

Spieker, Sven (2021): Destroy she said. In: Emese Kürti, Zsuzsa László (eds.), What Will Be Already Exists: Temporalities of Cold War Archives in East-Central Europe and Beyond. Bielefeld: transcript, pp. 35–47. *doi.org/10.1515/9783839458235-004*

Stiles, Kristine (2021): Collecting the Future. A Personal History of an Archive. In: Emese Kürti, Zsuzsa László (eds.), What Will Be Already Exists: Temporalities of Cold War Archives in East-Central Europe and Beyond. Bielefeld: transcript, pp. 21–34. *doi.org/10.1515/9783839458235-003*

Taylor, Diana (2003): The Archive And the Repertoire. Performing Cultural Memory in the Americas. Durham and London: Duke University Press. *doi.org/10.2307/j.ctv11smzlk*

Tlostanova, M. (2015): Can the post-Soviet think? On coloniality of knowledge, external imperial and double colonial difference. In: Intersections. East European Journal of Society and Politics, Vol. 1. No 2. pp. 38–58. *doi.org/10.17356/ieejsp.v1i2.38*

Tlostanova, Madina (2020): Dekolonial'nost' bytija, znanija i oshhushhenija: sbornik statej (Decoloniality of being, knowledge and feeling: collection of articles). Almaty: Centr Sovremennoj Kul'tury "Celinnyj".

Van der Ryn, Micah G. (2017): Samoan Tā–Vā (Time–Space) Concepts and Practices in Language, Society, and Architecture. In: Pacific Studies Special Issue. Vol. 40, No. 1/2, pp. 212–244.

Wolińska, Kasia (2021): Welcome to Danceolitics. In: Kasia Wolińska (ed.) Danceolitics. Berlin: Uferstudios GmbH, pp. 4–23.

"Things that Death Cannot Destroy": The Afterlife and Performativity of Photographic Images (Linda Fregni Nagler, Cristina Baldacci

Whatever their support may be, images not only travel but also act in time and space, generating specific social and cultural experiences that change according to different contexts, times and audiences (Gell 1998; Mitchell 2005; Bredekamp 2018; Osborne 2018). As images, photographs have their afterlife as cultural artefacts, too. Especially as artistic and anthropological objects, they pertain to all effects to material culture and are not mere representations of the objects to which they refer.

To address this issue from a particular perspective, the ongoing magic lantern slides collection and performance *Things that Death Cannot Destroy* (2009–today), by the Italian artist Linda Fregni Nagler (born in Stockholm in 1976), will be taken as a main case study *(fig. 1)*.[1]

Fig. 1 — Linda Fregni Nagler, Things that Death Cannot Destroy, *Part 1, 2010, Teatro Franco Parenti, Milan. Courtesy of the artist*

Magic lantern slides may seem ambivalent images. Being imprinted on glass, therefore possessing accentuated materiality, but then projected onto a screen or a wall in order to be seen, they give the illusion of immateriality. In the late eighteenth century – that is, before the actual invention of photography, when images were still hand-painted or reproduced with traditional printing techniques on slides – magic lantern slides ushered in a (sub)genre: that of *phantasmagoria* (Grossi and Pinotti 2022; Wynants 2020).

Hence, one key concept that will be addressed here, is the materiality and the performativity of photographs, as well as the performativity of both the image presentation device – the magic lantern – and the presentational form in which the slides are arranged: namely, a montage that produces what might be called an atlas of images in motion. As Fregni Nagler re-organises the slides of her collection (which currently counts about 4,000 specimens) every time she performs a new projection episode, *Things that Death Cannot Destroy* repeats a similar but always different visual narrative, which also generates a new circulation and reception of images – that is, a set of counter-narratives – bringing up another key concept: reenactment.

An object that "lacks all 'certainty'" except the physical presence

Speaking of the materiality of photographic images means taking into consideration at least three different aspects: the plasticity of the image itself, the presentational form to which an image is inevitably bound, and the physical traces that an image carries with itself, due to usage and time (Edwards and Hart 2004: 3).

As art historian Geoffrey Batchen wrote, photographs *"have volume, opacity, tactility and a physical presence in the world"*, they are material artefacts, and as such they are entangled with specific embodied and sensory-affective relations (Batchen 1997: 2). Even today, when the materiality of images seems to dissolve into computational data and algorithms, digitally produced photographs still need a material support or physical device in order to be seen and circulated (Sassoon 2004; Ackerman et al. 2020).

Against all expectations, their materiality is still an essential trait forming a firm point in a cloud of uncertainty – so well expressed by Régis Durand, the former director of the Centre National de la Photographie and of the Jeu de Paume in Paris, in the footsteps of Roland Barthes:

"Photography seems to call for so many different ways of viewing. It is not even clear that it exists (and how) as a medium. Is the medium the paper print, the ordinary print we use for our snapshots? Or is it the artist's print, which can be put up on the wall, matted and framed, or kept loose in a portfolio? Or is it the photograph as printed on a page of a magazine, or in a book? The object

lacks all "certainty" (to use Barthes's word), making the phenomenological reading of it problematic and plural." (Durand 1995: 146)

Forming part of the material turn introduced by anthropology in cultural studies, the magic lantern is a suitable example to attest the full status of images as objects that undergo *"a continuing process of production, exchange, usage, and meaning"* (Edwards and Hart 2004: 4). Besides being the most important and popular means of entertainment, education and propaganda in Europe across the nineteenth century, magic lantern slides are among the longest lasting supports for photographic images. Once secured on slides, photographs are de facto endowed with hapticity and objecthood.

However, the magic lantern has only recently (more or less in the last decade) attracted scholarly interest from different disciplinary perspectives,[2] re-emerging from pre-cinema history where it was long relegated, together with other optical devices. It was essentially with the shift towards Media Archaeology – starting from the 1980s – that film and media studies opened up the discipline to a social history approach, focusing attention on both local (cinema) cultures and audiences, and intermedial relations. This change of view produced a new interest in what was actually shown and to whom; that is, in the objects as artefacts and documents, and in their audiences, from a cultural perspective.

To say it with photography scholars Elizabeth Edwards and Janice Hart:

"some forms of materiality emerge from specific performative desires for the image. Photographs […] are made for a reason for a specific audience, to embody specific messages and moral values […]. While this applies equally to image content, it is […] essential to see material forms in the same way. For instance, to print in platinum, which is one of the most stable and permanent of photographic processes, as opposed to the volatility and inherently unstable chemistry of silver-based prints, speaks to a desire for permanence." (Edwards and Hart 2004: 10)

The same might be said of magic lantern slides, although, being made of glass, they can easily crack. Nonetheless, they continue to carry the images printed on them, ensuring permanence. This is also thanks to the special way in which they are constructed: each slide receives first the emulsion (or photograph), then the matte and finally a piece of cover glass. Next, to keep it together and preserve it from dust and other harmful elements, the slide is taped all the way around. Usually, tinting is added by hand, given that most magic lantern slides were produced far before the invention of the colour film.

Things that Death Cannot Destroy, the title Fregni Nagler chose for her work, puts a particular emphasis on the materiality of magic lantern slides. An emphasis that the artist stresses even more when collecting and showing slides of architectural buildings that should have lasted over time, but in fact perished. What remains are the images carried by the magic lantern slides. To give an example, the twin hangars for airships at Orly Airport were destroyed by an Allied bombardment in 1944 *(fig. 2).* Curiously enough, their creator, Eugène Freyssinet, had won the building competition established in the early 1920s because of the (supposed) stability and resistance of his project.

Fig. 2 — Linda Fregni Nagler [ARCH-013-ML], 29017 A Fr 0728 Pt A.h el: Orly, France. Aéroport. Hangar. Exterior. Front & side. 1916 (destroyed). Reinforced concrete. Hollow iron ribbed construction. Eugène Freyssinet, architect. The Art Institute of Chicago: Ryerson Library. Hand-coloured gelatin silver positive photograph on glass from the artist's collection. Courtesy of the artist

Fregni Nagler's work resumes the Warburgian idea that images do not die, because, being anthropological as well as artistic objects, they have their own afterlife *(Nachleben)*[3]. The materiality of images, which always need a support to be displayed, is fundamental for Fregni Nagler. As a photographer and collector, she has a passion for early prints. Besides magic lantern slides produced between 1860 and 1940, she fervently collects daguerreotype, calotype, ambrotype, tintype and albumen prints of the same period, with all the marks and imperfections that time leaves on paper, plates and slides, increasing the beauty and uniqueness of images as objects.[4]

Each of her projects begins with a passionate search for those images that were born with "burning desire" (Batchen 1999) in the nineteenth century as surprising, quasi alchemical, experiments between art and science. Every day she collects and saves these objet-trouvés from dispersion (she first purchased vintage prints at flea markets, then started to buy them over the Internet) by recreating her own private taxonomy and archive in the studio – although she is perfectly aware that every classification is in itself arbitrary, tentative, incomplete, inclined to a perfection that cannot be reached. Confining the real in predefined categories is always an act of force, a fictitious representation that is affected by the choices of a specific creator and the canons of a given epoch. This is why Fregni Nagler also ironically plays with the classifications she invents – such as the one named "FOCE", which refers to those "forgotten celebrities" who were once famous and whom photography somehow rescues from oblivion.[5]

The magic lantern performance as "an encyclopaedic journey"

If Fregni Nagler's archive gathers curious images-objects that she collects and orders according to her own criteria, the magic lantern slides of *Things that Death Cannot Destroy* comprise a personal and slightly ambiguous atlas of images *(Bilderatlas)* – ambiguous in the double sense of enigmatic and arbitrary. The slides the artist selects from her collection for the different presentations are carefully choreographed and projected in a sequence of pairs by using two large antique magic lanterns, which play a leading role in the performance, together with the artist herself and her assistant, who insert and remove the slides *(fig. 3)*.[6]

Fig. 3 — Linda Fregni Nagler, Things that Death Cannot Destroy, *Part 9, 2019. Teatro dell'Arte, Triennale, Milan. Courtesy of the artist*

As a result, the images emerge from the dark, revealing unexpected formal associations. The sudden amazement that the montage of images produces is increased by a narrator's voice, which adds mystery and characterises the storytelling as both visual and audio. The voiceover simply reads the inscriptions on the (paper or fabric) passepartouts of the slides. These give fragmentary and incomplete information about the content, origin, date and copyright of the images, while the author's name is in most cases missing. Anonymity is a recurring feature of magic lantern slides. The images they carry were chosen for didactic, scientific, commemorative, entertaining and propagandistic purposes, so not much attention was given to their artistic value, although many of them possess aesthetic qualities, and others can sometimes be attributed to well-known artists and photographers.

Things that Death Cannot Destroy combines the erudition of the amateur pastime and the wonder of both the *Wunderkammer* and the cinema of the origins, as well as the irony of the surrealist divertissement and the uncanny amusement of the freak show. When, two by two, the projected images come out of the dark, that same cathartic effect – which was probably experienced by our non-digitised ancestors at the time of proto-photography and pre-cinema – is reenacted in the present. The artist's magic lantern performance shows the most astonishing matches: a Libyan woman, with a sewing machine, and a giraffe; a wood pigeon's nest and two conjoined black girl twins; a set of Great Horned Owl young and a group of Chinese women; a Lilliputian human being and a Ruby-throated Hummingbird (both smaller than the finger of one hand); a nest of blue winged teal and a man walking down the Descending Passage of the Great Pyramid; and so on and so forth *(fig. 4 & 5)*.

Fig. 4 — Linda Fregni Nagler (left) [ETN-053-ML],
Libyan Woman with Sewing Machine. *Hand coloured gelatin silver positive photograph on glass from the artist's collection.*

(right) [NATHIST-009-ML] Department of Public Education. Hand-coloured gelatin silver positive photograph on glass from the artist's collection. Courtesy of the artist

Fig. 5 — Linda Fregni Nagler (left) [UCC-010-ML] A.5261-14 82 842.83, Nest of Blue-Winged Teal. *Hand coloured gelatin silver positive photograph on glass from the artist's collection.*

(right) [EGY-024-ML] 44, Great Pyramid: Walking Down Descending Passage (Figure – Professor J. Edgar). Lecture – The Pyramid Portrayal of Creation. Slide (Copyright): Morton Edgar, 224 W. Regent St., Glasgow, Scotland. *Hand-coloured gelatin silver positive photograph on glass from the artist's collection. Courtesy of the artist*

Yet, this montage of images is not only a study of unusual formal associations, it is also a critical gesture. Appropriating historical slides and 'returning' them in the present with a presentational mode that mimics the traditional magic lantern performance subverts the original educational and entertainment purposes by prompting a meditation on the photographic gaze and on the cultural stereotypes produced by photography as a (Western and male-dominated) medium. Fregni Nagler's gesture may not be as manifestly political as the restitution that the German filmmaker Harun Farocki accomplishes with his critical montage of images, which Georges Didi-Huberman (2009) took as the artistically best example and so eloquently described – the intellectual legacy he pursues stretches between the twentieth and twenty-first centuries, beginning with Walter Benjamin, Bertolt Brecht, Aby Warburg and culminating in himself – as *"a montage of thought accelerated to the rhythm of anger in order to better, to calmly denounce the violence of the world"* (Didi-Huberman 2009: 46). Nonetheless, it is likewise the conscious, ethical act of taking images from the archives of history and returning them to others (the spectators) through a montage that dampens the artist's authorship – but not her engagement – in favour of the power of images by themselves.[7]

In the wake of Warburg, Fregni Nagler's juxtaposition of images becomes a knowledge device, fostering *"the idea that the meaning of something depends on the context in which it is found, and, more specifically, on its position within a sequence or a system"* (Menegoi 2018: 90). *Things that Death Cannot Destroy* is first of all an exercise in looking – not by chance: an author that she holds dear is John Berger, with his pivotal book *About Looking* (Berger 1980). Looking is an act that is never neutral and, thus, never the same. This also explains Fregni Nagler's daily practice of re-photographing the (anonymous) pre-existing images she collects as both a conceptual and aesthetic gesture. Her aim is to go beyond visual clichés and iconographic conventions and reveal what photographs usually hide – instead of showing – about their modes of production, circulation and reception, about the people who commissioned them and their social context.

With her magic lantern performance, Fregni Nagler invites the audience to undertake a (visual) "encyclopaedic journey" (2017) that reveals collecting, archiving and exhibiting to be culture-specific gestures:

"Every photograph, though belonging to very different contexts, is connected to the preceding one, the visual path developing into a sort of cadavre exquis. This choreography, together with variations in cultural interpretation, raises issues around the staging of the human figure, social categorization, censorship and copyright. In this personal and ambiguous encyclopedia, what is legible is not History, but a bringing together of many pieces of a mosaic that may be combined in infinite variations." (Fregni Nagler 2017: n. p.)[8]

Since its invention, photography has reflected "the aesthetic conditioning of different social groups", "the power and gender dynamics at work in society at large" (especially in institutional contexts), the desire for "a tool of mass visual reproduction" (Menegoi 2018: 87), in a time – first the nineteenth and then the twentieth century – when Western culture had a growing need to classify and archive everything, an urge that after almost two centuries is still not fulfilled.

Moreover, *Things that Death Cannot Destroy* raises questions about the readability of images – especially when considering the ambiguous correlation between photographs and their informative inscriptions, which are spoken by a narrator during the slide projection. This raises questions about the afterlife and performativity of images, as, for each new projection/performance, they are reenacted from the past and become visible again, in a new here and now. And it dwells on the relationship between image and word, photography and its inscription: a text that adds information, which is sometimes useful, sometimes misleading. The inscription on a photograph – or in this specific case on a magic lantern slide – speaks also of an attempt at naming, thus, at classifying and knowing.

In his *Little History of Photography,* Walter Benjamin had already questioned the importance of the inscription. Without it – he commented – "all photographic construction must remain arrested in the approximate" (Benjamin 1931: 257). Around the same time, Warburg underlined the communicative connotation of images with his famous motto "Das Wort zum Bild"[9] (the word to the image). Fregni Nagler reaffirms this attitude in her own peculiar way.

With his *Bilderatlas,* named after *Mnemosyne,* Warburg wanted to show that forms, especially minor ones, survive their own death by contaminating each other. And they do this by travelling across time and by impressing themselves as lasting signs in cultural memory. He saw these archetypal signs, his well-known *pathos formulas (Pathosformeln),* resurfacing in the history of art and, more in general, in the history of images, without any hierarchy; that is, without any distinction between high and low culture. This is one of the reasons why throughout the twentieth century – and still today – his *Bilderatlas* has become an important aesthetic and epistemic tool, not only for theoretical thinking but also for artistic practice – as the atlas-form allows a continuous review of history, of knowledge and of the world through images.

Reenacting images "on the brink of extinction"

As temporary performances, magic lantern projections can only be repeated through reenactment, a practice that seems to have recently become quite popular in contemporary performing and visual arts. On the one hand, contemporary reenactments of historical projections revive the past with a certain nostalgic desire, as if to re-appropriate history or even be possessed by it. On the other hand, they manifest the present, since *"a performance does not only represent reality, it also produces reality. It engenders a situation that inscribes the [contemporary] spectator in certain values, conventions and imaginaries"* (Vanhoutte 2004: 251–252), bringing together past and present. Yet reenactments of historical magic lantern performances both perpetuate a canon and transgress it. While it is evident that they present both the past and an outdated visual device, they are not limited to *"merely animating a historical artefact, they intentionally constitute new work that explicitly incorporates contemporary genres, technologies, and styles"* (Vanhoutte 2004: 254). From this perspective, re-stagings of magic lantern performances of the nineteenth and early twentieth century are *"not so much concerned with the image of history, but rather with the theoretical assumptions that inform our understanding of history and of performance"* (Vanhoutte 2004: 254), as well as of the outdated visual apparatus and its representational modes.

Especially when reenactment is related to art practice, as well as museum practice, curatorship or art history and therefore with all activities that deal with the production, circulation, reception and preservation of artworks/images, it becomes an act of interpretation and critique. Reenactment challenges a whole range of apparently 'antithetical' relations between past and present, original and copy (cf. originality, copyright), repetition and variation, authenticity and aura, presence and absence, canon and appropriation, durée and transience. It also includes a strong educational commitment, well expressed by curator Dieter Roelstraete during the remake of the legendary *When Attitudes Become Form* exhibition (Bern, 1969) in 2013 at the Fondazione Prada in Venice:

"Both remake and reenactment represent a type of renegade art history in action, anxious to keep in living memory that which is always in danger of being forgotten, marginalized, swept aside [...]. Remakes and reenactments, then, perform a reconstructive educational role that ensures the perpetuation of an 'other' art history outside the confines and constraints of canon and mainstream alike – one that truly is written by the (remaking, reenacting) artists firsthand." (Roelstraete 2013: 424)

It may be useful, at this point, to propose a definition of reenactment as both an act of critique and a tool for knowledge production, where the prefix "re-" in its hovering between back and again creates complex patterns of temporal and spatial relations and therefore provides a keystone for building a different relation with the past, one that helps de-canonise pre-established (art)historical or (art)critical interpretations. With all of this said, reenactment may be described as:

"1) *the act of (re)appropriation or* Aneignung, *in Paul Ricoeur's words 'the process by which one makes one's own* (eigen) *what was initially other or alien* (fremd)';
2) *an exercise of (re)interpretation in the sense of working-through or* Durcharbeitung *(from the verb* durcharbeiten), *to use Freud's famous expression, which Jean-François Lyotard later exhumed;*
3) *a process of (re)construction, given that the event or object to be reactivated is often chosen precisely because it was left unfinished, or got lost or altered as an artefact or memory;*
4) *a gesture of (re)mediation in the sense of the term given by Jay Bolter and Richard Grusin, that is, reworking and transposing not just from one time and/or setting to another, but also from one support, idiom, or medium to another;*
5) *the act of (re)circulating images across time, space, the media, and later (re)contextualizing them."*

(Baldacci 2022: 178)

Concerning the circulation or migration of images and their spatial, temporal and semantic (re)contextualisation Fregni Nagler's work is particularly meaningful. Her collection, classification and display of photographs produced between the nineteenth and the early twentieth century have but one constant feature: anonymity. Even when an 'author' is mentioned, it refers almost always to a commercial photographer or studio, rarely to a big name. With her predilection for vernacular images (Chéroux 2021), the artist goes against the modernist tradition of a history of photography intended as a succession of authors, among whom mainly Western men. She prefers minor histories, which still need to be retraced and told.[10]

For her the meaning and fascination of those forgotten artefacts lie precisely in the gap between now and then, the contemporary viewer's gaze and the (outdated) visual codes of their alter ego in the past. However, it is not just a fascination with the objects themselves, but also with what they (re)present: people, places, animals and architecture that all no longer exist. It is photography that brings them back as "phantoms",[11] as images that speak of a double fragility: first, the instability of the medium, photography, and of their different supports, which give objecthood to the images, making them susceptible to deterioration; second, the uncertainty of the represented subject that reveals its presence *in absentia* or, in the words of Barthes, seems to be there but actually "has been" and can "never be repeated existentially", it "has occurred only once" (Barthes 1981: 4). In the case of the photographs collected by Fregni Nagler, this crucial aspect is accentuated by their anonymity, by their being *"images that double the stakes in photography's gamble with duration: traces of vanished creatures, but on the brink of extinction themselves"* (Menegoi 2018: 90).

They somehow survive only through their visual reenactment and re-mediation. Let us take the example of one of Fregni Nagler's favourites, the Flower Vendor or *Flower Seller*, a recurring image that has become a cliché in the tradition of Japanese photographic prints. Fregni Nagler has collected several variations of the *Flower Seller* printed on different supports and has re-used them in her work. As a magic lantern slide the *Flower Seller* is reenacted in *Things that Death Cannot Destroy;* as a vintage Japanese print it is first re-photographed and then increased in size and hand-painted before being re-printed *(fig. 6)*.

Fig. 6 — Linda Fregni Nagler (left), Things that Death Cannot Destroy, *Part 9, 2019. Teatro dell'Arte, Triennale, Milan. (right) Artist at work on* Flower Vendor *(YS_FS_LFN_001), 2018. Hand coloured gelatin silver print, cm 123,2 × 156,7, framed. Courtesy of the artist*

With this and other Japanese leitmotifs, such as the Mount Fuji landscapes, the artist plays on the variants of pre-existing images both producing and circulating "after-images". Behind the act of re-photographing, enlarging and colouring by hand (by herself or with the help of her studio assistants) those stereotyped images lies not only the idea of its visual appropriation and reenactment, but also that of its materiality, of its migration from one medium to another – a process that makes an image return as the same but also as always different, over and over again.

ACKNOWLEDGEMENT Thank you to Linda Fregni Nagler for the ongoing exchange of ideas and valuable advice on her work, and to Ralph Nisbet for the English proofreading and editing.

---

1   Linda Fregni Nagler's work, in addition to being particularly significant for the issues addressed here, was shown at the Museum für Kunst und Gewerbe in Hamburg a few months after the "Material Goods" conference (as her first solo exhibition in Germany). See Linda Fregni Nagler. *Fotografie neu ordnen: Blickinszenierung* (30 June 2023–7 January 2024), where, with a comparative attitude distinctive of her practice, she combined two series of her own work *How to Look at a Camera* (2019), depicting two groups of subjects, the "Tapada Limeña" (ca. 1850) and "Back to Camera" views from original tintypes (ca. 1860) – which she translated into photogravures – together with selected photographs from the museum collection.

2   See, in particular, the cultural heritage approach developed by the Dutch research project A Million Pictures, which among other outputs produced a conference, *A Million Pictures: History, Archiving and Cultural Re-Use of Educational Lantern Slides* (Utrecht University, 29 August–1 September 2017); an edited volume (Dellmann and Kessler 2020); and a website, *a-million-pictures.wp.hum.uu.nl/*.

3   In 2016 Fregni Nagler was among a bunch of contemporary artists (Andy Hope 1930, Albert Oehlen, Tal R, Elfie Semotan, Sarah Lehnerer, Olaf Metzel, Christian Vind, Jannis Marwitz, Jochen Lempert, Matt Mullican, Peter Weibel) who were invited to compose a panel *(Bildertafel)* "after Warburg" – which she did, using photographic reproductions from her collection. The occasion was the huge reconstruction and

exhibiting of the *Bilderatlas* at zkm–Zentrum für Kunst und Medien in Karlsruhe in 2016 (Forschungsgruppe Mnemosyne | 8. Salon, 2016), which was followed, in 2020, by the remake at hkw Haus der Kulturen der Welt in Berlin (Ohrt and Heil 2020).

4   The artist showed part of her collection of anonymous prints (997 images), classified under the title *The Hidden Mother*, at the Venice Art Biennale in 2013 – it was then also reproduced as a book (Zanot 2013).

5   In this curious repertoire, one finds Fridtjof Nansen (1861–1930), the Norwegian explorer, scientist, diplomat and humanitarian, who – among other things – led the team that made the first crossing of the Greenland interior in 1888; helped establish neuron doctrine; and became Nobel Peace Prize laureate in 1922. Another almost forgotten past celebrity is Emilio Aguinaldo (1869–1964), the Filipino politician and revolutionary responsible for the birth of the first Philippine republic in 1897.

6   Major presentations of the work were held – among other places – in Rome (Teatro Valle Occupato, 23 April 2013), Stockholm (Moderna Museet, 11 and 12 September 2015) and Milan (Teatro dell'arte, Triennale di Milano, 3 April 2019).

7   Particularly significant was the episode experienced by Fregni Nagler during the preparation of her exhibition at the Museum für Kunst und Gewerbe in Hamburg. The artist was invited to display her work *Girls from the Southern Seas* (a photographic survey and restitution of women's body done by a woman) alongside a series of photographs of 'non-Western women' belonging to the museum collection. But, after a fervent discussion among the museum staff, who feared that the press and public opinion could misunderstand the work as somehow perpetuating a colonial gaze, she was asked to change the selection. Thus, the show turned into another project (see footnote 1). Doesn't the fact of not being allowed to 'return' photographs from the museum's collection and one's own work because of a 'cautious' institutional attitude somehow go against the very act of being able to see, exhibit and, therefore, let people know? Is it better to keep images hidden in the archives until the political-cultural situation allows them to be shown without harmful consequences (until when and for whom precisely)? Isn't not showing them at all a much greater damage? Allow me to briefly mention this episode here, not just to put it on record, but also to debunk the critique that emerged about the artist's work during the discussion after my presentation at the "Material Goods" conference in Hamburg, on 3 February 2023. On that occasion, the artist's montage of images in *Things that Death Cannot Destroy* appeared controversial to some participants as it does not follow a distinct decolonial approach in which her position emerges in a literal way. Cancel culture also subtly hides behind the fear, and consequent denial, of exhibiting, especially if those that worry are museums and cultural institutions.

8   This is a quote from the introduction of a printout that the artist realised in a few exemplars in June 2017 thinking of a publication that would translate *Things that Death Cannot Destroy* from "a visual art performance into printed matter".

9   This motto was pronounced by Warburg during a conference at the Handelskammer in Hamburg in 1928 (Warburg, Notizheft Handelskammer, The Warburg Institute, Archives, 12.27 u. 98.3.1; see Diers 2023).

10 Fregni Nagler worked for several years at a research and curatorial project dedicated to the nineteenth-century explorer and inventor Hercule Florence (1804–1879), one of the brilliant proto-photographers, who worked in pseudo-isolation in colonial Brazil, and to whom history has paid little attention (Fregni Nagler and Raimondi 2017).

11 This was a term particularly dear to Warburg when referring to the afterlife of images; see Didi-Huberman 2016.

REFERENCES

Ackerman, Ada, Barbara **Grespi** & Andrea **Pinotti** (2020): Mediatic Handology? In: Cinéma & Cie, Vol. XX No. 35, pp. 7–28; *riviste.unimi.it/index.php/cinemaetcie/article/view/16535* (14/07/2023).

Baldacci, Cristina (2022): Re-Presenting Art History: An Unfinished Process. In: Cristina Baldacci, Clio Nicastro and Arianna Sforzini (eds.), Over and Over and Over Again: Reenactment Strategies in Contemporary Arts and Theory. Berlin: ICI Berlin Press, pp. 173–182; *doi.org/10.37050/ci21_18*.

Barthes, Roland (1981): Camera Lucida: Reflections on Photography. Trans. by Richard Howard. New York: Hill and Wang (orig. French ed. 1980).

Batchen, Geoffrey (1999): Burning with Desire: The Conception of Photography. Cambridge (MA): MIT Press.

Batchen, Geoffrey (1997): Photography's Objects. Albuquerque: University of New Mexico Art Museum.

Benjamin, Walter (1931 [2005]): Little History of Photography. In: Michael W. Jennings, Howard Eiland and Gary Smith (eds.), Walter Benjamin: Selected Writings, Volume 2, Part 2, 1931—1934, trans. by Rodney Livingstone and others. Cambridge (MA): Harvard University Press, pp. 507–530.

Berger, John (1980): About Looking. New York: Pantheon Books.

Berger, John (1972): Ways of Seeing. London: Penguin Books.

Bredekamp, Horst (2018): Image Acts: A Systematic Approach to Visual Agency. Trans. by Elizabeth Clegg. Berlin and Boston: De Gruyter (orig. German ed. 2010).

Chéroux, Clément (2021): The Importance of the Vernacular. In: Since 1839… Eleven Essays on Photography. Trans. by Shane B. Lillis. Toronto and Cambridge (MA): Ryerson Image Centre/MIT Press, pp. 131–155.

Dellmann, Sarah and Frank **Kessler** (eds.) (2020): A Million Pictures: Magic Lantern Slides in the History of Learning. Barnet (London): John Libbey.

Didi-Huberman, Georges (2009): How to Open Your Eyes. In: Antje Ehmann & Kodwo Eshun (eds.), Harun Farocki, Against What? Against Whom?. London: Koenig Books, pp. 38–50.

Didi-Huberman, Georges (2010): Remontages du temps subi. L'œil de l'histoire, 2. Paris: Minuit.

Didi-Huberman, Georges (2016): The Surviving Image. Phantoms of Time and Time of Phantoms: Aby Warburg's History of Art. Trans. by Harvey Mendelsohn. State College (PA): Penn State University Press.

Diers, Michel (2023): Porträt aus Büchern. Stichworte. In: Engramma 198; *engramma.it/eOS/index.php?id_articolo=4904* (23/07/2023).

Durand, Régis (1995): How to See (Photographically). In: Patrice Petro (ed.), Fugitive Images: From Photography to Video. Bloomington: Indiana University Press, pp. 141–151.

Edwards, Elizabeth and Janice **Hart** (eds.) (2004): Photographs, Objects, Histories: On the Materiality of Images. New York and London: Routledge.

Forschungsgruppe Mnemosyne and **8. Salon** (ed.) (2016): Aby Warburg: Mnemosyne Bilderatlas. Zurich & Karlsruhe: Kartoffelverlag/UFBP/ZKM.

Fregni Nagler, Linda and Cristiano **Raimondi** (eds.) (2017): Hercule Florence: Le Nouveau Robinson. Milan and Monaco: Humboldt Books/Nouveau Musée National de Monaco.

Gell, Alfred (1998): Art and Agency: An Anthropological Theory. Oxford: Clarendon Press.

Grossi, Giancarlo and Andrea **Pinotti** (2022): Introduction: The Image Between Presence and Absence. In: AN-ICON. Studies in Environmental Images, No.1, pp. 4–16; *doi.org/10.54103/ai/17909*.

Menegoi, Simone (2018): Towards a Minor Photography: The Work of Linda Fregni Nagler. In: Vincenzo de Bellis (ed.), Linda Fregni Nagler: Yama no Shashin. Milan: Humboldt Books, pp. 85–90.

Mitchell, W.J.T. (2005): What Do Pictures Want? The Lives and Loves of Images. Chicago: The University of Chicago Press.

Ohrt, Roberto and Axel **Heil** (eds.) (2020): Aby Warburg. Bilderatlas Mnemosyne: The Original. Berlin: Hatje Cantz.

Osborne, Peter (2018): The Distributed Image. In: Picture Industry: A Provisional History of the Technical Image 1844-2018. Arles and Annandale-On-Hudson (NY): LUMA/CCS Bard, pp. 772–775.

Roelstraete, Dieter (2013): Make it Re-: The Eternally Returning Object. In: Germano Celant (ed.), When Attitudes Become Form: Bern 1969/Venice 2013. Milan: Fondazione Prada, pp. 423–428.

Sassoon, Joanna (2004): Photographic Materiality in the Age of Digital Reproduction. In: Elizabeth Edwards and Janice Hart (eds.), Photographs, Objects, Histories: On the Materiality of Images. New York and London: Routledge, pp. 186–202.

Vanhoutte, Kurt (2004): Re-enactment and the Magic Lantern Performance: Possessed by History. In: Elizabeth Edwards and Janice Hart (eds.), Photographs, Objects, Histories: On the Materiality of Images. New York and London: Routledge, pp. 251–262.

Wynants, Nele (2020): Dissolving Visions: From Slide Adaptation to Artistic Appropriation in Magic Lantern Practices. In: Sarah Dellmann and Frank Kessler (eds.), A Million Pictures: Magic Lantern Slides in the History of Learning. Barnet (London): John Libbey, pp. 263–274.

Zanot, Francesco (ed.) (2013): Linda Fregni Nagler: The Hidden Mother. London and Monaco: MACK/Nouveau Musée National de Monaco.

Multiple Materialisms: Situating Dance between Enactivist and New Materialist Discourses

Timmy De Laet

Introduction: lines and lineages

Unfolding an Archive (2022) is the first solo performance Zoë Demoustier created as an associate choreographer at *Ultima Vez,* the renowned Brussels-based dance company founded by Wim Vandekeybus.[1] Demoustier draws for this piece from the archive of her father, Daniel Demoustier, who worked as a war journalist and cameraman for over twenty years. While he was shooting images of violent conflicts, political upheavals and ecological catastrophes at different corners of the world, Zoë Demoustier was growing up in Belgium with her mother and her younger brother and sister. The performance begins with a recorded phone call in which she asks her father about the wars he covered as a journalist, but he does not seem to be able to remember it all clearly. When she appears on stage, she begins drawing various white-coloured lines on the black floor using a stick that slowly releases a sandy substance. The intricate web of seemingly random lines that emerges could suggest the borders of the countries where her father has worked, or the lifelines of all the people he has witnessed dying. However, what at first seem clear demarcations increasingly become rather abstract lines of lineage as we rarely get to see any footage of the historical realities housed in this archive. These realities are mainly transmitted through an ingenious soundscape that figures as a sonic backdrop for Demoustier's dancing. Rather than visual imagery, Demoustier uses sound and choreographic movement to draw spectators into the archival world that not only extends far beyond her own body but also includes documents – both materialised and immaterial – that nonetheless are a part of what her body as an archive is able to incorporate.

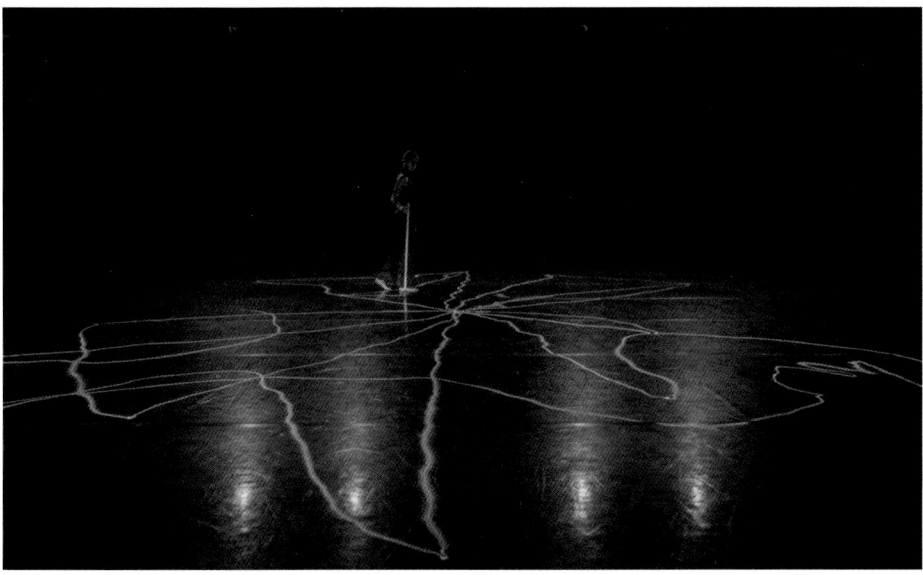

Fig. 1 (previous page) — Unfolding an Archive *by Zoë Demoustier*
Photo Tom Herbots, courtesy of the artist

The lines we see drawn on the stage visualise the entangled network of recollections, mnemonic residues and sonic traces that make up the archive Demoustier is unfolding and which in one way or another are all related to each other. As Demoustier explains in an interview:

> *"The archive is visualised by a map that I draw on the theatre floor as a kind of forensic investigation. The map is subjective: 'home' is in the middle [...]. Every location is linked to a sound and a movement. Whenever I arrive at a new spot, I search for where the visual memories [...] are located in my own physical archive. Gradually an interplay develops between the locations, the sounds and the movements. The archive gets shaken up and new connections are made."* (Demoustier 2022a: paragraph 4)

What Demoustier describes as her "subjective map" is not intended to conjure up ghostly traces of choreographic steps, movements or sequences once performed on what Marvin Carlson would refer to as the "haunted stage" (Carlson 2001). Instead, the lines are indicative of the connections Demoustier is seeking to find with the archive left by her father as well as with the memories housed in her own body (or what she calls her "own physical archive"). In this regard, it is meaningful that

Fig. 2 — Unfolding an Archive *by Zoë Demoustier*
Photo Tom Herbots, courtesy of the artist

the clearly demarcated lines will become blurred by Demoustier's dancing throughout the piece, much like how memories tend to become hazy as time passes by. This perhaps straightforward yet ingenious set-up of *Unfolding an Archive* is emblematic of how the piece invites us to reconsider how exactly dance is able to reactivate archival materials and what implications this has for our understanding of the materiality of the archive, memory and dance. *(Fig. 2)*

Questions surrounding the role of archives in dance and performance have been attracting increasing attention from both practitioners and scholars for several years now. Especially the emergence in the late 1990s and the early 2000s of what came to be known as "choreographic reenactment" played an important part in this renewed interest in how live performing arts could withstand their own presumed ephemerality by engaging differently – and probably more complicitly – with their material remains. While the term "reenactment" is not undisputed, it is generally used for inventive reinterpretations of dance works from the past, which often also take a critical stance towards the historiography of dance (Franko 2017). Strictly speaking, Demoustier's performance does not fit within the "genre" of choreographic reenactment, given that it is not a recreation of a past dance work but rather a form of documentary dance.

My aim in this contribution, however, is not to get involved in a terminological debate about which practices could be categorised under these labels and which others arguably not. Instead, I want to approach Demoustier's *Unfolding an Archive* as embodying a confrontation between two allegedly "new" theoretical discourses that might help to gain a better understanding of how dance can be conceived of as a deeply material practice extending beyond the dancing body. More specifically, and as I will demonstrate, Demoustier's piece can be read as appealing, on the one hand, to enactivist frameworks in cognitive science, and new materialist discourses in the humanities, on the other hand. Taking this observation as my starting point, I will assess what both strands of research might have to offer to dance studies and dance practice, and vice versa.

To this end, I will first take a critical look at the concept of the body-as-archive, which not only returns in Zoë

Demoustier's *Unfolding an Archive* but is also central in current artistic and scholarly discourses, often as a result of the rise of choreographic reenactment. However, by tracing how this notion of the body-as-archive can lead to a monistic type of thinking that effaces the differences between the body and the archive, I will argue that enactivist approaches within cognitive science can help to rectify this fallacy. In a second movement, I will dig a few layers deeper by showing how the basic tenets of enactivism invite, if not require, a profound reconsideration of materialism as a theoretical concept. The fact that matter is somewhat of a blind spot within enactivism will lead me to gauge the potential flaws and promises of new materialist discourses for dance studies.[2] Ultimately, then, this contribution aims to push Demoustier's artistic proposal further through a primarily methodological exploration that shows how purportedly "new" theoretical paradigms always need to be situated within a wider intellectual horizon if they are to invigorate dance scholarship.

From the body-as-archive to enactivist dance archives

The choreography that Zoë Demoustier performs in *Unfolding an Archive* demonstrates that her own body plays a central, though not exclusive, role in creating what she calls her "subjective map". As such, her performance relates to the discourse on the body-as-archive, which seeks to foreground bodily capacities of archivisation as a supplement to the historical information contained in archival artefacts, documents, notations, recordings, relics, and so forth. Whilst elevating the body to the status of a primary resource for dance history, the main drawback of a notion like the body-as-archive is that it runs the risk (even when hyphenated) of reinforcing a monistic mode of thinking that eclipses how the body interacts with the archive (and vice versa), effacing instead any distinction between both categories. As I will argue later in this contribution, this monistic view is precisely one of the main flaws of some strands within new materialist discourses. Within dance studies, an exemplary instance of this approach can be found in André Lepecki's much-cited essay "The Body as Archive", in which he claims that *"in dance re-enactments there will be no distinctions left between archive and body. The body is archive and archive a body"* (Lepecki 2010: 31). Other leading scholars, such as Diana Taylor and Rebecca Schneider, are more cautious in keeping a certain differentiation between the archive and the body. While Taylor argues that *"the archive and the repertoire exist in a constant state of interaction"* (Taylor 2003: 21), Schneider takes recourse to intermediality in order to mark the jump from one medium to another in processes of embodied transmission (Schneider 2011). On a closer look, however, neither Taylor nor Schneider specify how exactly the relational interactions between the archive and the body take shape in practice.

While the theoretical interventions by Lepecki, Taylor and Schneider have found a widespread resonance within dance and performance studies, there is a lack of perhaps more empirical accounts that give concrete substance to the interactions between embodied practice and materialised archival remains without lapsing into a monistic understanding of the body-as-archive. At the same time, one might question whether it is really the empiricism that is lacking, or whether it is rather a matter of developing theoretical frameworks more apt at capturing the complex dynamics between the body and the archive. One avenue that could yield new insights into these matters might be found in neuroscience and philosophy of mind – more specifically, in enactivist models of cognition. Even though enactivism is primarily an interpretative framework for better understanding the workings of the mind and does not directly deal with either dance or the archive *per se,* it may help us to get a better grasp of how the materiality of the archive operates in tandem with embodied practice, thereby undoing the latter's presumed intangibility. By extension, enactivism may offer useful perspectives for articulating how dance in general is a fundamentally expanded – or, to put it in Foucauldian terms – "dispersive" practice that exceeds by far the privileged role commonly granted to the body as the sole and primary medium of dance. In this respect, and as I will explore in more detail below, the relational dynamics foregrounded by enactivism necessitate a critical reconsideration of the (im)materiality of dance against the backdrop of both new and historical materialisms as they have been theorised within and beyond dance studies.

While it is obviously impossible to cover within the scope of this contribution all different strands of research that go under the banner of enactivism,[3] a brief look at some of its basic assumptions should help to clarify what exactly an enactivist perspective entails. Broadly speaking, enactivism is a school of thought within cognitive science that emerged from the early 1990s onwards, proposing a fundamentally different way of looking at how the human mind functions. Shaun Gallagher, one of the main proponents of enactivism, provides a concise statement of this view in his 2017 book *Enactivist Interventions: Rethinking the Mind,* when he writes:

"*Enactivist approaches to cognition suggest that, at least in basic (perception- and action-related) cases, cognitive processes are not just in the head, but involve bodily and environmental factors. This view clearly poses a challenge to what has been the standard science of cognition, especially to cognitive neuroscience, and to any science that claims to provide full and exclusive explanations in terms of one factor, e.g., neural processing.*" (Gallagher 2017: 1)

What enactivism opposes are two basic orthodoxies within cognitive science. On the one hand, it rejects the idea that the human mind is restricted to only those processes happening in the brain (or what Gallagher refers to as "neural processing", which is sometimes also called "internalism" [Wheeler 2015: 458]). On the other hand, it refutes the assumption that human cognition works with perceptual representations of the outer world or of one's own experiences, rather than with things-in-themselves (which is sometimes called "representationalism" [Wheeler 2015: 458]). As an alternative to these standard theories of cognition, enactivism holds that *"cognition is not simply a brain event"* and neither a matter of representational content, proposing instead that cognition *"emerges from processes distributed across brain-body-environment"* (Gallagher 2017: 6).

The seminal work that basically launched enactivism within cognitive science was the 1991 book by Francisco Varela, Evan Thompson and Eleanor Rosch, titled *The Embodied Mind: Cognitive Science and Human Experience.* Drawing on phenomenology, evolutionary biology, psychology and even Buddhist philosophy, Varela and his co-authors introduced the term "enaction", which gradually morphed into the slightly more general label of "enactivism". In her introduction to the 2016 revised edition, Eleaonor Rosch clarifies what they meant by this notion of "enaction":

"*Whereas most embodiment research focuses on the interaction between body and mind, body and environment, or en-*

vironment and mind, enaction sees the lived body as a single system that encompasses all three." (Rosch 2016: xlviii)

Based on the three components singled out by Rosch (body, mind and environment), the so-called enactivist approach would eventually grow into what is currently known as "4 E cognition" or "4 E cognitive science", with the 4 Es referring to the idea that cognition is embodied, embedded, extended and enactive. More specifically, the first two Es postulate that cognition is embodied because it is not only a matter of the mind but also located in the body outside of its neural processes, while it is also deeply embedded within a larger social, cultural and natural environment. The second two Es make a more radical claim. For if cognition is extended, it means that any object, tool or instrument we use (the typical examples here are computers, smartphones but also glasses) are not merely functional supplements but constitutive parts of our cognitive system. The fourth E, which stands for enactive, means that cognition is literally enacted and can therefore only emerge from our interactive engagement with the outer world (see Young and Jennings 2022: 420).

One of the most fascinating aspects of Zoë Demoustier's dance piece *Unfolding an Archive* is that it almost literally enacts the basic tenets of enactivism. As her dancing body serves as a clear focal point within the piece, it foregrounds the embodied dimension of the archival functions that dance can assume. However, the white lines we see drawn on the stage also stress how Demoustier's body-as-archive is not limited to its own corporeality but also intimately embedded within a larger environment of echoes, sounds and images that, strictly speaking, belong to a world outside of the performance space but are nonetheless an intrinsic part of the work as it unfolds. At the same time, the importance of the soundscape, which at times appears to put her body into motion, highlights how the sound recordings are an extended yet constitutive part of the archival world she is creating on stage. And, of course, this archival world only comes into being because it is enacted – or should we say, "re-enacted"? – through her embodied performance that revolves around the interaction with the sounds, images and lines drawn on the floor. As such, what Demoustier creates by pulling together these various means of expression is a prime example of what we could call an "enactivist dance archive".

Even though it is not hard to identify these correspondences, it is not my intention to suggest that Demoustier's dance piece is simply a neat illustration of what enactivism in cognitive science aims for, nor do I want to imply that the principles of enactivism can be seamlessly applied to dance. On the contrary, Demoustier's case is most interesting because of the blind spots it brings to light, which appear to be pertinent to both cognitive science and dance studies. For if Demoustier's dancing body shows itself as one actant within a so-called "enactivist dance archive" that relies on the interactive relationships between its different components, we are immediately confronted with the double-sided question as to who is acting upon what, and vice versa, what is acting upon whom? In other words, where are we to locate the agency within the interactive relationships that define this enactivist perspective on dance's archival potential? Does this agency reside only in the dancing body, or is there also an agential force emanating from the material world surrounding that body?

Framing these questions in this manner quite immediately leads us to the growing interest (both within and beyond dance studies) in theories of so-called "new materialism", given that exactly these strands of research have been concerned with articulating the agency of matter, albeit in various and – as I will show – sometimes incompatible ways. Nonetheless, situating dance between enactivism and new materialist discourses might be helpful in extending the relationist framework proposed by enactivist views on cognition to dance, with specific attention to the multiple materialisms that one could discern in choreographic practices as well as dance scholarship.

New materialist matters

Oddly enough, despite the explicit insistence on organisms acting as embedded and extended entities within a material environment, matter remains one of the most elusive elements among enactivist views on cognition. As Lambros Malafouris argues, cognitive enactivists fail to realise that *"it will be a new type of sociomaterial practice-based explanation of cognitive phenomena that is needed",* if they are to succeed in the "theoretical shift" they are pursuing (Malafouris 2018: 761). What in his view is missing is a robust account of "material culture", which for him includes not only physical objects but also "the practices, techniques and the social skills it embodies" (Malafouris 2018: 762).

Probably due to his unique profile as a cognitive archaeologist, Malfouris is one of the the few who advocates a more sustained attention to the role of matter in enactivist interpretative frameworks. He finds promising support for this endeavour in the theories of so-called "new materialism". New materialist discourses have become one of the most prominent trends within twenty-first century's critical thought, as they emerged across a wide range of domains (including geography, anthropology, sociology or political theory), while also gaining ample attention within dance and performance studies.[4] However, because the influential work of authors such as Rosi Braidotti, Manuel DeLanda, Karen Barad or Jane Bennett has often been lumped together, "new materialism" began to function as an umbrella term, obscuring the important and fundamental differences between the distinct theoretical positions that go behind it.[5] Despite this plurality, one of the key assumptions that unites new materialist discourses is that matter is not inert but has its own kind of agency, which also determines how we, as humans, live our lives. Or, as Diana Coole and Samantha Frost put it, because new materialisms position *"materiality [as] always something more than 'mere' matter",* it entails that *"the human species is being relocated within a natural environment whose material forces themselves manifest certain agentic capacities"* (Coole and Frost 2010: 9–10). Consequently, new materialism – and related theories such as Object-Oriented Ontology (also known as "triple O" or "OOO") or speculative realism – have played a major role in opening our eyes to the idea that matter matters. The important implication of this perspective is that humans are not the sole centre of the world and that we should move beyond the anthropocentric humanism deeply entrenched within Western thinking, or what Graham Harman calls "onto-taxonomy" (Harman 2020).

The attractiveness of new materialisms for dance scholarship is probably not surprising, given that they seem to offer a firmer foothold to dance, whose material basis has long been overlooked precisely because dance has generally been regarded as the most ephemeral (and therefore the presumably most immaterial) art form of all. Partly in response to choreographic reenactment, however, the prevalent discourse on dance's ephemerality has taken a U-turn, giving rise instead to questions on how dance and performance might remain. While it could be argued that this has been nothing less than a paradigm shift, this fundamental change now appears to be moving into a second stage, as issues about the function of matter (in the broad sense of the term) in relation to the enduring nature of choreography are increasingly foregrounded. Dance scholar Danielle Robinson, for example, discusses her specific approach to choreographic reenactment by drawing on new materialism, which prompts her to ask *"what would happen if we started paying more attention to the materiality of dance as well as dance's material conditions?"* (Robinson 2021: 234). Indeed, since documents, writings, notations, sketches, drawings, photographs, objects, props, costumes and so forth are increasingly recognised as playing a constitutive role in the creation of choreography rather than merely serving as secondary derivatives, there is a greater interest in what the materiality of dance actually consists of – also beyond the dancing body.

In this respect, new materialist discourses offer convenient frameworks to account for the role of matter and materiality (and even theoretical materialisms) in dance practice and scholarship. However, it is also important to reckon with the challenges – if not flaws – that come with this purportedly "new" paradigm, not in the least when dance scholars take recourse to it. At least three major pitfalls can be identified in the attempt to incorporate new materialisms into dance studies. First, there is the difficulty of finding a balance between the agency of material conditions (as highlighted by new materialisms) vis-à-vis the agency of dancing subjects (as habitually privileged by dance studies). Second, it is necessary to come to terms with the implications of new materialist discourses, which despite their internal variations have a tendency to posit monistic ontologies at the expense of acknowledging the different, multiple, and relational "intra-actions" – to use Karen Barad's famous term (Barad 2007: 33) – between the constituent parts and agencies within specific materialistic systems, including choreography.[6] Third, there is an urgent need for scholarly rigour that historicises new materialisms by situating this varied field of research in its proper intellectual historical context through transversal readings of preceding paradigms, which is in fact what some new materialists explicitly call for.

In the following, I will address each of these challenges by referencing a few samples of dance scholarship drawing on new materialisms while also taking into account some vehement criticisms that have been levelled against new materialist discourses. Confronting both angles will allow me to assess what is needed for a productive crossover between new materialist discourses and dance studies in order to think through the materiality of dance as well as the role enactivism might play in this.

Challenge 1: going beyond dance's body humanism

Given the focus of new materialism on the agency of matter, one would assume that adopting a new materialist perspective on dance leads to a recalibration of the hitherto privileged role of the dancing body as the prime medium of dance, or what Rudi Laermans calls the "body humanism" prevalent in choreographic practices or dance discourses (Laermans 2015: 222). Yet, this is not necessarily the case. Earlier, I referred to Danielle Robinson, who asks after the materiality of dance in the context of her research on choreographic reenactment. It is arguably symptomatic that her account is still centred on the dancing body. Outlining her method, which she terms "empathic attunement", Robinson explains that it *"attempts to bring together the subjectivity of the researcher with the subjectivity of the people connected with a particular source"*, noting that *"such a process would <u>emphasize the people</u> behind, within, and around dance objects"* (Robinson 2021: 235; emphasis added). Thus, and despite her avowed reliance on new materialist theories, Robinson seems to be interested mainly in the humanistic dimensions that arise from revisiting dance's material traces. In a similar vein, Lizzy Le Quesne's discussion of the Skinner Releasing Technique (SRT) in her 2018 article "Learning to Dance in the Twenty-First Century" is explicitly framed within new materialist thinking, but she, too, seems to locate the agency of matter primarily in the dancer's body. When she describes how SRT stimulates a *"practice of actively handing oneself over to unfolding kinaesthetic urges that seem to arise in and move the body in unfamiliar ways"*, it is difficult to see how the new materialist perspective on this technique leads her beyond the dancer's own body, despite her assertion that it is *"a practice of the agency or dynamism of matter"* (Le Quesne 2018: 85).

Examples like these show that the alliance between new materialist discourses and dance studies does not always lead to a thorough and fully sustained dialogue that would question some of the most ingrained key assumptions governing the discourse on dance. Even when the body is perceived as moving beyond its own subjective control, a new materialist framework would require taking into account the entire material infrastructure and intersubjective relationalities affording this experience. To explore this further, possible convergences between new materialisms and cognitive enactivism might be beneficial, precisely because the interactions between body, brain and environment are central to the latter.

Challenge 2: monistic ontologies

Whereas some new materialist approaches to dance hold on to the prevalence of the body, others run the risk of reinforcing the critiques sometimes raised against new materialisms. It has been argued, for instance, that new materialists tend to obscure the different agential capacities of human subjects vis-à-vis non-human materials by attributing agency to both. In this vein, Katherina N. Hayles sharply criticises the frequent use of the notion of "force" in new materialist discourses. She argues more specifically that *"the overall aim of decentering the human and celebrating the nonliving as fully capable of agency"* leads to a lack of *"further specification about the different kinds of agencies and forces"*, which in turn reveals that *"the preference for one kind of force over another is an ideological choice, not an empirical conclusion"* (Hayles 2017: 195). Susanne Lettow raises similar concerns over the lack of differentiation between distinct types of agencies, particularly in Karen Barad's theorisation of agency. She notes that *"no room is left for conceptualizing structural differences between human and nonhuman forms of agency, and neither can we conceptualize differences or relations of power and domination among humans"* (Lettow 2017: 111). The common ground in the critiques by Hayles, Lettow and others is that new materialisms ultimately posit a monistic ontology that levels out all distinctions between human and non-human forms.[7] The potential flaw of such frameworks is, therefore, that they eclipse the relational dynamics between the constituent parts of the ecosystems they attempt to describe.

Even though these critiques have been countered, and in some cases convincingly so (e.g., Bianchi et al. 2021: 9; Klitgård 2021: 204–207),[8] dance scholars have not always adequately considered the monistic viewpoints that are sometimes implied by certain strands within new materialist discourses. Elise Nuding, for example, draws on Karen Barad's expanded definition of "bodies" (Nuding 2020: 50) when discussing a choreographic technique she called "sounding score", contending that *"the manifold bodies of the dance – score, sounding lines, my body, bodies of sound and movement, body of language, body of space – are co-implicated in each other's emergence"* (Nuding 2020: 52). This emergence, she concludes, ensures *"the body of the dance becoming through the material-discursive affective timespacemattering of the dancing bodies"* (Nuding 2020: 53). Here too, Nuding is using Barad's terminology and, in spite of her detailed account of sounding score, one is left wondering how exactly the intra-actions between time, space and matter are at play within the coming-into-being of the dance. When a concept such as "timespacemattering" is transferred to dance,[9] its relational implications should be fleshed out through the "raw data" engendered by dance, rather than to suffice with the idea that, for example, discursive language and embodied experience are entangled. Otherwise, the juxtaposition of fundamental categories such as time, space and matter results in a monistic viewpoint that does not always accord with the relationality that is sometimes central to new materialist thinking.

It is, however, not difficult to see why the jargon of new materialist discourses offers a rich vocabulary for dance studies. Both fields share an ardent struggle against some of the most entrenched dualisms in Western culture that oppose body to mind, language to experience, humans to matter, etc. Yet, an interdisciplinary encounter like this one becomes problematic when either the implications of, or distinctions between, certain strands of new materialist thinking are not completely taken into account, or when they are not pushed beyond their own limitations. Paula Kramer, for example, fails to recognise the key distinctions between Graham Harman's object-oriented ontology and Jane Bennett's vitalist materialism, when she frames her discussion of the relationalities between moving bodies and natural environments within outdoor dance practices in the context of both thinkers.

A relatively short yet meaningful debate between both Harman and Bennett, however, does reveal how their theoretical stances are not only different, but even incommensurable. This incompatibility is mainly based on Harman's "flat" ontology, which embraces "the Kantian thing-in-itself" as something that exists "regardless of any relations with outside things" (Harman 2017: 244), as opposed to Bennett's "positive ontology", which contends that things only become what they are because they are a part of a "dense network of relations" (Bennett 2010: x, 13).[10] Differences like these show how cautious one should be in adopting new materialist viewpoints when considering dance. In other words, before making the interdisciplinary leap to dance studies, it is important to identify the various strands within so-called "new materialism" and to what extent they actually fit (or do not fit) together.[11]

Challenge 3: historicising materialisms

While it is crucial for dance studies to connect with recent developments within various fields of research (both within and outside the humanities), it is equally important not to restrict dance scholarship to allegedly "new" tendencies. Instead, these trends should be historicised by taking into account the intellectual traditions to which they relate and situating them in a larger history of ideas – or, what in German is more aptly called, *Ideengeschichte.* Indeed, some of the most well-known proponents of new materialist discourses have openly questioned the "newness" of so-called "new" materialisms. As Karen Barad, for instance, states in a conversation with Daniela Gandorfer:

> *"The call for a new domain of thought (as if thought should have domains) was not mine and I have critiqued the use of 'new' in 'new materialisms' since its founding, both for the use of 'new' in its reliance on a progressivist notion of temporality and the discontinuity implied from the presumed 'old' materialism of Marx."* (Barad and Gandorfer 2021: 62, endnote 19)[12]

As a philosophical term, "materialism" has a long history that dates back to the Ancient Greeks and continues to the present. In this respect, Barad's reference to Marx is meaningful, as one of the most influential instances of materialism (whether "new" or "old") is, of course, Marx's historical materialism.

The role of Marxism, however, is heavily contested within new materialist discourses: while some of its proponents (such as not only Karen Barad but also Diana Coole and Samantha Frost) acknowledge the continuities with this intellectual history, others explicitly distance themselves from Marxist historical materialism (see, e.g., de Landa in Dolphijn and van der Tuin 2012: 40–41; Bennett 2001: 119–121).[13] Despite the fundamental differences between these two positions, it would be hard not to deal with Marx's legacy at all. This is especially the case when we are to follow Rick Dolphijn's and Iris van der Tuin's suggestion that new materialism can only *"create a remarkably powerful and fresh 'rhythm' in academia today"* if it *"says 'yes, and' to all intellectual traditions"* and *"continues to rewrite the history of philosophy"* (Dolphijn and van der Tuin 2012: 89, 110; original emphasis).

In *Marx in Motion* (2020), Thomas Nail succinctly states that the main criticisms levelled at Marx's historical materialism in contemporary theory (including but not limited to new materialisms) pertain to his alleged historical determinism, economic reductionism and anthropocentrism (Nail 2020: 2–5). While each of these principles certainly stands in stark contrast with the main tenets of new materialist discourses, we need to question to what extent they are the result of a caricatured image of Marx we inherited and which does not do justice to the complexity of his thought. Furthermore, if "transversality" (as claimed by Dolphijn and van der Tuin [2012: 100]) is indeed a hallmark of new materialist thinking,[14] it is necessary to pursue rather than foreclose a more intense commitment to tracing the intellectual history that gave rise to new materialist discourses in our present days. In this respect, Susanne Lettow makes a convincing argument that the broad ontological claims advanced by new materialism should not be replaced but rather recalibrated by what she calls the "praxeological dimensions" that can be found in Marx's historical materialism (Lettow 2017: 108). Indeed, the emphasis that Marx places on "practice" offers a perhaps unexpected entrance for dance studies to forge a bridge between new and historical materialist discourses.

One might be surprised to discover in Marx's writings a multiplicity of terms and thoughts that are, in fact, choreographic in nature. Already his early work, and more specifically the first of his so-called "Theses on Feuerbach", makes a forceful statement on what materialism in his opinion should entail, which resonates strongly with contemporary dance discourses:

"The chief defect of all hitherto existing materialism (that of Feuerbach included) is that the thing, reality, sensuousness, is conceived only in the form of the object or of contemplation, but not as sensuous human activity, practice, not subjectively. Hence, in contradistinction to materialism, the active side was developed abstractly by idealism – which, of course, does not know real, sensuous activity as such." (Marx [1845] 1998: 569; original emphasis)

Marx opposes the tendency of idealistic thought to objectify human nature (as he saw epitomised in the work of Ludwig Feuerbach), proposing instead to look at the sensuous dimensions of human activity as they unfold in practice. The terms "sensuous" and "practice" are particularly crucial here, not only due to their choreographic resonance, but also because they suggest that Marx is after a worldview that takes into account the enacted, extended, embedded and embodied layers of being (as enactivism proposes) relative to the entanglement of human beings with the material world surrounding them (as most strands within new materialist discourses suggest). Moreover, when Marx together with Friedrich Engels claims that materialism *"does not explain practice from ideas but explains the formation of ideas from material practice"* ([1845] 1998: 61), we are right at the core of what contemporary choreography is often seeking to establish.

Conclusion: revisiting materialisms

While creating *Unfolding an Archive*, Zoë Demoustier initially drew her subjective map on the stage using a mixture of cement and concrete powder. But after hearing that this compound could be unhealthy, she started using aquarium sand and clay powder. Preparing this substance grew into a ritual that helps her to concentrate, while its materiality remained central to the piece. As she explains in an interview, the sand became the unifying tissue of the work:

"That sand connects it all, because no matter how different the places from my father's war reports were, if you look at them for hours, they all look the same. After a while, you can no longer see whether the dust is kicking up from the rubble in Kosovo,

Iraq, or Rwanda." (Demoustier 2022b: paragraph 3; translation by Timmy De Laet)

From this perspective, Demoustier's *Unfolding an Archive* could be seen as an attempt to materialise the immateriality of her own personal memories of the times her father was absent, while his work as a war reporter was in itself already aimed at materialising the conflicts and catastrophes he was witnessing. Precisely because Demoustier's piece moves into the blurry zone between matter and immateriality, it invites us to reconsider how dance scholarship has been engaging with newly emerging areas of research, such as enactivism or new materialist discourses. My aim in this contribution was to take up this invitation by showing how the relational dynamics put forth by enactivism could provide a valuable framework for expanding the materiality of dance beyond the dancing body and even beyond the material remains that dance may leave behind. At the same time, the lack of a robust theorisation of materiality within enactivism led me to explore how dance scholars turned to new materialist discourses in order to account for the material dimensions of dance as opposed to its presumed ephemeral immateriality.

Fig. 3 — Unfolding an Archive *by Zoë Demoustier*
Photo Tom Herbots, courtesy of the artist

As this contribution took its impetus from Zoë Demoustier's *Unfolding an Archive,* it sought to acknowledge the value of this particular performance as what Mieke Bal – following art philosopher Hubert Damisch – would call a "theoretical object" (Bal 2010: 7) and also to treat it as such. Consequently, my discussion of Demoustier's work led to a mainly methodological exploration into how dance studies is engaging with new developments within the humanities (and beyond). This endeavour showed that new materialist discourses should be treated carefully, primarily due to the risk of slipping into monistic ontologies as well as the fallacy of mixing distinct strands of thinking that are sometimes incommensurable. It also resulted in the claim that dance scholarship might benefit from a more consistent historicisation of the theoretical frameworks it is keen to adopt. In this regard, new materialisms should be considered more often in conjunction with their historical predecessors, such as Marx's historical materialism.

In the same way that supposedly "new" materialist discourses are not actually new, importing Marx into dance studies is not entirely novel in itself either. In this sense too, dance scholarship should do well in revisiting its own legacies. One of these (more recent) legacies that fused dance studies with Marxist theory can be found in the work of Randy Martin, who passed away at the early age of 57.[15] In his 1998 book *Critical Moves: Dance Studies in Theory and Politics,* Martin almost presciently wrote about the need for *"terms that can more fully articulate the body's materiality"* in order to start conceiving of the body *"not as a unity but as an economy with its own internal and nonreducible effectivities"* (Martin 1998: 210). The note accompanying this passage further clarifies that Martin is not upholding an essentialised conception of the body. Here, he tellingly refers to Marx, for whom *"a nature or a society that simply exists as a given is not subject to practice and therefore becomes a mere idealization"* (Martin 1998: 249–252; emphasis added). Again, we see how, for Marx, practice is key to avoid lapsing into an unwarranted immaterialisation (or what he refers to as "a mere idealization") of matter, which not only applies to the body but also extends to nature or social relationships.

Both enactivism and new materialist discourses can be seen as delivering the critical terminologies Randy Martin was calling for already in the late 1990s. However, as I have argued, these new developments also come with their own challenges. One of the lessons we should learn from Martin's work is that historicising one's own presumed contemporary position within a larger horizon of critical thinking can help to avoid some of the pitfalls that may not be immediately apparent from within one's own contemporaneity. Therefore, returning to Marxism does not mean reviving the fallacies of this particular tradition, but rather critically assessing the presuppositions of new tendencies before they turn into traditions themselves. This amounts to a transhistorical approach that connects so-called "older" traditions with allegedly "new" developments. Most importantly, as Zoë Demoustier's *Unfolding an Archive* demonstrates, dance may be the most effective avenue to achieve this, precisely because choreography holds the potential to draw lines – both literal and metaphorical – between one's personal histories, present positionality and future aspirations. As such, it shows how the new can only be new in hindsight of the old while awaiting what will have been. Acknowledging this relationality is key to conceptualising any kind of materiality.

ACKNOWLEDGEMENT

Research for this contribution has been made possible through a grant provided by the Research Foundation Flanders – FWO (grant ID: W000320N).

1. *Ultima Vez* provides structural support to new upcoming artists as a part of their so-called "Ulti'Mates" program. Next to Zoë Demoustier, other choreographers currently involved in this programme are Lukah Katangila and Seppe Baeyens. For more information, see: ultimavez.com/new-makers (29/07/2023).

2. By taking this focus on enactivism in relation to materialism, my approach differs from the one Shay Welch develops in her 2022 book *Choreography as Embodied Critical Inquiry*. As one of the few dance scholars connecting enactivist models of cognition to dance, Welch details how the production of meaning and knowledge through dance is in line with how enactivism *"positions the core of meaning-making within the body-brain-environment dynamical system"* (Welch 2022: 130). Instead of trying to uncover the epistemological dimensions of dance through enactivism, I rather use it as a framework for a critical account of materiality as a notion that emerges frequently in dance discourses and choreographic practices.

3. For a useful overview of what they call "the varieties of enactivism", see Ward, Silverman and Villalobos 2017.

4. While Alison D'Amato claims that new materialist discourses *"remain under-acknowledged with respect to dance"* (D'Amato 2021: 70), quite some dance scholars have been engaging with different strands from within new materialisms. It is obviously impossible to give an exhaustive account, but a few notable examples might include: Kramer 2012; Le Quesne 2018; Domm 2019; Nuding 2020; Hunter 2021; Robinson 2021; Ruhsam 2021; D'Amato 2021; Foellmer 2022; Frischkorn 2023. Throughout this contribution, I will return to some of these references in more detail.

5. Precisely because of the divergent – and, as I will show, sometimes incommensurable – theoretical positions labelled together under "new materialism", Diana Coole and Samanta Frost use the pluralised version of the term for their seminal 2010 edited volume *New Materialisms*. They explain their choice as follows: *"If we pluralize these new materialisms, this is indicative of our appreciation that despite some important linkages between different strands of contemporary work and a more general materialist turn, there are currently a number of distinctive initiatives that resist any simple conflation, not least because they reflect on various levels of materialization."* (Coole and Frost 2010: 4) In this contribution, I will also acknowledge this plurality by using the terms "new materialist discourses" or "new materialisms".

6. Within new materialist discourses, Karen Barad is one of the most prominent voices advocating a deeply relational understanding of materialism (as opposed to the more monistic tendencies in other new materialisms), which is epitomised in her concept of "intra-action". As Barad explains, "the neologism 'intra-action' signifies the mutual constitution of entangled agencies" (Barad 2007: 33). In this sense, she differentiates "intra-action" from "the usual 'interaction,' which assumes that there are separate individual agencies that precede their interaction" (Barad 2007: 33).

7. For similar critiques, see Möser 2021 and Poyares 2021.

8. I should add that Diana Coole did introduce the notion of "agentic capacity" to differentiate between "potency", "reflexivity" and "responsibility" as three different modes of agency (see Coole 2013). I want to thank Susanne Foellmer for bringing this text to my attention.

9. It should be noted, however, that Barad actually uses the term "spacetimemattering" (see, e.g., Barad 2007: 179).

10. For the debate between Jane Bennett and Graham Harman, see Bennett 2012 and Harman 2014. Here, Harman reiterates his refusal of relationism as a fundamental property of objects: *"[…] despite what Bennett says, objects for me are by no means the sole locus of all the acting, since objects insofar as they are aloof do not act at all: they simply exist, too non-relational to engage in any activity whatsoever"* (2014: 100; original emphasis).

11 For an insightful overview of the different strands within new materialisms, see Gamble, Hanan and Nail 2019 and "Part 1: Varieties of Materialism" in Lemke 2021: 19–78.

12 Karen Barad refers here to a keynote lecture she delivered at a conference on "What's New About New Materialisms" at the University of California on 4 May 2012, titled "Nothing is New, Nothing is Not New". In their editorial introduction to *New Materialisms,* Diana Coole and Samantha Frost endorse a similar historicising point of view, claiming that *"in labeling these essays collectively as new materialisms, we do not wish to deny their rich materialist heritage. Many of our contributors indeed draw inspiration from materialist traditions developed prior to modernity or from philosophies that have until recently remained neglected or marginalized currents within modern thinking. From this perspective their interventions might be categorized as renewed materialisms"* (Coole and Frost 2010: 4).

13 This split between anti-Marxist new materialisms and a renewed historical materialism serves as the starting point for the edited volume *Materialism and Politics* (Bianchi et al. 2021). As asserted by the editors, the objective of their book *"is not to propose a reconciliation or a synthesis of these different materialist tendencies, but to portray their great variety and even contradictions without excluding the possibility of an encounter between them"* (Bianchi et al. 2021: 2). For a revealing critique of the new materialist rejection of Marx's historical materialism, see Choat 2018.

14 According to Rick Dolphijn and Iris van der Tuin, the transversality of new materialist discourses stems from its "immanent gesture" to seek for intersections between "academic (neo-)disciplines", "paradigms" and "the linear spatiotemporalities conventionally assigned to epistemic trends (for instance 'new materialism' versus Marxist historical materialism as practiced by Benjamin for instance)" (Dolphijn and van der Tuin 2012: 100).

15 The impact of Randy Martin's work on dance studies, including the ways in which he imported Marxism into dance scholarship, was the topic of a special issue of *Dance Research Journal,* edited by Mark Franko and André Lepecki (2016).

REFERENCES

Bal, Mieke (2010): Of What One Cannot Speak: Doris Salcedo's Political Art. Chicago: The University of Chicago Press.

Barad, Karen (2007): Meeting the Universe Halfway: Quantum Physics and the Entanglement of Matter and Meaning. Durham and London: Duke University Press.

Barad, Karen and Daniela **Gandorfer** (2021): Political Desirings: Yearnings for Mattering (,) Differently. In: Theory & Event, Vol. 24, No. 1, pp. 14–66, DOI: 10.1353/tae.2021.0002.

Bennet, Jane (2001): The Enchantment of Modern Life: Attachments, Crossings, and Ethics. Princeton and Oxford: Princeton University Press.

Bennett, Jane (2010): Vibrant Matter: A Political Ecology of Things. Durham and London: Duke University Press.

Bennett, Jane (2012): Systems and Things: A Response to Graham Harman and Timothy Morton. In: New Literary History, Vol. 43 no. 2, pp. 225–233, DOI: *doi.org/10.1353/nlh.2012.0020*.

Bianchi, Bernardo, Emilie **Filion-Donato**, Marlon **Miguel** and Ayşe **Yuva** (2021): From "Materialism" towards "Materialities". In: Bernardo Bianchi, Emilie Filion-Donato, Marlon Miguel and Ayşe Yuva (eds.), Materialism and Politics (= Cultural Inquiry, Vol. 20), Berlin: ICI Berlin Press, pp. 1–18.

Carlson, Marvin (2001): The Haunted Stage: The Theatre as Memory Machine. Ann Arbor: The University of Michigan Press.

Choat, Simon (2018): Science, Agency and Ontology: A Historical-Materialist Response to New Materialism. In: Political Studies, Vol. 66 No. 4, pp. 1027–1042, DOI: *doi.org/10.1177/ 0032321717731926*.

Coole, Diana and Samantha **Frost** (eds.) (2010): New Materialisms: Ontology, Agency, and Politics. Durham and London: Duke University Press.

Coole, Diana (2013): Agentic Capacities and Capacious Historical Materialism: Thinking with New Materialisms in the Political Sciences. In: Millenium: Journal of International Studies, Vol. 41, No. 3, pp. 451–69.

D'Amato, Alison (2021): Movement as Matter: A Practice-Based Inquiry into the Substance of Dancing. In: Dance Research Journal, Vol. 53 No. 3, pp. 69–86.

Demoustier, Zoë (2020a): An Archive, Near and Far. Interview by Elowise Vandenbroeck for KVS (Koninklijke Vlaamse Schouburg), *kvs.be/en/pQ7B4uZ/een-archief-van-ver-en-dichtbij* (01/02/2023).

Demoustier, Zoë (2020b): "Ik wil niet mijn hele leven in mijn dansbubbel blijven. Interview by Tom Peeters, 31 October, *bruzz.be/culture/theatre-dance/choreografe-zoe-demoustier-ik-wil-niet-mijn-hele-leven-mijn-dansbubbel* (13/09/2023).

Dolphijn, Rick and Iris **van der Tuin** (2012): New Materialism: Interviews & Cartographies. Ann Arbor: Open Humanities Press.

Domm, Daniela Perazzo (2019): Im/possible Choreographies: Diffractive Processes and Ethical Entanglements in Current British Dance Practices. In: Dance Research Journal, Vol. 51, No. 3, pp. 66–83.

Foellmer, Susanne (2022): Choreographie im Modus relationaler Handlungsmacht: New Materialism, komplexe Systeme und die Frage nach Agency. In: Sabine Huschka and Gerald Siegmund (eds.), Choreographie als Kulturtechnik. Berlin: Neofelis, pp. 139–164.

Franko, Mark and André **Lepecki** (eds.) (2016): Randy Martin and Dance Studies. Special issue of Dance Research Journal, Vol. 46 No. 3.

Franko, Mark (ed.) (2017): The Oxford Handbook of Dance and Reenactment. New York: Oxford University Press.

Frischkorn, Moritz (2023): More-Than-Human Choreography: Handling Things Between Logistics and Entanglement. Bielefeld: transcript.

Gamble, Christopher N., Joshua S. **Hanan** and Thomas **Nail** (2019): What is New Materialism? In: Angelaki, Vol. 24 No. 6, pp. 111–134, DOI: *doi.org/10.1080/0969725X.2019.1684704*.

Gallagher, Shaun (2017): Enactivist Interventions: Rethinking the Mind. New York: Oxford University Press.

Harman, Graham (2014): Materialism is Not the Solution: On Matter, Form, and Mimesis. In: The Nordic Journal of Aesthetics, No. 47, pp. 94–110.

Harman, Graham (2017): Object-Oriented Ontology: A New Theory of Everything. London: Penguin Books.

Harman, Graham (2020): The Only Exit from Modern Philosophy. In Open Philosophy, Vol. 3, No. 1, 132–146, DOI: *doi.org/10.1515/opphil-2020-0009*.

Hayles, Katherine N. (2017). "The Cognitive Nonconscious and the New Materialism". In: Sarah Ellenzweig and John H. Zammito (eds.), The New Politics of Materialism: History, Philosophy, Science. London and New York: Routledge, pp. 181–199.

Hunter, Victoria (2021): Site, Dance and Body: Movement, Materials and Corporeal Engagement. Cham: Palgrave Macmillan.

Klitgård, Mathias (2021): Notas hacia una noción materialista del tiempo. In: Helena López, David Gutiérrez and Jorge Alberto Palomino (eds.), Lecturas interdisciplinares de los cuerpos: discursos, emociones y afectos. México: Universidad Nacional Autónoma de México, pp. 187–218.

Kramer, Paula (2012): Bodies, Rivers, Rocks and Trees: Meeting Agentic Materiality in Contemporary Outdoor Dance Practices. In Performance Research, Vol. 17 No. 4, pp. 83–91, DOI: *doi.org/10.1080/13528165.2012.712316*.

Laermans, Rudi (2015): Moving Together: Theorizing and Making Contemporary Dance. Amsterdam: Antenna / Valiz.

Lemke, Thomas (2021): The Government of Things: Foucault and the New Materialisms. New York: New York University Press.

Lepecki, André (2011): The Body as Archive: Will to Re-Enact and the Afterlives of Dances. In Dance Research Journal, Vol. 42 No. 2, pp. 28–48.

Le Quesne, Lizzy (2018): Learning to Dance in the Twenty-First Century: Skinner Releasing Technique as Technology of Becoming, within a New Materialist Frame. In: Journal of Dance & Somatic Practices, Vol. 10 No. 1, pp. 79-93, DOI: *10.1386/jdsp.10.1.79_1*.

Lettow, Susan (2017): Turning the Turn: New Materialism, Historical Materialism and Critical Theory. In Thesis Eleven, Vol. 140 No. 1, pp. 106-121, DOI: *10.1177/0725513616683853*.

Malafouris, Lambros (2018): Bringing Things to Mind: 4Es and Material Engagement. In: Albert Newen, Leon de Bruin and Shaun Gallagher (eds.), The Oxford Handbook of 4E Cognition. New York: Oxford University Press, pp. 755–771.

Martin, Randy (1998): Critical Moves: Dance Studies in Theory and Politics. Durham and London: Duke University Press.

Marx, Karl ([1845] 1998): Theses on Feuerbach. In: Karl Marx and Friedrich Engels, The German Ideology. New York: Prometheus Books, pp. 569–574.

Marx, Karl and Friedrich **Engels** (1998): The German Ideology. New York: Prometheus Books.

Möser, Cornelia (2021): Materialism, Matter, Matrix, and Mater: Contesting Notions in Feminist and Gender Studies. In: Bernardo Bianchi, Emilie Filion-Donato, Marlon Miguel and Ayşe Yuva (eds.), Materialism and Politics (= Cultural Inquiry, Vol. 20), Berlin: ICI Berlin Press, pp. 203–214.

Nail, Thomas (2020): Marx in Motion: A New Materialist Marxism. New York: Oxford University Press.

Nuding, Elise (2020): "Unsound Bodies: Mapping Manifols in/of the Dance." In Sarah Whatley, Imogen Racz, Katerina Paramana and Marie-Louise Crawley (eds.), Art and Dance in Dialogue: Body, Space, Object. Cham: Palgrave Macmillan, pp. 39–58.

Poyares, Marianna (2021): Theory's Method? Ethnography and Critical Theory. In: Bernardo Bianchi, Emilie Filion-Donato, Marlon Miguel and Ayşe Yuva (eds.), Materialism and Politics (= Cultural Inquiry, Vol. 20), Berlin: ICI Berlin Press, pp. 345–363.

Robinson, Danielle (2021): Feeling with, Moving Toward: Empathetic Attunement as Dance Reconstruction Methodology. In: Clare Parfitt (ed.), Cultural Memory and Popular Dance: Dancing to Remember, Dancing to Forget. Cham: Palgrave Macmillan, pp. 229–242.

Ruhsam, Martina (2021): Moving Matter: Nicht-menschliche Körper in zeitgenössischen Choreografien. Bielefeld: transcript.

Rosch, Eleanor (2016): Introduction to the Revised Edition. In: Francisco Varela, Evan Thompson and Eleanor Rosch ([1991] 2016): The Embodied Mind: Cognitive Science and Human Experience. Revised edition. Cambridge, MA and London, England: The MIT Press, pp. xxxv–lv.

Schneider, Rebecca (2011): Performing Remains: Art and War in Times of Theatrical Reenactment. London and New York: Routledge.

Taylor, Diana (2003): The Archive and the Repertoire: Performing Cultural Memory in the Americas. Durham and London: Duke University Press.

Varela, Francisco, Evan **Thompson** and Eleanor **Rosch** ([1991] 2016): The Embodied Mind: Cognitive Science and Human Experience. Revised edition. Cambridge, MA and London, England: The MIT Press.

Ward, Dave, David **Silverman** and Mario **Villalobos** (2017): Introduction: The Varieties of Enactivism. In: Topoi, Vol. 36 No. 3, pp. 365–375, DOI: *10.1007/s11245-017-9484-6*.

Welch, Shay (2022): Choreography as Embodied Critical Inquiry: Embodied Cognition and Creative Movement. Cham: Palgrave Macmillan.

Wheeler, Michael (2015): The Revolution will not be Optimised: Radical Enactivism, Extended Functionalism and the Extensive Mind. In: Topoi, Vol. 36 No. 3, pp. 457–472, DOI: *10.1007/s11245-015-9356-x*.

Young, Benjamin D. and Carolyn Dicey Jennings (eds.) (2022): Mind, Cognition, and Neuroscience: A Philosophical Introduction. New York and London: Routledge.

Con-
tributo

Aleida Assmann studied English Literature and Egyptology at the universities Heidelberg and Tübingen. From 1993 to 2014 she held the chair of English Literature and Literary Theory at the University of Konstanz, Germany. She taught as a guest professor at international universities (Rice University, Princeton, Yale, Chicago or Vienna). Main areas of her research are history of media, history and theory of reading, cultural memory, with special emphasis on Holocaust and trauma. The Max Planck Research Award allowed her to establish a research group on 'memory and history' (2009–2015). Together with her husband Jan Assmann she received the Peace Prize of the German Book Trade in 2018. Currently she is directing a research group at the University of Konstanz on the topic 'Civic Strength'.

Cristina Baldacci is an Associate Professor in History of Contemporary Art at Ca' Foscari University of Venice, where she is also affiliated with THE NEW INSTITUTE Centre for Environmental Humanities (NICHE). At NICHE she is the PI of the Ecological Art Practices research cluster. Her research interests focus on archiving and collecting as art practices; reenactment and other 're-' strategies in contemporary arts and theory; art and Climate Change; archives and the Anthropocene – all topics on which she has extensively published (see, among others, the monograph *Archivi impossibili: Un'ossessione dell'arte contemporanea*, 2016, and the co-edited volumes *Over and Over and Over Again: Reenactment Strategies in Contemporary Arts and Theory*, 2022; *On Reenactment: Concepts, Methodologies, Tools*, 2022).

Jonathan Burrows is a choreographer, based in the UK. His main artistic focus is an ongoing body of pieces with the Italian composer Matteo Fargion, also living in the UK, with whom he continues to perform around the world. Their work includes *Both Sitting Duet* (2002), *The Quiet Dance* (2005), *Speaking Dance* (2006), *Cheap Lecture* (2009), *The Cow Piece* (2009), *Body Not Fit For Purpose* (2014) and *Rewriting* (2021). Burrows is the author of *A Choreographer's Handbook* (Routledge 2010) and *Writing Dance* (Varamo Press 2022), and he is currently Associate Professor at the Centre for Dance Research, Coventry University, UK.

Franz Anton Cramer has been Research Associate in the project "Choreographies of Archiving" directed by Gabriele Klein (2020–2023), as part of the Cluster of Excellence "Understanding Written Artefacts" at Hamburg University. Prior to that, he has realised research and archival projects at the University of Leipzig (Dance Archives), CN D (Centre national de la danse in Paris), Berlin (Tanzplan Deutschland / Dance Heritage), and University of Salzburg. From 2006 to 2010 he was co-director of the BA Programme Contemporary Dance, Context, Choreography at the Inter-University Centre for Dance in Berlin.

Annet Dekker is Assistant Professor Cultural Analysis, and Archival and Information Studies at the University of Amsterdam. She is also Visiting Professor and co-director of the Centre for the Study of the Networked Image at London South Bank University. She has a long career as a researcher and curator for international organisations and festivals. She publishes regularly in numerous collections and journals and is the editor of several volumes, most recently, *Documentation as Art: Expanded Digital Practices* (Routledge, 2022, with Gabriella Giannachi) and *Curating Digital Art. From Presenting and Collecting Digital Art to Networked Co-Curating* (Valiz 2021). Her monograph, *Collecting and Conserving Net Art* (Routledge 2018) is a seminal work in the field of digital art conservation.

Timmy De Laet is an Associate Professor of Theatre and Dance Studies at the University of Antwerp and a Lecturer at the BA and MA Dance program of the Royal Conservatoire Antwerp (Belgium). He is the co-founder and coordinator of "CoDa | Cultures of Dance – Research Network for Dance Studies" (funded by the Research Foundation Flanders – FWO, grant ID: W000320N). He is the Associate Editor of the *European Journal of Theatre and Performance* and has worked as a dramaturge with Sidi Larbi Cherkaoui for the productions *3S* (2020) and *Vlaemsch (chez moi)* (2022). Timmy's research focuses on the reiterative nature of dance in relation to archivisation, documentation and historiography. His writings on these topics have been published in journals such as *Dance Research, Muséologies* and *Performance Research,* as well as in various anthologies, including *The Oxford Handbook of Dance and Reenactment* (2017) and *The Routledge Companion to Dance Studies* (2020).

deufert&plischke have been working as an artist duo on the intersection of dance, society and media since 2001. Their works are created through choreography, photography, text and video and constitute unconditional commitments to the participatory process. In their more than 20 years together as artistwin, Kattrin Deufert and

Thomas Plischke have cooperated with each other and with others from the beginning – their performances and transdisciplinary works are always created in dialogue, question the hierarchy between artists and audiences and create new spaces in which there is room for participants' imagination. deufert&plischke curate festivals, their formats and series travel around the world. For all the complexity on and off stage, collaboration remains as the core principle and a consistent aesthetic in which a playful confusion is always recognisable. The artistic duo brings their audience to action and reflection and shows like no other how entertaining unreadability can be. For several years now, deufert&plischke have been living and working as an artist family with their two children Moritz and Simon. In 2020, they founded *Spinnerei Schwelm,* a venue for contemporary art in the small town of Schwelm in North Rhine-Westphalia.

Lou Forster is a curator, art historian and dramaturge. He works at the intersection of dance and human sciences. In 2014, he initiated an ambitious project about the choreographer Lucinda Childs. He curated the first retrospective exhibition about her work and supported the donation of her papers to the Centre national de la danse in Pantin. He is currently writing his dissertation at the School for Advanced Studies in the Social Sciences (EHESS) in Paris. From 2018 to 2022, his knowledge about dance benefited from the research program "Chorégraphies" of the Institut national d'histoire de l'art (INHA) where he works as PhD fellow. He graduated from Kinetography Laban at Conservatoire national de musique et de danse de Paris in 2020. In 2010, he founded with the choreographer Lenio Kaklea, ABD, a curatorial platform to develop projects that explore the intersection of dance, research and critical theory.

Gabriele Klein is Professor of Ballet and Dance ("Hans van Manen Chair") at the University of Amsterdam since 2022. From 2002 to 2023 she held the chair of Sociology of Human Movement, Sports, Dance and Performance Studies at Hamburg University. From 2022 to 2023 she was a Research Fellow at the Käte Hamburger Centre "global dis:connect" at LMU Munich. She is PI of the Cluster of Excellence "Understanding Written Artefacts" at Hamburg University. Her English publications include books like *Dance (and) Theory* (2013, with G. Brandstetter), *Emerging Bodies* (2011, with S. Noeth) and *Pina Bausch's Dance Theater. Company, Artistic Practices, and Reception* (2020).

Sybille Krämer was Full Professor for Philosophy at the Freie Universität Berlin. Since her retirement in 2018 she has been guest professor at the Institute for Culture and Aesthetics of Digital Media at Leuphana University Lüneburg. She was a member of the German Scientific Council (2000–2006), the European Research Council (2007–2014), the 'Senat' of the German Research Foundation (2009–2015) and Permanent Fellow at the Wissenschaftskolleg zu Berlin (2005–2008). In 2016 she received an Honorary Doctorate from the Linköping University/Sweden. Her research areas include mathematics and philosophy in the 17th century, social epistemology, philosophy of language and writing, performative studies, media and cultural techniques, digitality and history of computation, and testimony and witnessing.

Bojana Kunst is a philosopher, dramaturge and performance theoretician. She works as a professor at the Institute for Applied Theatre Studies in Justus Liebig University Gießen, where she is leading an international master programme Choreography and Performance. She worked as a researcher at the University of Ljubljana and the University of Antwerp, and as a DAAD-professor at Hamburg University, Performance Studies (2009–2012). She lectured and organised seminars, workshops and laboratories in different academic institutions, theatres, artistic organisations across Europe, and works continuously with independent artistic initiatives, artists, groups and activists. Her research interest is contemporary performance and dance, arts theory and philosophy of contemporary art. She published *Artist at Work. Proximity of Art and Capitalism* (2015) and *The Life of Art. Transversal Lines of Care* (2021, in Slovenian and German).

Axel Malik began his unique form of daily writing in 1989. The writing process yields highly individual sign-like characters that never repeat themselves. These characters do not have an external reference or semantic content. Yet writing they are – a form of writing that a priori defies 'reading' in any traditional sense. Malik has been presenting his art in installations in archives and libraries, public interventions and writing performances. He was artist in residence at the cluster of excellence "Understanding Written Artefacts" at Hamburg University.

Sasha Portyannikova is a dance artist, curator and teacher. She graduated from Vaganova Ballet Academy (MA 2013), cofounded the dance cooperative Isadorino Gore with Dasha Plokhova (2012), and became

Fulbright Visiting Scholar (2018). Her scholarly interests include social choreography, post-Soviet dance research and decolonial practices. In 2020 she published the book *Manual for the Practical Use of a Dance Archive* together with Dasha Plokhova (in Russian). Since 2019 she curates the project *Touching Margins* together with Nitsan Margaliot and Anna Chwialkowska, which has become an educational platform for dance professionals from diverse backgrounds to elaborate upon different aspects of dance history decolonisation.

Sasha Waltz is a choreographer, dancer and director. She studied dance and choreography in Amsterdam and New York. Together with Jochen Sandig she founded the company Sasha Waltz & Guests in 1993 and is cofounder of the Sophiensæle (1996) and the Radialsystem (2006). From 2000 to 2004 she was a member of the artistic direction of the Schaubühne am Lehniner Platz in Berlin and in the season 2019/20 she was director of the Berlin State Ballet together with Johannes Öhman. In her current choreographic work Waltz focuses on the condensation of collaborative processes, such as the synchronous development of choreography and music (e.g. *Kreatur,* 2017). In 2021 Sasha Waltz was awarded the French cultural order "Commandeur de l'ordre des Arts et des Lettres".